TOMORROW'S SCOTLAND

Edited by Gerry Hassan
and Chris Warhurst

Lawrence & Wishart
LONDON 2002

Lawrence and Wishart Limited
99a Wallis Road
London
E9 5LN

First published 2002

British Library Cataloguing in Publication Data.
A catalogue record for this book is available from the British
Library

ISBN 0 85315 947 5

Text setting Derek Doyle and Associates, Liverpool
Printed and bound by Bookcraft, Midsomer Norton

Contents

To Jules Feiffer, and the
idea of Jaytalking

Future Scotland: the making of the new social democracy

GERRY HASSAN AND CHRIS WARHURST

The English once fled to Gretna Green to get married in a hurry. Now there are other enticements drawing them north. Scotland is becoming a social magnet, attracting English people who want better care for their elderly, better university education with grants and no student fees, higher levels of hospital staffing, improved ratios of teachers to pupils in schools. And it's no longer a matter of taking the high or the low road north: Scotland just has better roads.

> Douglas Fraser and James Cusick, *Sunday Herald*[1]

Scotland was a new and confident country, flexing its autonomous muscles. Scottish culture was great, Scottish youth were great. Scottish authors basked gaily in their Scottishness.

> David Aaronovitch, *Paddling to Jerusalem*[2]

There is also a tendency to use the word Tory as a lazy shorthand for incorrigible villainous arsehole, the cancer in the body of Scottish society. I've nothing against this practice philosophically, mark you (and Iain Banks is apt to do it, too); it's just that once you've come across it once or twice, it does get a bit transparent.

> Charles Jennings, *Faintheart*[3]

Devolution will have major consequences for Scotland and its future, as well as for the wider UK. Scotland is slowly becoming a different place from the rest of the UK: a society and body politic with a different set of priorities, debates and policies. At least that is the way it is meant to be. English perspectives on Scotland such as the ones quoted above tend to acknowledge the fundamental change that has been embarked upon. Douglas Fraser and James Cusick are describing 'the land of milk and honey' view from England, which sees Scottish social democracy as a Scandinavian model of politics and public spending, one much envied by English progressives, with their anxieties about

'Middle England' and 'The Third Way'. In David Aaronovitch's account, Scots identity and culture are seen as something secure and confident, allowing the Scots to have pride in their achievements without engaging in constant self-analysis – a perspective which has gained new impetus post-devolution, and is in reality motivated more by English insecurities than Scottish certainties. The third perspective, articulated by Charles Jennings in his *Faintheart* tour north of the border, sees Scotland as a land obsessed with defining itself by what it is not: anti-Tory and anti-English.

What is interesting about most English explanations of Scottish devolution is the extent to which its far-reaching and progressive aspects have impressed them. What is strange from a north of the border perspective is that this sense of Scotland becoming a different country, in which a progressive majority develops its own priorities without having to worry about the reaction of 'Basildon Man' or 'Worcester Woman', is not reflected in Scottish debates. This chapter will attempt to explain this dislocation between policy and story, which is a reflection of the ambiguity at the heart of Scottish devolution, and of the failure of Scots political and civic leaders to articulate a narrative about the purpose of devolution.

BACK TO THE FUTURE?: THE PARABOLA OF SCOTTISH DEVOLUTION

Several different perspectives shaped the establishment of the Scottish Parliament. First, there was the normalisation perspective, stressing that Scotland should take its rightful place on the world stage of nations. The second perspective, the restoration view, emphasised the return to Scotland of its Parliament after a 292-year hiatus. The third perspective, the radical democratisation view, regarded the creation of the Parliament as the first step in the process of democratising Scotland.[4] The dominant strands in this debate were those which emphasised conservation and preservation, and saw the Scottish Parliament as maintaining the internal status quo of public life; it was largely outside Scotland, in groups such as Charter 88, that devolution was seen as a radical democratising initiative north of the border.

Two years after devolution a set of different stories has unfurled. The first story is that of civic Scotland. In this story, the Parliament is civic Scotland's creation, via the Convention; and it articulates a narrow group of vested interests through the use of phrases such as 'popular sovereignty' and 'the settled will of the people'. Second is the story of Nationalist Scotland, which dismisses the Parliament as a 'toy-town' institution, not worthy of its name. And despite all the good intentions of the SNP leadership towards devolution, this cynical view is widely found in the SNP grassroots, as well as in some left-wing circles suspicious of anything touched by New Labour. A third story suggests that the Parliament is a souped-up Labour council of well-remunerated councillors. Iain Macwhirter, Scotland's respected political commentator, dismayed at Old Labour habits, goes further, regarding the Parliament as the voice of South Lanarkshire Council.[5] Fourth, some right-wing critics see the Parliament as the embodiment of the labourist Labour-SNP tax-and-spend politics that dominate Scotland. This worldview sees the first two years, with the abolition of Section 28/Clause 2a, and Mike Watson's bill to outlaw foxhunting, as representing the embodiment of 'the most politically correct state in the Western world'.[6]

These contradictions exist because a coherent social democratic story of events is absent from these formative years of devolution. This absence is not surprising. Although there is a social democratic consensus in Scotland, it is rarely defined and seldom discussed. The words 'social democracy' are rarely spoken out loud in Scottish public life. This is, in part, because Scottish social democracy is dominated by the forces of Labour, SNP and civic Scotland, and shaped by the divisions within it.[7]

Devolution's added value has been its promise of a 'new politics' in both processes and policy. Such a new politics would involve new methods of consultation, and a policy agenda that could take account of broader socio-economic realities – for example a public health agenda that acknowledged the impact of social inclusion and the multi-faceted nature of poverty. However, if we look at this 'new' approach in a historical context, it becomes apparent that it is 'new' only in relation to the aberration of Thatcherism; it is offering a return to pre-1979 Scotland, when policy was shaped by consultation with a host of dense networks around the Scottish Office.[8] What is occurring now with the Scottish Parliament is a return to the social democratic mindset of 1950s and 1960s Scotland – a model which undoubtedly worked then, but which is not relevant to today's problems. Given the rhetoric and hopes around the Parliament, this in itself is a contributory factor in the widespread sense of disappointment. We believe that the widespread sense of disappointment about devolution is partly caused by this slipping backwards into the mindset of an earlier era. The difference between the rhetoric of the 'new politics' and the reality of the first two years of devolution has produced a Scottish version of *Back to the Future*: and thus has arisen the parabola of Scottish devolution.[9]

AFTER DONALD: THE HENRY MCLEISH INTERREGNUM

Scottish politics moved more quickly than anyone would have foreseen. A new group of leaders is now emergent, following the resignation of Alex Salmond and the death of Donald Dewar in 2000, and the resignation of Henry McLeish in 2001.

In his brief period as First Minister, McLeish attempted to develop a distinct and populist agenda. In August 2001 he attempted to offer an interpretation of the changes of the first two years, redefining them as something more coherent: the governance of Scotland had been transformed into a 'new paradigm'.[10] A few weeks later he identified a series of themes with which he wanted his administration associated:

- What matters is what works
- Government should work to improve people's lives
- The interests of consumers should be put before those of producers
- We are stronger together, weaker apart
- Building for the long-term
- We must balance rights and responsibilities
- The rights of individuals must be protected.[11]

These seven credos of McLeish were startling in their blandness. It was hard to imagine anyone in democratic politics in Scotland – from the far-left to the further extremes of right-wing Thatcherism – who would contest these points. However, McLeish's credos, although on one level bland, do contain subtle nuances, identifying the territory and boundaries of his administration: he was attempting to stand within the traditions of the Scottish consensus, yet at the same time to differentiate his administration from certain parts of it. He also attempted to develop his own distinct public sector reform agenda, defining Thatcherism as 'a state of political war' on public services, which he then contrasted to the contemporary 'death of ideology':[12] a post-ideological, value-free politics.

John Swinney's first year as SNP leader saw the emergence of a similar agenda. At the 2001 SNP conference he crystallised the post-Salmond agenda, developing a more populist cutting edge on the tax-raising powers of the Parliament, while still paying homage to the old shibboleths of independent nationhood, and seeing the devolved institutions as an 'incomplete Parliament'. The SNP' s response to public sector reform has been to interpret it as an assault on Scotland's traditions: 'first it was the poll tax, now it's privatisation. Tory or New Labour – it doesn't matter, Scotland is still the favourite guinea pig'. Swinney attacked Labour's support of PFI as 'anti-Scottish and anti-public sector'.[13] Such an attack puts the SNP squarely into the camp of the producer and vested-interest defence of public sector employment, rather than that of public service. And it attempts to claim the Scottish consensus as the sole property of the SNP, branding New Labour as privatising what Thatcher would not even dare.

This positioning has to be seen in the context of the SNP's transformation over the last decade into a serious social democratic and modernising nationalist movement – albeit with limitations within both. The SNP's adoption of a social democratic mindset has coincided with a moment of crisis for the traditional centre-left throughout the world, post-1989, post-Cold War. In coming late to this tradition, the SNP has adopted unquestioningly a set of assumptions and beliefs that social democratic parties the world over are moving away from: that government and the state are good; that the public sector always works as a force for progress; that public spending is always a virtue. Thus the SNP has adopted a set of assumptions that could be called 'Old Labour' or 'old social democracy', defining vested-interest Scotland as the voice of the people.

THE THIRD MAN: THE COMING OF JACK MCCONNELL

Jack McConnell was elected First Minister on 22 November 2001. In a speech on the day of his election he talked of a Scotland where young people still leave school without qualifications or self-confidence: 'This is what makes me angry. And it needs to change. Lewis Grassic Gibbon said that anger is at the root of all change – but anger must be balanced. Too much anger and you're incapable of change, not enough and you don't really want it.'[14]

McConnell reflected on the lessons and mistakes of the first two years: 'We've spent too much time on politics and not enough on government, although the civil service machine has found it difficult to move from government to politics and there's sometimes been a clash.' He was only too aware of the pressure to be seen doing something on every issue, with little effect: 'ministerial announcements distributing dollops of cash around the country, without much sign three months later of any difference.'[15] The day after his dramatic ministerial reshuffle he was similarly blunt: 'Since July 1999, the Executive has amassed a formidable number of strategy documents, action plans, committees and targets through which we have sought to define our direction. There is also a considerable volume of review activity going on across portfolios.'[16]

In a debate on the Scottish Executive's priorities in January 2002, McConnell laid out five priority areas: health, education, transport, crime and jobs; in each listing achievements and areas where more could be done. He again acknowledged that time and energy had been wasted in the first two years of the Parliament. Revealingly, despite his recognition of the importance of a 'knowledge-based, wealth creating economy', the new agenda was about public services, delivery and closing 'the opportunity gap' between those who succeed and fail.[17] Gone are the managerial mantras and buzzwords taken from the new economy gurus.

The response of McConnell's opponents to this agenda was disappointing if predictable. Swinney, not surprisingly, pronounced government delivery of public services to have been a failure, and dismissed 'another relaunch of the Scottish Executive'.[18] His alternative was the usual mix of managerialism and catch-all opposition politics. He did not offer a distinct SNP message, not only failing to invoke the uplands of a new Scotland under independence, but also omitting a detailed case for a better, fairer Scotland. His only convincing comments came in his closing remarks, when he attempted to dissociate the Parliament from the Executive:

> The Parliament has proved itself: it dragged the Executive kicking and screaming into a commitment to deliver free personal care for the elderly; it voted democratically for a tie-up scheme for Scotland's fishing industry; it shone a light on the cronyism of the Labour Party that has corroded Scottish politics and, with the SNP in the lead, it exposed the scandal of closed waiting lists. The Scottish Parliament has proved itself; the problem is that the Executive has failed to deliver on any of its policy commitments to the people of Scotland.[19]

McConnell has come to the leadership at the relatively young age of 41, though he has been in the public eye for more than a decade, first as leader of Stirling Council and then as General Secretary of the Scottish Labour Party, before stints as Finance and then Education Minister. In this period, the nearest McConnell has come to developing a detailed manifesto for change was in his contribution to *A Different Future*.[20] Here he recognised that the Labour Party's concept of modernisation was rooted in the experience of losing elections in the 1980s, and the triumph of Thatcherism; and that there was now a need to evolve, as historical circumstances changed: 'We have to move onto the next stage of modernisation, what has been called "modernising the modernisation", reappraising the left's message in light of the complexities and uncertainties of the modern world ... Modernisation is not a retreat from the politics of the left; on the contrary it is the lifeblood that will keep the left relevant'.[21]

Modernisation, then, is not a value-free process, nor 'was it an end in itself'; instead it is the means by which 'Scotland can become a fairer and more successful country for all her citizens'.[22] McConnell concluded his essay with a reference to the disconnection that has become widespread in the UK post-1997 and in Scotland post-1999: 'Government in the twenty-first century is about being creative, innovative and pushing traditional boundaries. It is, ultimately, about taking risks. And perhaps, the biggest risk is to fail to capture the imagination of the public at large'.[23]

DEVOLUTION, DISAPPOINTMENT AND THE FORCES OF CONSERVATISM

Numerous commentators have noted the high expectations Scots had of their Parliament pre-devolution.[24] At the time of the 1997 referendum, Scots expected a lot of this imaginary body, but support had already fallen by the time of the first Scottish Parliament elections in 1999, and fell considerably in the first year of devolution.[25] In 1999, 41 per cent of voters believed that the Parliament had the most influence over the way Scotland was run, compared to 39 per cent saying Westminster. After one year of devolution, when asked where power actually lay, 66 per cent replied Westminster and 13 per cent the Scottish Parliament; when asked which institution should have the most influence the preferences reversed: 72 per cent chose the Scottish Parliament and 13 per cent Westminster.[26]

Complex factors have produced this outcome. One is what Joyce Macmillan has called the 'fantasy Parliament' view, where, pre-devolution, various groups and individuals could project onto this body their dream wishes and hopes for the Parliament. Not unexpectedly, the real Parliament has fallen significantly short of this fantasy, leaving a sense of palpable loss.[27] However, the political agenda that has been advanced by the Scottish Executive and main players in the Parliament has also been influential: for in spite of all the progressive measures adopted by the Parliament, and the enlightened programmatic plans of the Executive, the Parliament's model of politics has been one influenced by a managerialist approach; it has sometimes seemed value-free, and more concerned with adopting a business and corporate-friendly politics than with remembering the groups who first supported the Parliament.

Findings from the *2000 Scottish Social Attitudes Survey* confirm this view. According to Lindsay Paterson, the 1997 referendum brought together two views of devolution: the liberal reformist view, found mainly in Labour and Lib Dem voters, and the social democratic case, located among the SNP and other nationalists.[28] These two differing perspectives were already falling apart by the time of the first Scottish Parliament elections, and have further separated in the first years of devolution. Those people who are liberal reform-minded in Scotland tend to have extensive social capital, good jobs and good education – professional Scotland. This group, while holding a Scottish identity, are more British-orientated. They are supportive of the Parliament and the UK state – seeing the two as working for the benefit of people. Social democrat Scotland includes the excluded of Scotland: people who lack strong social capital (including trade union links), have less secure or poorly paid jobs and little education. They have a much stronger Scottish identity and they have become rapidly disillusioned with the Parliament.

Paterson concludes this analysis with the observation that whereas in the 1980s and 1990s the main divide in Scottish politics was between a left-of-centre and nationalist consensus, and those who did not fit into it, things are now different. Socialism and nationalism – the narratives of the 1980s consensus – are now, post-devolution, the voices of the socially excluded, whereas the professional classes have now become the greatest upholders of the limited politics on offer.

This sense that included, networked Scotland has gained most from devolution is reinforced by a number of commentaries about how the Scottish Parliament works in practice. In the first year of devolution, Peter Lynch put forward the view that consultation had not gone beyond 'the usual suspects', with 'the development of "clientistic" relations with some subject committees and their main pressure groups'.[29] This view has more recent support. Joyce Macmillan has argued that business and corporate groups view the new mechanisms of consultation as working well, allowing them access to give evidence, lobby ministers and press the pressure points of the new political system to advance their interests.[30]

Research by Ailsa Macintosh on the consultation process on one parliamentary bill, the Education Bill, from draft bill to final Act, has shown the limitations of 'the new politics'. Examining the experience of seven organisations giving evidence at the draft stage of the bill, she found a variety of experiences. Voluntary organisations such as Save the Children and the umbrella group Children in Scotland found the consultation process encouraging and felt listened too, but representatives from the Church of Scotland and Catholic Church felt more disappointed, while St Mary's Episcopal Primary School in Dunblane, the only self-governing school in Scotland, felt extremely disillusioned. The last three bodies all felt consultation was less than transparent, with the Executive engaging in a 'pre-determined agenda', 'hidden decisions' and 'political stone-walling'.[31] Macintosh concludes: 'A wider range of voices is now being heard, but cultural and political traditions still set limits on the debate, perhaps on the imagination ...'[32]

Scottish politics under devolution has changed significantly in terms of personnel. Both Donald Dewar and Henry McLeish clearly represented both a beginning and an ending – a beginning in the establishment of a new Parliament and political system, and an ending of the Westminster-dominated era of Scottish politics. Both individuals personified this sense of transition, looking both to the past and the future. Dewar was a significant Scottish and British politician for over two decades, respected by the political elites in both arenas. In many respects, he personified the ambiguities and contradictions within Scottish devolution more acutely than any other senior Scottish politician: the shift from Westminster to a Scottish-focused politics, and the conservative impulse at the heart of devolution. McLeish was a less significant Scottish and British politician, who tried to emphasise his difference from Dewar, stressing a more populist, politically sensitive and different set of priorities from Westminster.

McConnell's election as First Minister clearly marks a break with his predecessors: he is clearly a beginning. He is a Scottish born and created politician, who has spent his political career advancing a distinctive and radical Scottish agenda. McConnell's political agenda has been the subject of many analyses viewing him as a conservative Labour politician and a creature of Lanarkshire politics.[33] This view is wide of the mark on a number of levels. McConnell's style has always been one of many paradoxes: he has advanced a modernising perspective in Scottish Labour, while aware of the traditions of the labour movement; he has known how to work within the old machine politics, without being a prisoner of it. And he has advanced a managerial version of politics, focusing on results, while also being aware that a reforming politics needs to articulate a sense of vision and values. McConnell will attempt to provide a bridge between the old and new: the pre-devolution hopes and expectations of home rule, and the need to develop a more detailed, deliverable post-devolution agenda. If this approach is successful, it may address the dislocation at the heart of devolution between included and excluded Scotland.

NEW SCOTLAND, NEW UNION?

Devolution has produced political change in a number of ways. It has changed the political environment and has forced the political parties to develop distinctive Scottish agendas and priorities. All the main political parties now have Scottish-developed leaders. In the future, these leaders will be elected by party members, giving them a very different mandate from Westminster-orientated politicians. There has already been controversy about the nature of Labour's two selection processes: the limited franchise that elected McLeish in October 2000 against McConnell and the election of McConnell in November 2001 without a contest.

The political parties will eventually have to develop different Scottish and UK agendas, certainly more so than they managed in the 2001 general election. For example, Labour's famous five point pledge card in 2001 saw three of the five pledges in devolved areas, while the SNP campaign was run by John Swinney, who was not standing at the Westminster election (his face presented on the front cover of the party manifesto in an attempt to raise his profile).

In terms of electoral politics, we have only had two examples of devolution elections: the first Scottish Parliament elections in 1999 and the 2001 UK general election. These elections have produced significant differences. In the former, the SNP clearly positioned themselves as a serious threat to Labour and a potential competitor for power; in the latter, the SNP vote fell and Labour's historic dominance was entrenched. Different party systems seem to be evolving between the two: the Scottish Parliament has a four party system with two smaller micro parties, whereas Westminster has a one party dominated system.

Scottish politics is different from British politics and this difference has a variety of consequences. The *2000 Scottish Social Attitudes Survey* shows that Labour's courting of the centre ground has produced dividends for the party both in Scotland and England, the largest party with voters on the left and centre. However, there is a complication for Scottish Labour in that its biggest rival on both the left and centre is the SNP, whereas on the right it is the Conservatives. In England, the Conservatives are Labour's main rivals on the centre and right. This difference has profound consequences: 'being in the centre in Scotland requires Labour to pay attention to leftwards pressures, whereas being on the centre in England forces attention to the right.'[34] The political dynamic of Scottish and English politics will, if this positioning remains the case, further differentiate.

Many challenges remain in the new Scottish environment. One is the need to develop Scottish ideas, policy and legislation. The first two years of devolution have seen the Scottish Parliament too reliant on Westminster. For example, the Scottish Parliament has provision to allow the UK Parliament to lead and initiate legislation in devolved areas – known as the 'Sewel Convention', after Lord Sewel who devised this mechanism during the passing of the Scotland Act.[35] The Sewel Convention was meant to be used sparingly, but in the first two and a half years of devolution it has been used 31 times. Thirty Holyrood Acts have been passed during the same period.[36]

MSPs have voted to allow Westminster to legislate in numerous devolved areas, such as the extension of the Food Standards Agency to Scotland, reducing the age of consent for gay men, plans to register paedophiles extended to Scotland and new race relations laws for police and council workers. According to Fraser Nelson: 'using Westminster as a good ideas catalogue has democratic drawbacks. House of Commons legislation has a nasty habit of mutating several times over by the time it reaches the final draft. The end result is rarely what MSPs first ordered.'[37] Sometimes legislation does not happen at all, given the way Westminster works: the ban on tobacco advertising is a good example. A Sewel Resolution was passed by the Scottish Parliament in January 2001: the Tobacco Advertising and Promotions Bill was expanded to include Scotland, only to be dropped from the 2001 Queen's Speech. Nelson argues that what 'started as expediency is descending into abrogation':[38] a practice that is damaging accountability and the democratic debate in Scotland, as well as the potential for devolution. It could set a dangerous precedent which could be abused by a future Tory Government legislating in Scotland; although this should require a Scottish Parliamentary vote, this is only a convention, not law.

Another example of over-dependence has been the extent to which numerous Scottish Executive initiatives copy Westminster policy. This emulation exists across a range of policy areas, with the Scottish Executive modifying earlier Westminster policy announcements: mobile phone mast regulations, generic medicine pricing, the National Cancer Plan and free central heating for pensioners are but a few examples. This, as with the propensity to offload legislative responsibility via the Sewel Convention, has profound consequences for the state of devolution: 'Scotland's civil servants have spent all their careers applying Whitehall policy north of the border. They are doing it still, only now policy is left in quarantine at the border before a kilt is pinned on it.'[39] Scottish policy cross-border traffic is also a one-way road, with the Scottish Executive plagiarising Whitehall. The only example of policy travelling south is the example of the Scots abolition of tuition fees and Westminster reappraisal of its policy.

What ties Sewel and Scottish Executive copying of Whitehall is the promotion of a limited, conservative version of devolution, whereby the potential for change is being constrained. The democratisation of Scottish policy debates – something intrinsic to the fate of devolution – is harmed by these actions, and there are fundamental consequences for the question of who has power and influence in Scotland, aiding as they do the existing civil service machine at the expense of politicians.

In practice, the Scottish Executive has not delivered on the hopes of reinventing government, whether joined-up or holistic. Instead it has shown traditional Westminster and Whitehall characteristics: exhibiting a top-down politics combined with a constant sense of instability – a jockeying for position and the moving of ministers and responsibilities back and forth in areas such as sport, tourism and transport. In addition, there has been a slow, inexorable expansion of the payroll vote, allowing the Executive to dominate the Parliament to a degree surpassing Westminster.

The extent of institutional change and instability in the Executive is illustrated by the fact that after Jack McConnell's 'Night of the Long Knives' in November 2001, an astonishing 34 ministers had served in some form or another as a minister within the first two and a half years: nearly half of the combined Labour and Lib Dem vote. Of Labour's 56 MSPs elected in May 1999, an incredible 28 have served in some ministerial capacity;[40] of the 16 Lib Dems, six have held office. Only one minister, Jim Wallace, Deputy First Minister and Justice Minister, has held the same post throughout this period.[41] These figures illustrate the problems for Scottish Executive ministers attempting to get on top of their briefs and departments, let alone develop long-term or innovative policy. This is a politics whereby the main continuities and control remain firmly in the hands of the civil service. One positive way of looking at this situation is that a large group of expertise – twelve ex-ministers – ten Labour, two Lib Dems – sit on the backbenches and could provide a valuable resource to assist Parliament and the wider policy communities in learning about the workings of government and devolution.

Despite these developments, Scottish devolution is judged to be a success by those outside: 'the land of milk and honey' portrayed by the BBC's *Newsnight* and the social democrat consensus envied by English progressives. The Scottish experience internally has been a varied one but, viewed externally, it still offers the potential to act as a catalyst to reconstruct the British state. Anthony Giddens, Tony Blair's guru and architect of 'The Third Way', has acknowledged this case in *Where Now for New Labour?*. In it he states: 'The differing experience of devolution in Scotland, Wales and London creates a strong case that, if regional government in England were to be established, it should be given serious powers which should include legislative and tax-raising powers.'[42]

In an illuminating passage no doubt unwelcome in No 10 or No 11 Downing Street, Giddens reflects on the pragmatic case for the Union, and what might happen if it breaks up: 'Countries can divide without any such conflicts at all. The break-up of Czechoslovakia, for instance, happened in a peaceful way. The same would be true if Scotland declared its independence from the UK.'[43] Giddens is, of course, against such an outcome, but such calm analysis is to be welcomed when contrasted to the Labour unionist views held by people such as Gordon Brown and Douglas Alexander – on Scotland's incapacity to govern itself or run an efficient economy and public services – or the fundamentalist Nationalist case that Scotland must be independent to be free and prosper. Politics post-devolution have to move beyond this stale rhetoric and acknowledge that Scotland's place in the Union and the question of independence are, like most issues in politics in advanced capitalist democracies, no longer matters of black and white, but of different shades of grey.

In any case, the politics of independence become more ambiguous as the EU develops. What is the difference between a maximalist devolution settlement and independent statehood in a world with the euro? In a devolution where Scotland had full fiscal autonomy and the right to legislate in any areas bar defence and foreign affairs, the difference is in degree, not principle. Complete Scottish independence – an Autarkic Scotland – is a non-starter, held onto only by a few unreconstructed Nationalists at the fringes of the SNP. The issue for modern nationalists and social democrats is not whether 'independence' is a good or bad thing, but what constitutional settlement can aid the advancement of a 'good society'. Such an approach involves a pragmatic outlook far-removed from the wild men of Labour unionism and fundamental Nationalism, but instead involves working out what the principles of the 'good society' are, and looking at whether a new kind of Union can be made, one in which Scotland is comfortable, and which aids progressives in England, Wales and Northern Ireland too.

SCOTLAND'S THREE TOMORROWS

Scottish politics and devolution have a number of potential different future scenarios. One is a technocratic, managerial, post-ideological politics defined by the Blairite mantra 'what works is what works'. The outcome is claimed to be value-free policy. It is a scenario with which Henry McLeish's brief administration had a lot in common. It is also a model currently being applied to public sector reform. In this sector the limits of the notion of 'value-free' are starkly revealed, as marketisation continues – though it is the service not the institutions that are now being privatised.

Another scenario is a politics obsessed with constitutional issues, in which arguments over the Barnett formula, fiscal autonomy and electoral systems become the obsession of the political classes to the marginalisation, even exclusion of everything else. A variety of issues are potentially manifest in this scenario, from the debate on retaining a

129-seat Scottish Parliament, to the debate on electoral reform for local government, and the prospect of a SNP-led administration and the threat of the 'neverendum' (continual referendums on Scottish independence). This scenario dominated Scotland pre-devolution, and infused the Dewar and McLeish administrations.

The third scenario would see social democratic Scotland find a new voice and confidence to develop a politics that lives up to the hopes of people pre-devolution and the demands of the twenty-first century. That absent social democratic account of devolution, that we earlier suggested is needed, would advocate a less institutionally dominated politics and a genuine politics of self-government, focused on communities and individuals, not the constitution. Its development, articulation and diffusion are the challenge to Jack McConnell and social democrats in all parties.

For this to happen, Scotland has to tell a different story about itself. This story has to have an internal perspective that acknowledges current economic, social and political realities, as well as seeking to outline the purpose of devolution as a means, not simply an end. It should be honest about what Scotland is, envision what it can become, and offer guidance on the steps needed to get there. This has to involve breaking with the myths and complacencies which define the dominant internal story of Scotland. It has to challenge the hold of Red Clydeside and with it the belief that Scotland is a socialist nirvana, and the urban kailyard conformity which passes for political fashion in cultural and intellectual circles. A new internal story is required to refashion the external image of Scotland with its pernicious use of tartan and shortbread. A modern Scotland has to define itself versus the old, and has yet to speak internationally.[44]

To shift Scottish politics into a new stage of development, and towards the kind of country we want, involves a social democratic politics and vision linked to a sense of time-scales. One of the legacies of socialist thought is the conflict between immediate action, and priorities and time-scales that demand that 'the next Labour Government' bring about 'a fundamental and irreversible shift in wealth and power' in one term. Scottish social democracy needs to tap into these debates, developing a link between policy, programmes, vision and a sense of what a different Scotland should look like in twenty years time. The Scottish Executive might reply that they have such a vision in documents such as the Social Justice programme, with its laudable aim of abolishing child poverty in twenty years; but this is an example of how far removed we are from developing a different future Scotland.[45] The Social Justice document, for all its worthy aims, is filled with managerial and micro-measures, and seems to assume that child poverty can be abolished by elite decree, without a national debate let alone a crusade that engages and challenges people.

A more radical way of developing and thinking about policy would differentiate policies for the short, medium and long-term. Short-term policies – over the life of one Parliament – would respond to immediate problems and build support for progressive change, while 'be[ing] consistent with middle-term theories about how to achieve long-term goals, such as an egalitarian society'. Middle-period strategies are 'the period of trying to change attitudes and values, both by persuasion or by the removal of institutions whose main function is to maintain privilege'. Policies here 'require at least a generation simply because of the need for attitudinal change'.[46] Finally, long-term values have to be articulated and developed about the kind of society social democrats and progressives want. Bernard Crick summarises these three approaches into the following schema:

- Short-term tactical reforms within the system to build a basis of popular confidence for advance
- Middle-term strategies to change the system
- Long-term persuasion to work a new system in a new spirit.[47]

Whatever the future for Scotland, we need to recognise that politics, let alone devolution, will not exclusively dominate popular concerns. In the last year, what filled the media in Scotland as much as everywhere else was the cult of celebrity and an obsession with money and consumption – pop icon Madonna marrying film producer Guy Ritchie at Skibo Castle and christening her child at Dornoch Cathedral, and the arrival of Prince William at the University of St Andrews.

However, just as we acknowledge that across the Western world politics does not dominate everything, so we reject the anti-political argument that poses the end of history, ideology and every 'ism' that has ever been invented. We believe that the fate of Scottish politics and devolution is interwoven with bringing a sense of progressive and social democratic values into politics.

In the last three years we have contributed widely to the Scottish policy debate. *A Different Future* examined a progressive agenda of distinctive and innovative thinking and solutions around the new Parliament. *The New Scottish Politics* assessed the first year of the new Parliament and how the new institutional arrangements worked. *Tomorrow's Scotland* examines how devolution has affected the wider Scotland. It addresses two main themes. First, it assesses the change that devolution has brought to Scotland across a range of areas: political parties, institutions, policy and identity, and an analysis of the potential for future change. Second, it addresses the possibilities of developing a more relevant and radical progressive politics, which matches the challenges of contemporary Scotland. To progress this agenda we offer twelve characteristics for a new Scots social democratic politics:

- We need to acknowledge the passing of the old social democracy, celebrating its strengths: its promotion of egalitarianism, sense of community and public service; while acknowledging its weaknesses: its anti-entrepreneurialism, lack of social inclusion, paternalism and producer-domination.
- The new social democracy has to take the best from the old but strike out onto new terrain: being anti-paternalist, citizen-focused, consumer-sensitive, entrepreneurial and democratising.
- Politics has to recognise the diverse and pluralist nature of Scotland. We have to develop a different kind of politics from that of twentieth century Scotland, recognising that political loyalties are much weaker and voters more volatile than in the past. All parties are now popular minorities and have to engage with the public in a different kind of way, with government contingent and listening, based on dialogue and negotiation.
- We need to develop a politics that is not over-crowded in the middle ground, but allows other perspectives to grow. Scottish politics for too long has been shaped by a consensual centrist politics, which saps radicalism and heresy. We need greater political choice, encouraging a genuine centre-right perspective in Scottish politics and radical left thinking beyond the stale certainties of the Scottish Socialist Party. It is only through choice and diversity that a creative and dynamic centre-left politics can prosper.
- We have to develop a public sector reform agenda about more than greater public spending or the (de)merits of PFI and PPP. An efficacious balance has to be established between producers and consumers, even if that is discomfiting to particular trade union interests. We need to find a new public sector ethos – a partnership for change and democratisation involving employees and users.
- It must challenge vested interests, whether they support privilege or producer interests. So far, the vested interests challenged under devolution have all been marginal – Scottish Opera and Hampden Park, for example – but for far-reaching progressive change we need to challenge the entrenched interests in education, health, law, business, and local and national government.
- It has to be about a less institutionally dominated public life. For

too long Scots' solutions to any problem have involved setting up a new quango or agency – in reality doing little more than aiding the management of decline. Scottish devolution was meant to produce a more accountable political culture, but so far has increased the institutional clutter of public life.

- We have to articulate a vision of a different kind of society and reinstitute the idea of progress as a central part of the political ideal. Policy has to be less determined by managerial assumptions and the belief in value-free, ideologically neutral solutions. Centre-left policy thinking should be anchored in a distinct vision about the kind of society we want to bring about, based on developing the notion of the 'good society' and wider self-government for individuals and communities.

- The Scottish Parliament has to become the primary political institution in the country, and for this to happen it has to stop acting like a part-time legislature, passing the buck to Westminster whenever it can.

- We also need to develop a politics that is less focused on 'devolution' or 'independence'. The Parliament must also accept that it is not the only political institution in the country: wider governance is critical for, and conducive to, a different Scotland. Parliament must simultaneously lead, listen and respond to public opinion.

- We have to stop thinking of Scotland as a homogenous entity, which usually means the Central Belt. We have to recognise the differences and inequalities between Glasgow and Edinburgh, urban and rural, Highland and Lowland. In particular, the importance of Glasgow as Scotland's first city has to be underlined; it produces one-third of Scottish GDP but faces massive challenges in terms of poverty, health and funding, as well as governance.

- Finally, we have to recognise that, although there are differences of degree in some matters, Scotland is not that exceptional from other advanced capitalist societies. The problems and policy challenges we face are not that different from elsewhere. As a consequence, we should be developing Scottish-specific policies that are not afraid to adapt ideas and practices from elsewhere; informed by an understanding of what Scotland is now and the vision of what we want Scotland to be in the future.

A Scottish social democracy that embraced and progressed towards these twelve points would significantly revitalise Scottish politics. However, for this revitalisation to happen, we need to acknowledge the wider environment in which Scotland finds itself. Across the globe, traditional politics are in trouble and the relevance of politics as a force for change is under attack. This problem is compounded in Scotland by the gap between the high expectations pre-devolution and the mixed record of delivery by Dewar and McLeish, by Labour's institutional dominance and the lack of credible alternatives from either the SNP or the Conservatives.

The problem with Scottish politics goes deeper than any short-term factors. There has been a lack of grass roots, citizen-led initiatives in Scotland for most of the post-war period. With honourable exceptions, there was no New Left tradition (Upper Clyde Shipworkers excepted) or Thatcherite revolution (the poll tax being the exception that proves the rule).[48] This lack of political imagination in late twentieth century Scotland is particular cause for concern at a time, when, on Colin Crouch's analysis, contemporary politics are in a state of 'post-democracy' across the Western world. The old political structures of party loyalty, membership and activism have withered, and been replaced by a new elite-driven politics, of party leaderships, corporate and public affairs interests, whereby the old democratic structures of the party no longer work, and governments listen more carefully to elite concerns than to those who are meant to sustain them. Crouch has argued that in many ways this represents a return to a tradition of pre-democratic politics, similar to the politics of the nineteenth-century era of restricted franchise, but because we have passed through a high point of democratic politics from 1945-70, politics are still informed by the democratic spirit: thus, this is an age of 'post-democracy'.[49]

This narrowing of the political can be seen in what has been called the privatisation of public life, and in its corollary, the publicisation of private life.[50] The decline of traditional political culture and its marginalisation by a post-1968 popular culture driven by emotional empathy and finding similar reference points has strengthened the politics of 'post-democracy'. There is something more subtle and more profound at work here than just the tabloidisation and dumbing down of public life.

This is all relevant to Scotland and Scottish devolution, because it affects the chances of progressive politics making a difference to peoples' lives. Scottish politics operates in the same climate of 'post-democracy' and public/private discourse, limiting the capacity of politics to recreate itself into something new. Combined with the historic absence of New Left and Thatcherite perspectives, we should recognise how far we have come and how far we still need to go. We have experienced a partial revolution in the last few years, in setting up the new institutions of devolution; but we need to move on to the next stage, developing the politics and vision to change Scotland. If we are to succeed, we need a new approach to politics: one that recognises that for too long Scottish politics have been dominated by politicians, institutions and top-down processes, for all the myths of 'popular sovereignty'; and that we need to take Scotland back into the hands of the people. This requires an approach which will be citizen-led, focusing on people as individuals and as both producers and consumers; which champions a politics which expands from the narrow politics of devolution (about structures and processes) to the wider goal of self-government. Such a task will require new ideas and political forces which are prepared to challenge what has passed for the status quo for too long. We believe that Scotland can have a major role in creating the new social democracy. It has already done so at a UK level, playing a leading part in ending the old centralist, unitary-state social democracy. It is time to develop a politics which changes and challenges Scotland, and advances a philosophy for celebrating the diversity and divergent polity of the UK.

NOTES

1. D. Fraser and J. Cusick, 'The Land of Milk and Honey', *Sunday Herald*, 14.1.01.
2. D. Aaronovitch, *Paddling to Jerusalem*, London: Fourth Estate 2000, p10.
3. C. Jennings, *Faintheart: An Englishman Ventures North of the Border*, London: Abacus 2001, p152.
4. G. Hassan and C. Warhurst, 'New Scotland?: Polices, Parties and Institutions', *Political Quarterly*, April-June 2001, Vol. 72 No. 2, pp213-26.
5. Tom McCabe, the Business Manager of the Parliament from 1999-2001, was previously leader of South Lanarkshire Council from 1995-99, leading commentators such as Iain Macwhirter to see some of the Parliament's more Old Labour actions as being similar to the practices of South Lanarkshire Council.
6. A. Cochrane, 'The Smack of Weak Government', *Spectator*, 15.9.01.
7. See the chapters by Lindsay Paterson and Jim McCormick in this book on the nature of Scottish social democracy.
8. L. Paterson, 'Scottish Democracy and Scottish Utopias: The First Year of the Scottish Parliament', *Scottish Affairs*, Autumn 2000, No. 33, pp45-61.
9. This analysis borrows from the analysis of Colin Crouch's writing on 'post-democracy'. See: C. Crouch, 'The Parabola of Working Class Politics', in A. Gamble and T. Wright (eds), *The New Social Democracy, Political Quarterly Special Issue*, London: Blackwell 1999, pp69-83.
10. H. McLeish, 'Devolution and After: The Longer View', Speech to Glasgow University, 20.8.01.
11. H. McLeish, Speech at a Centre for Scottish Public Policy Conference, *A Different Scotland: The Scottish Parliament Two Years On*, Royal Society of Edinburgh, 15.9.01.

12. *Ibid*.
13. J. Swinney, SNP Annual Conference Address, Dundee, 21.9.01.
14. J. McConnell, *Scottish Parliament Official Report*, 22.11.01, Col 4150.
15. Quoted in A. Jaspan and D. Fraser, 'I Grew Up in the 70s, Wore Clogs and an Afghan Coat', *Sunday Herald*, 25.11.01.
16. J. McConnell, Scottish Executive News Website, 28.11.01.
17. J. McConnell, *Scottish Parliament Official Report*, 9.1.02, Col 5135.
18. J. Swinney, *Scottish Parliament, op. cit.*, 9.1.02, Col 5138.
19. *Ibid*, Col 5141.
20. See D. Fraser, 'The Jackobite Uprising', *Sunday Herald*, 18.11.01.
21. J. McConnell, 'Modernising the Modernisers', in G. Hassan and C. Warhurst (eds), *A Different Future: A Modernisers' Guide to Scotland*, Edinburgh: Centre for Scottish Public Policy/The Big Issue in Scotland 1999, p69.
22. *Ibid*, p68, both quotes.
23. *Ibid*, p74.
24. See D. Denver, J. Mitchell, C. Pattie and H. Bochel, *Scotland Decides: The Devolution Issue and the Scottish Referendum*, London: Frank Cass 2000, p200.
25. A. Brown, D. McCrone, L. Paterson and P. Surridge, *The Scottish Electorate: The 1997 General Election and Beyond*, London: Macmillan 1999; L. Paterson, A. Brown, J. Curtice, K. Hinds, D. McCrone, A. Park, K. Sproston and P. Surridge, *New Scotland, New Politics?*, Edinburgh: Polygon 2001; J. Curtice, D. McCrone, A. Park and L. Paterson (eds), *New Scotland, New Society?: Are Social and Political Ties Fragmenting?*, Edinburgh: Polygon 2002.
26. P. Surridge, 'Society and Democracy: The New Scotland', in J. Curtice et al, *New Scotland, New Society?, op. cit.*, p140.
27. J. Macmillan, Speech to a Centre for Scottish Public Policy Conference, *A Different Scotland: The Scottish Parliament: Two Years On*, Royal Society of Edinburgh, 15.9.01.
28. L. Paterson, 'Social Capital and Constitution Reform', in J. Curtice et al, *New Scotland, New Society?, op. cit.*, pp29-31.
29. P. Lynch, 'The Committee System of the Scottish Parliament', in G. Hassan and C. Warhurst (eds), *The New Scottish Politics: The First Year of the Scottish Parliament and Beyond*, Edinburgh: Stationery Office 2000, p72. Also see: B. K. Wintrobe, *Realising the Vision: A Parliament with a Purpose*, London: The Constitution Unit 2001, pp51-69.
30. J. Macmillan, 'Will Scottish Devolution Make A Difference?', in B. Crick (ed), *Citizens: Towards a Citizenship Culture, Political Quarterly Special Issue*, London: Blackwell 2001, pp36-46.
31. A. Macintosh, 'An Accessible Parliament?', University of Edinburgh MSc Dissertation, September 2000, p54.

32. *Ibid*, p68.
33. J. Macmillan, 'Can This Bruising New Pragmatism Work?', *The Scotsman*, 17.1.02; I. Macwhirter, 'Muddles on the Mound', *Sunday Herald*, 30.12.01.
34. L. Paterson, 'Governing from the Centre: Ideology and Public Policy', in J. Curtice et al, *New Scotland, New Society?*, *op. cit.*, p213.
35. M. Russell and R. Hazell, 'Devolution and Westminster', in R. Hazell (ed), *The State and the Nations: The First Year of Devolution in the United Kingdom*, London: Imprint Academic 2000, pp187-90; R. Masterman and R. Hazell, 'Devolution and Westminster', in A. Trench (ed), *The State of the Nation 2001: The Second Year of Devolution in the United Kingdom*, London: Imprint Academic 2000.
36. *The Scotsman*, 30.1.02.
37. F. Nelson, 'MSPs let powers drift back to Westminster', *The Scotsman*, 29.10.01.
38. *Ibid*.
39. F. Nelson, 'Is this Devolution or Just Duplication?', *The Times*, 26.6.01.
40. This figure of 28 Labour MSPs elected in May 1999 having held ministerial office includes the late Donald Dewar and Sam Galbraith, who resigned his seat in March 2001.
41. Jim Wallace has, of course, had three spells as Acting First Minister, twice in 2000 and once in 2001. Ross Finnie, his Lib Dem companion in the Scottish Executive, has had a marked degree of continuity as well, being Rural Affairs Minister since May 1999, but had water added to his portfolio after the famous Wendy Alexander 'tantrum' in March 2001, and, more significantly, environment added in November 2001, after the sacking of Sarah Boyack.
42. A. Giddens, *Where Now for New Labour?*, London: Fabian Society/Policy Network 2001, p45.
43. *Ibid*, p47.
44. See the chapter by Janice Kirkpatrick in this volume on the absence of Scotland from the international stage.
45. Scottish Executive, *Social Justice: a Scotland Where Everyone Matters*, Edinburgh: Scottish Executive 1999; Scottish Executive, *Social Justice: a Scotland Where Everyone Matters: Milestone Sources and Definitions*, Edinburgh: Scottish Executive 1999.
46. B. Crick, *Socialist Values and Time*, London: Fabian Society 1984, pp36-37.
47. *Ibid*, p37.
48. Hassan and Warhurst, *New Scotland?*, op. cit., pp225-26.
49. C. Crouch, *Coping with Post-Democracy*, London: Fabian Society 2000, pp49-55.
50. M. Bunting, 'From Socialism to Starbucks: The Decline of Politics and the Consumption of Our Inner Self', *Renewal: The Journal of Labour Politics*, Vol. 9, No. 2/3, 2001, pp23-32.

The paradoxes of Scottish Labour: devolution, change and conservatism

GERRY HASSAN

The Scottish Labour Party has been involved in the process of initiating a widespread constitutional reform programme at a UK level since 1997; and after decades of campaigning, the Scottish Parliament has been established. This has changed dramatically the role of Scottish Labour, bringing it into coalition government with the Liberal Democrats; however, it also carries with it the potential to evolve into a more competitive and pluralist politics, which in the future may be less Labour-orientated.

In the hundred and fourteen years of Scottish Labour's existence, its electoral fortunes have fluctuated – as have those of the Labour Party in the UK – but the Scottish Labour Party has gradually strengthened its position as the leading party in Scotland. It has contributed across the spectrum of Scottish public life, producing a range of national leaders who have played significant roles in Scotland and Westminster. The party has been crucial to the politics of the Union, developing a vital role in representing Scottish and British interests, emphasising Scotland's contribution to the Union and the Union's contribution to Scotland. The establishment of the Scottish Parliament brings new opportunities and challenges: to its electoral position, its leadership and its ability to advocate both Scottish and British interests.

Surprisingly, the Scottish Labour Party has been relatively ignored by contemporary political analysis.[1] Most studies of Scottish Labour have looked at it historically – its origins, the contribution of the ILP, Red Clydeside – or at its relationship with Scottish nationalism. This reflects the orthodoxies of political analysis, which emphasise the primacy of Westminster politics and ignore the territorial dimension of political parties.[2] This chapter looks at Scottish Labour in a number of ways: it examines its contribution to Scottish politics; looks at its role as a sub-section of British Labour; views it as a case study of territorial politics; and addresses the paradoxes inherent in Scottish Labour's championing of devolution.

ELECTORAL PERFORMANCE

Scottish Labour has been the dominant party in terms of electoral performance for most of post-war politics. In the period of 1945-70 it averaged 47.3 per cent of the vote and had a stable vote as characterised by the two party politics of that era. Its vote fluctuated between a high of 49.9 per cent (1966) – still Scottish Labour's best result – and a low of 44.5 per cent (1970) – a difference of 5.4 per cent. In the period of 1974-2001, it has averaged 40.0 per cent – ranging from a high of 45.6 per cent (1987) to a low of 35.1 per cent (1983) – a range of 10.5 per cent. These two eras are characterised by very different political environments: the first period saw a two-party system where the Conservatives in three elections polled more votes than Labour, and overall polled an average of 3.8 per cent less than Labour. The second period saw a more pluralist politics defined by four party competition whereby Labour's vote declined slightly, but its main competitor switched between the Conservatives and SNP; Labour's lead widening over the former to 15.0 per cent and an impressive 20.1 per cent over the latter.[3]

Table 1.1:
Scottish and English Labour voting performance 1945-2001

	1945	1950	1951	1955	1959	1964	1966	1970
Scotland	47.6	46.2	47.9	46.7	46.7	48.7	49.9	44.5
England	48.5	46.2	48.8	46.8	43.6	43.5	48.0	43.4

	1974(1)	1974(2)	1979	1983	1987	1992	1997	2001
Scotland	36.6	36.3	41.5	35.1	42.4	39.0	45.6	43.2
England	37.6	40.1	36.7	26.9	29.5	34.0	43.5	41.4

Source: Kellas, *The Scottish Political System*, 4th edn. 1989; Hassan and Lynch, *The Almanac of Scottish Politics*; House of Commons Research Paper 01/54

Scottish Labour's support in 1997 (45.6 per cent) was higher than at any election since 1966 and lower than at every election in 1945-70 bar one (1970); its 2001 vote (43.2 per cent) was lower than any of these. However, due to the distortions of the first-past-the-post electoral system, Labour returned a record number of MPs in 1997 (56) and 2001 (55).[4] Scottish Labour's level of support has in recent years on several occasions been significantly higher than the party's vote in England overall. This rose to its highest gap in the 1987 election (13.9 per cent), before slowly falling at each subsequent election reaching a mere 1.8 per cent in 2001 – the smallest gap between Labour in Scotland and England since 1974. It is not so much Labour's strength that has allowed it in recent years to increasingly dominate Scottish politics; it is more a question of Conservative weakness and decline, and a growing gap between their vote in Scotland and in England.

Over the post-war period, Labour in Scotland has secured higher levels of support than in England in ten out of sixteen elections (see Table 1.1.). In only five elections did Labour in England win higher support and in one it was the same (1950). This masks differences between the two eras. During 1945-70, Labour won across England an average 46.1 per cent – only 1.2 per cent less than the Scottish party; but over the period 1974-2001 the English average was 36.2 per cent – 3.8 per cent lower than the Scottish party. The Scottish party seems to have managed better the shift during the post-war period to a multi-party system.

However, the Scottish party's electoral dominance of Scotland is not as strong as it first seems. The party has never won a majority of the popular vote – something the Scottish Tories did in 1955 and the Liberals managed for most of the nineteenth century. The Welsh Labour Party, in comparison, has won over 50 per cent of the vote in eight out of the sixteen post-war elections.[5] Although the party made an electoral break-through in the 'Red Clydeside' contest of 1922, it was not until the 1959 election that it achieved a lead over the Conservatives in seats, and not till 1964 in votes. Since the decline of the Conservatives, Labour has elected MPs and MSPs across a whole swathe of urban, industrial and post-industrial Scotland, with little electoral competition – the SNP too seems unable to win in Labour areas. Other parts of Scotland – the Highlands and Islands, North East Scotland and Scottish Borders – are more impervious to Labour's appeal and more open to the SNP and Lib Dems.

Scottish Labour's heartlands are clustered in the Central Belt, and in particular in the West of Scotland. This latter area shapes the party's politics: Labour's dominance and lack of serious opposition produces a more majoritarian and traditional form of labourism. Other areas such as Aberdeen and Edinburgh, where the party has faced more competition and serious challenge, have produced a less traditional politics. One indication of this is that the 'new left' currents of the Labour Co-ordinating Committee and Scottish Labour Action have tended to come from outside the West of Scotland – from Edinburgh, Stirling and outside the Central Belt. Glasgow and its surrounding areas have contributed relatively little to this reformist agenda.

Scottish Labour's dominance does not necessarily come from its levels of electoral support. When we examine Scottish Labour's levels of representation (see Table 1.2) we can note a discrepancy between Scottish Labour's popular support and its representation. The Westminster election saw Scottish Labour win over three-quarters of Scotland's representation while receiving just over four-tenths of the vote. The party also gains a benefit from the local government electoral system, although this was smaller in the 1999 elections than previously. At the two levels at which proportional representation has been intro-duced Scottish Labour receives levels of representation much closer to its popular support, although in both it gains sizeable bonuses. In the Scottish Parliament this is because Labour is so dominant in the 73 FPTP seats that it is impossible to rectify the imbalance in a 129 seat Parliament.

Table 1.2:
Scottish Labour Representation at different levels of government

	% Votes	Seats	% Seats	% Lab over-rep
Local Government (1999)	36.6	545	47.5	+10.9
Scottish Parliament (1999)	38.8	56	43.4	+ 4.6
UK Parliament (2001)	43.2	55	77.5	+34.3
Euro Parliament (1999)	28.7	3	37.5	+ 8.8

PARTY IDENTITY AND ORGANISATION

Origins
The Scottish Labour Party has a distinctive history, going back to Keir Hardie's Scottish Labour Party of 1888, which wound up the year after the establishment of the ILP in 1893.[6] A separate Scottish Workers Parliamentary Committee was formed months before the LRC (the fore-runner of the modern Labour Party) began in 1900;[7] the Scottish Committee then ceased in 1909, leaving behind no structures for devel-oping a Scottish agenda, and in 1915 the Scottish Advisory Council was set up – a body subordinate to the British party.[8] This became known as the Scottish Council of the Labour Party – and is how the party was known until 1994. The 1918 party constitution formalised the Scottish party's 'regional' status, and established a centralised party structure in which trade union interests predominated.

On one level the Scottish Labour Party had been nationalised and incorporated into the British party – a highly centralised, formalised structure which allowed for little differentiation. However, on a more informal level, the Scottish party retained the discretion and freedom to invoke a distinctly Scottish agenda, symbols and language. This implicit understanding between Scottish and British Labour was to sustain itself for most of the twentieth century.

Doctrine and ethos of Scottish Labour

The distinction between formal and informal structures has a wider significance in Labour than in other parties; in the Labour Party beliefs coalesce into a sense of 'doctrine and ethos'.[9] It is perhaps easier to define the meaning of doctrine than of ethos. They could be defined as follows:

> Doctrines are what people usually have in mind when they talk of the ideology of the party; they can be coherent statements of a position; they can lead to policies. Labour's doctrines commonly do, and these policies are then recorded in the Reports of the Labour Party Conferences. They can be accepted, rejected, enacted into law, contemptuously ignored, but they are always explicit. An ethos is not so hard and fast nor so easy to describe. By the ethos of the party I have in mind what an earlier age might have called the spirit of the party; its traditions and habits, its feel. The ethos is not explicit, it is not laid down in the rules …[10]

Scottish Labour's doctrine and ethos have allowed the party to differentiate itself from British Labour.[11] Its doctrine has traditionally been shaped by a left view, with Scottish Labour Annual Conferences often taking positions significantly to the left of the British party. However, these have often been on issues of emotional symbolism, rather than practical policy. The party's ethos operates on two different levels. First, it has invoked 'the radical heritage' of the Scottish Liberal Party of the nineteenth century, including disestablishment, temperance, land reform and home rule.[12] Second, while in policy terms the party has acted in a conservative way, particularly in local government, in terms of culture and values the Scottish party has prided itself on its radicalism and maintenance of labour movement traditions. This can be seen in the way Scottish Labour's electoral success in the 1980s was presented as a validation of the party compared to the deficiencies of English Labour, or the suspicious attitude many had to the creation of New Labour, seeing it as superfluous in Scotland.

Autonomy and policy-making

Historically, Scottish Labour has had differing degrees of autonomy: beginning as the separate Scottish Labour Party, becoming the Scottish Council for most of its history, before changing its name in 1994 to the

Scottish Labour Party (the name of Keir Hardie's party of 1888 and Jim Sillars' of 1976). From the 1918 Labour Party constitution, the Scottish party was seen as a 'regional' party – the equivalent of the English North East – important to Labour in delivering MPs to Westminster, and with some degree of differentiation, but, formally speaking, with little autonomy over policy, finances and party bureaucracy.

Scottish Annual Conference for most of the post-war period was relatively anodyne, dominated by self-important local council dignitaries. Party conference was restricted in the subjects it could debate, concentrating on the economy, housing and education. This eventually changed; in 1968 a resolution was passed abolishing the veto on non-Scottish subjects, and in 1972 the constitutional rule change was passed bringing this into effect.[13] In the next two decades Scottish Conference was to be transformed, as some of the most intractable problems on the planet were debated, from poll tax non-payment to Palestine, from the autonomy of the Scottish party to fighting apartheid.

In the 1980s Scottish Conference became a crucial site in the battle for greater autonomy for the party, spearheaded by the Scottish Labour Action pressure group. After Labour's third election defeat in 1987, SLA advanced debates on party autonomy, 'the dual mandate' and poll tax non-payment – debates that Donald Dewar would have been happy avoiding.[14] SLA also pioneered creative thinking on a Scottish Parliament, leading Labour debates on electoral reform and gender representation. It thus helped to develop a climate where new ideas could be debated, but it did not succeed in its core aims: calls for party autonomy were always defeated by the leadership, or through remitting back. Thus, Labour came to power in 1997 committed to devolution in government, but with a centralist party structure.

The Scottish party's policy-making processes have undergone radical change with the advent of the Scottish Policy Forum in 1998, as a result of the 'Partnership into Power' consultation. The Forum is made up of 88 delegates and ex-officios from CLPs, trade unions and local authorities, and MPs, MSPs and MEPs, who meet several times a year. According to Lesley Quinn, Scottish Labour Secretary: 'The SPF produces detailed policy reports that are discussed, debated and voted upon at Scottish Conference. These reports replace the composites that were previously debated.'[15]

The Forum develops policy from a two-year rolling programme with policy commissions; the first were on crime, justice and legal affairs, education, enterprise and lifelong learning, and social inclusion. Quinn emphasises that these changes have not altered where power lies: 'the Scottish Labour Party annual conference remains the sovereign policy-making body within the Labour Party for the Scottish

Parliament manifesto. The SPF submits reports and policy recommendations, but party conference decides which policies go into the manifesto.'[16]

However, Quinn's comments disguise the extent to which policy-making has changed. The Policy Forum is widely seen by party members as a top-down process, involving greater centralisation and the party leadership managing relations with the party. With the advent of the Scottish Parliament, these processes have become ministerially focused and influenced, with ministers, advisers and parliamentary researchers becoming the key shapers of documents and debates at the Forum.

This has altered the role of conference. Reports from the Policy Forum now dominate conference, and the right of CLPs to submit resolutions outwith this process is restricted: resolutions in an area of a policy commission cannot be separately submitted, but have to be directed to the relevant policy commission. Scottish conference is now restricted to 'devolved matters, matters of shared responsibility, our work in the European Parliament and local government',[17] plus internal issues. Conference has become even more stage managed, with opportunities for genuine debate carefully controlled, and focused on ministerial debates. A study of the 2001 conference showed that 40 per cent of conference speakers were 'guests', rather than 'delegates': ministers, MPs and MSPs. It may turn out to be the case that the 1998 Scottish conference, which criticised the Labour government's welfare reforms as 'morally bankrupt', was the last example of old-fashioned Labour policy-making.

Membership
The Scottish party has traditionally been characterised by a relatively smaller party membership than the British party. And while the advent of New Labour produced a 59 per cent increase in GB party membership – from 264,000 in 1994 to 420,000 in 1997, Scottish party membership rose from 19,321 in 1993 to 30,371 in 1997 – a rise of 57 per cent.[18] But since the election of a UK Labour government, Labour's membership figures overall have started to slide and then terminally decline; GB membership fell from 420,000 to 259,000 – possibly falling as low as 229,000 (falls of 38 per cent and 45 per cent respectively).[19] Scottish party membership, on the other hand, after showing a similar rise has not experienced a similar fall, tapering off to 21,175 – a fall of 30 per cent.[20] Scottish constituency parties have traditionally been smaller than their GB counterparts, in part reflecting the smaller electorates in each constituency. But in the last four years the average British CLP has fallen from 655 to 357 members, whereas

Scottish CLPs have experienced a more measured decline from 422 to 294.[21]

We can only speculate at why British and Scottish membership has differentiated in the last few years. Both experienced a similar influx of new members around the electoral honeymoon of New Labour between 1994-97, but one would have to be sceptical about whether new recruits were joining for the same reasons north and south of the border. Across Britain, most of New Labour's new members contained a high percentage of Blairite recruits, who were fairly apolitical – attracted by the new shine of New Labour – and were inactive as local members.[22] Scottish members would have been joining in the context of wider cultural and national factors about New Labour and the constitutional question. In addition to the loss of the new members South of the border, British party membership now stands at a post-war low, indicative of the shallowness of New Labour's social base;[23] whereas Scottish membership has remained at a higher level pointing to different factors at work between Labour and its members. However, on another level – qualitatively – Scottish Labour membership seems as disengaged as the party at a GB level, in terms of activist levels, election campaigns and turnout in Scottish Labour Executive elections.

Representation

Scottish Labour is the leading party at every level of Scottish government. In the immediate post-war era, there was a tradition of Scottish constituencies often choosing non-Scots as Labour MPs: John Strachey, Emrys Hughes and Willie Hamilton, for example. However, from the 1950s and 1960s this began to cease, with consequences for the national prominence of Labour MPs. This became the era of the dour ex-councillor loyalist who went to Westminster and disappeared. This was reflected in the dire record of Scots MPs being elected to the Shadow Cabinet. Of the 29 MPs elected to the Shadow Cabinet between 1951-64 only one, Tom Fraser, was a Scottish MP (he represented Hamilton and served as Shadow Secretary of State for Scotland).[24]

The most glaring evidence of the low profile of Scottish MPs can be seen in the record of Glasgow Labour MPs. From the 1950s, the city became more and more Labour-orientated, going from eight Labour and seven Tory MPs to a mere two Tory seats in 1964. Labour MPs were drawn from a very select and narrow elite: male, manual workers, ex-councillors with a track record of a decade or more on the local council. Even by 2001, six of Labour's ten Glasgow MPs were ex-councillors and only one, Ann McKechin, was a woman. In the post-war period, only two Labour MPs from this group, Bruce Millan and

Donald Dewar, were elected to the Shadow Cabinet and served in Labour Cabinets: both were Secretary of State for Scotland,[25] and both were middle-class 'outsiders' to the city's Labour traditions.

This has changed in some respects with the Scottish Parliament. Only one of Glasgow's ten Labour MSPs elected in 1999 had previously been a councillor (Frank McAveety); subsequently Bill Butler, previously of Glasgow City Council, was elected for Glasgow Anniesland in a 2000 by-election. Five of Glasgow's MSPs were women – a revolution compared to previous levels. However, some things remained unchanged in the first two years, with Glasgow Labour MSPs holding very few ministerial posts. Under Donald Dewar, only he and McAveety, as Glasgow MSPs, held ministerial posts, while after Dewar's death, in Henry McLeish's Executive, Margaret Curran, a junior minister, was the only Glasgow MSP holding a post. Jack McConnell has presided over a swing towards Glasgow and the West, with Patricia Ferguson and Mike Watson, both Glasgow MSPs, appointed Executive ministers, while Curran retained her junior post.

Scottish Labour overall has changed much more profoundly than Glasgow and West of Scotland Labour. From the 1970s on Scottish Labour began to select more middle-class, professional candidates, and this was reflected in Shadow Cabinet elections between 1979-97. Of the 46 MPs elected to the Shadow Cabinet in Labour's years in opposition, 8 represented Scottish seats – Gordon Brown, John Smith, Donald Dewar and Robin Cook among them.[26] Thus, in the first Labour Government in eighteen years, six Scots Labour MPs sat in the Cabinet.[27] This signalled the highpoint of the Scottish party's influence on the British party – from a degree of dependency to influence at the centre of decisions; though many commentators have speculated that, with a host of Labour MPs now representing South of England seats, and the pressures of devolution, this will fall.[28]

LABOUR AND DEVOLUTION

Scottish home rule was part of Scottish Labour Party policy from its formation: it was one of Keir Hardie's five points in Mid-Lanark in 1888. Despite this, home rule has always played an uneasy part in Labour's programme; it was a legacy of Gladstonian liberalism, and out of place within the Fabian centralism which influenced Labour as it became a party of government. The problems of the economy and society were to be solved by the strong central state, the powers and expertise of Whitehall mandarins and a politics of regional planning and redistribution. This labourist Unionism grew in strength in the immediate post-war period. Labour's 1951 British Handbook, in a section entitled 'Scottish Devolution', claimed that, 'Scotland has a substantial measure of devolution in the present structure of government'. After outlining the Secretary of State's responsibilities, it continued:

> Scottish Local Government is a complete and separate structure. The Scottish Legal System is separate and distinct from that of England and Wales. Government Departments have senior and responsible Scottish representatives. Nationalised industries, such as coalmining, civil aviation and railways, have each a Scottish advisory or administrative council.[29]

Scottish Labour abandoned devolution in 1957-58, and only came back to it reluctantly in 1974 because of the electoral threat posed by the SNP.[30] Labour developed more distinctive devolution policies in the 1980s and 1990s, partly through the Scottish Constitutional Convention, but it was not until Labour came to power in 1997, and the publishing of the White Paper *Scotland's Parliament*, that Scotland's over-representation at Westminster was tackled.[31] Many commentaries emphasise the difference between Labour in the 1970s and 1990s, but there are similarities. In the 1970s, devolution emerged as a reactive policy in response to the threat of the SNP; whereas in the 1990s devolution was in part driven by Labour's desire to protect its dominance of Scotland. Thus, devolution was shaped in both periods by a conservative impulse to maintain the institutional and political hegemony of Scottish Labour. An important factor that has allowed Scottish Labour to adapt its position on this has been that whatever Labour's actual policy on devolution, it has always remained a central element of the party's ethos. The myths of Scottish Labour have presented its commitment to home rule as an unbroken tradition from Keir Hardie to John Smith, and this has allowed the party to downgrade it, or even oppose it, knowing that it is a part of its culture – similar to Lords reform, foxhunting or land reform.

LABOUR AND MULTI-LAYERED GOVERNANCE

The establishment of the Scottish Parliament has resulted in four layers of elected government: local government, Holyrood, Westminster and the European Union. Examining the terrain of national representatives, Scotland now elects 209 MPs, MSPs and MEPs – 113 of whom are currently Labour; and each Scottish voter now has a choice of seventeen national representatives: one MP, one FPTP MSP, seven list MSPs and eight MEPs (Scotland being one constituency for the Euro elections).

This environment can be viewed as a 'layered cake', where each level

of government has a range of responsibilities, or as a nexus of intercon-
necting relationships known as 'multi-level governance'. Devolution
resulted in Scottish Labour finally devising processes to elect a leader,
which revealed some of the tensions between Holyrood and
Westminster. Donald Dewar was elected Labour's first leader in
September 1998, with a 99.8 per cent vote, and Henry McLeish became
its second, narrowly defeating Jack McConnell in October 2000 by 44
votes to 36.[32] Jack McConnell was its third – elected Scottish Labour
leader with no contested election with 97.3 per cent of a mini-electoral
college.[33] Dewar was elected leader of all Scottish Labour, but McLeish
was elected leader of Scottish Labour in the Scottish Parliament – a
change that happened unnoticed. Thus, when Henry McLeish and
Helen Liddell, Secretary of State for Scotland, toured the country
speaking to party audiences in the 2001 election they spoke as equals –
something which caused surprise amongst those unaware of the previous change. McConnell's election as leader of Scottish Labour in the
Scottish Parliament has been much more widely publicised, as the party
attempts to get the balance right in Holyrood-Westminster relations.

a) Labour Group of MSPs

The Labour Group elected in May 1999 was strikingly different in one
respect from Westminster Scottish Labour – gender balance – with 28
men and 28 women, the result of twinning constituencies.[34] There were
continuities – the high number of ex-councillors: 23 out of 56 had local
government backgrounds (41 per cent) compared to 30 out of 56 at
Westminster. Fifteen former council leaders were elected – ten on the
Labour benches, while another ex-Labour leader, Dennis Canavan, was
elected as an independent. Labour MSPs were the youngest of all the
party groups – averaging 43 years old, as compared to SNP MSPs at 45
and Conservative and Lib Dems at 49: Labour MPs at Westminster
were on average six years older at 49 years.[35] One reason for this was
the large number of thirty-something Labour MSPs, who made up
over one-third of the Labour Group, compared to only 5 per cent of
MPs. A whole host of high profile thirty-somethings entered the
Scottish Executive, challenging previously deeply-ingrained Scottish
Labour notions about serving your time. Another change in the
recruitment patterns could be observed in the shift towards more
middle-class professions, away from working-class backgrounds –
only 2 Labour MSPs as opposed to 14 Westminster MPs came from
manual working-class backgrounds.[36]

Despite the rhetoric of 'new politics' Holyrood developed a top-
down set of processes, aided by the Scottish Executive having several
experienced parliamentarians, while the Labour Group contained a

number of political novices. The early days of the Parliament saw the Labour leadership under Donald Dewar negotiate a coalition agreement with the Lib Dems: this was fully debated and voted on in the Lib Dem Group, which split 13-3 in favour of the deal; Labour on the other hand had a general debate about coalition, but none on the specific deal and no vote: John McAllion, a long-standing supporter of PR, opposed entering a coalition.[37]

The politics of the Labour Group have since developed into a model that in some ways is less consultative than Westminster. Scottish Executive Ministers decide and determine policy, often with little discussion with Labour MSPs. There are still no formal mechanisms for Executive-MSP consultation despite the small numbers involved. Suggestions by Labour MSPs of setting up a 1922 backbench committee have been resisted by ministers. Despite this, an informal culture of being able to access and influence ministers has arisen, which has worked as a group of senior and influential backbench MSPs has emerged.

Divisions and tensions within the Labour Group were illustrated by the election process to choose a successor to Donald Dewar in October 2000 as Scottish Labour leader. After the Scottish party was nearly forced into having no contest at all, the Scottish Labour Group and Scottish Labour Executive combined in a mini-electoral college to narrowly elect Henry McLeish against Jack McConnell. This revealed that the Scottish party wished to retain some degree of influence over its affairs. It also indicated the complex political characteristics of the Labour Group at Holyrood. There are no simple left-right divisions, and the Campaign for Socialism declined to put up a candidate, knowing they would win a derisory vote, but there were other clear divisions: McLeish stood for a Labour establishment continuity agenda, while McConnell embraced a pro-autonomy, modernising agenda.

The election of Jack McConnell with no open contest in November 2001 revealed even more significant faultlines. First, Wendy Alexander put herself forward as the candidate of the 'Brownites' with the open support and patronage of Gordon Brown, only to withdraw before her campaign became public. This was because UK party chairman Charles Clarke intervened to ensure that the election would be held by OMOV. This reduced the ability of Gordon Brown and his allies to deliver trade union votes for their favoured candidate. No other 'Brownite' candidates put themselves forward; and nor did John McAllion or Malcolm Chisholm, respectively from the Campaign for Socialism and the soft left, both unable to get the seven MSP nominations.[38]

The party thus missed a historic opportunity to begin the process of democratising itself and holding a wider debate about the role and direction of the Labour-led Scottish Executive. McConnell's 33 Labour nominations out of Labour's 55 MSPs told an interesting picture of his support:[39] 7 out of Glasgow's 10 MSPs nominated him, and the three who did not (Curran, Lamont and McNeill) were all pro-feminist left MSPs, whereas only one of Edinburgh's five MSPs supported him. There was a sizeable majority of backbenchers for McConnell, but a mere 4 out of 33 nominations from existing ministers, all junior (Brankin, Gray, Peacock, Allan Watson). Describing McConnell's subsequent decisions on the Executive as the 'Night of the Long Knives' – the revenge of a faction – had some truth: the eight new ministers were all McConnell supporters, and the seven ministers sacked were all, with one exception, not allies.

b) Scottish Executive

The first Scottish Executive comprised nine Labour Ministers and two Lib Dem Ministers, the same balance reflected at a junior ministerial level. It contained a mixture of experienced politicians with a Westminster, or in some cases local government, background and a group with no experience of elected politics. This led to tensions, particularly in relation to the debate over abolishing Section 28/Clause 2a. 'The Big Mac' Group, comprising Henry McLeish, a Westminster MP since 1987, Jack McConnell, ex-leader of Stirling Council, and Tom McCabe, ex-leader of South Lanarkshire Council, urged compromise with the 'Keep the Clausers', against Wendy Alexander and Susan Deacon, neither of whom had held elected office. This was not an Old versus New Labour divide, but about different kinds of politics and working within the West of Scotland Labour culture.

The number of thirty-something ministers in the Scottish Executive from Labour reflected the promise the party had in the 1980s – Alexander, Boyack, Deacon, McConnell and, after McLeish became First Minister, Baillie and MacKay. The impact of so many high profile Labour women ministers was significant in a party that had for so long been a male bastion. The average age of the Labour part of the Executive reflected the generational sea-change in the party; it fell from an average of 42 years for Labour ministers (excluding the First Minister and Lord Advocate) in Dewar's Cabinet, to 40 under Henry McLeish. McConnell's dramatic reshuffle, whereby a host of thirty-somethings were sacked and Malcolm Chisholm and Mike Watson (both 52 years) promoted, raised the average Labour age to 44. It remains to be seen whether the 'disappeared' thirty-somethings, such as Baillie, Deacon and Mackay, have seen their political careers abruptly ended, or if they can at some point come back.

The Scottish Executive's coalition arrangements were often fraught, with Labour ministers, special advisers and MSPs often acting as a Labour administration, rather than the Labour-Lib Dem Partnership coalition: witness Henry McLeish's off the cuff remarks about 'a coalition of one party'. It was a learning curve for both Labour and Lib Dems, despite a decade of previous co-operation in the Convention; it was different for Labour, who had previously been used to governing on its own, and some saw it as 'having to give up some power', whereas the Lib Dems were gaining influence. On a number of issues, such as tuition fees and care for the elderly, Labour ministers had to be reminded this was a coalition of two parties. There were signs of tension between the two parties when, for example, the Executive lost a vote on a fishing tie-up scheme, due to Lib Dem defections and Labour absences. However, considering the culture shock involved in setting up a Scottish Executive, and Labour moving from a one-party culture to sharing power with another, the working of the coalition should be viewed as a qualified success.

c) Labour MPs
Westminster pre-devolution was the pinnacle of the Scottish Labour establishment, and the main avenue for career advancement and leadership. In post-war times, Scottish Labour has historically elected more and more MPs to Westminster, electing a high-point of 50 in 1987 and 56 in 1997. The recruitment patterns of Scottish Labour have changed as well to reflect this broader appeal.

The Scottish party has, at various times when Labour has been thrown back into its heartlands, formed the backbone of the party. In 1987 Labour's 50 MPs represented 26 per cent of the PLP – a post-war high, whereas the 56 of 1997 represented half that percentage – 13 per cent – in a PLP exactly twice the size (119 versus 209).

Devolution has raised all kinds of issues, such as how Labour MPs and MSPs work together to deal with constituency enquiries. Tensions and conflicts have arisen about the political direction of Labour in Holyrood and Westminster, most obviously manifest in Westminster MPs' concern about the quality of Holyrood Labour MSPs. This articulated itself in the Clause 28 debate, when Labour MPs such as Michael Connarty were uneasy that the electorate would vote in Westminster elections on the record of Labour MSPs at Holyrood.[40]

Westminster's role in Scottish politics will change significantly with the 2005 Boundary Commission, which will reduce the number of Scottish seats to 59 – proportionately the same as the rest of the UK. This change, written into the Scotland Act 1998, will cause difficulties for Labour, the dominant party in Scotland, with several sitting Central Belt MPs having to compete for a smaller number of Labour seats.[41]

d) Local government

Local government has been a key mechanism by which Labour has exercised influence over large parts of Scottish life. As with Westminster, Labour has been more and more successful in the post-war period, expanding its local council base, and securing new councils such as Edinburgh and Stirling which once had strong Tory traditions. During the 1979-97 period of Tory rule, Labour local councils provided an important part of the party's sense of resistance. Lothian Region attempted one of the rare instances of a hard left strategy of non-compliance with the Tory Government, in 1981-82;[42] while Strathclyde Region – then the largest authority in Western Europe – bypassed Westminster and engaged with the European Union, holding a referendum against water privatisation in 1993.[43] It was not surprising that in 1996 the Tory Government abolished the regional tier of Scottish local government.

Labour's dominance in terms of councillors is not reflected in the popular vote, with the party being a beneficiary of the FPTP electoral system. For example, in 1999 only three authorities were elected with over 50 per cent Labour vote: North Lanarkshire (55.23 per cent), South Lanarkshire (50.02 per cent), West Dunbartonshire (52.17 per cent). Twelve other authorities elected Labour majorities with less than half the popular vote – the most distortive being Glasgow, where on 49.6 per cent the party won 74 out of 79 seats. There are also several parts of Scotland where Labour's appeal does not extend. Leaving Orkney and Shetland aside, where Labour did not stand, there are two councils where the party polled under 10 per cent: Aberdeenshire (5.03 per cent) and Borders (5.35 per cent); a further six councils see Labour with under 20 per cent: Angus (19.30 per cent), Argyll and Bute (10.33 per cent), Dumfries and Galloway (17.49 per cent), Highland (15.40 per cent), Perthshire and Kinross (16.08 per cent) and Western Isles (13.94 per cent).[44] Labour areas of weakness are, without exception, rural councils, but some return Labour representatives at Holyrood and Westminster: Dumfries and Western Isles, for example.

The influence and profile of local government has suffered since devolution, as has the quality of Labour councillors and leaders, with a number of council leaders becoming Labour MSPs. Labour local council leaders have become more faceless, bureaucratic party politicians – Charlie Gordon in Glasgow and Donald Anderson in Edinburgh are examples. Glasgow, in particular, has faced a number of related political problems in funding and providing services in one of the most deprived areas in Western Europe. Sadly, the council's reaction under Gordon was a kind of last gasp labourism, which involved leaving COSLA. Change is coming in the form of the Kerley Committee proposals for PR in local government,[45] but they will not begin to touch the multi-dimensional political and socio-economic problems in Labour's West of Scotland heartlands, of which Glasgow is merely the most pronounced.

e) The European Union

The European Union has slowly grown over the last twenty years, playing a larger role in Scottish and UK politics. During the Tory years in Scotland, a whole host of institutional players, ranging from the Scottish Office to COSLA and the STUC, developed a European agenda and influence. European membership came increasingly to be seen in Scotland in the late 1980s and 1990s as a way of bypassing Westminster, and securing additional monies via EU structural funds and the CAP. At the same time, the establishment of Scotland Europa aimed to increase influence at the heart the EU, while the European Committee of the Regions was viewed as one mechanism through which social democratic Scotland could make itself heard and emphasise the minority status of the Tories.

Many of these European positives are now more open to question, with EU monies in jeopardy after the Central and Eastern European nations join. Devolution poses new questions about Scotland's influence in the EU, and who most effectively speaks for Scotland – the Scottish Executive or UK government, in relation to the role of ministers in the Council of Ministers.

Most of these issues appear academic while Labour is in office at Holyrood and Westminster, but will become more acute if the SNP run a devolved administration. Scottish Labour has also become less popular in Euro elections. In 1994 it was Scotland's leading party in Europe, winning six of the eight Euro seats on 42.5 per cent of the vote; however in 1999, with a new PR system, Labour saw its MEPs halved to three and its vote tumble to 28.7 per cent – the worst national performance by Labour in post-war times – a signal of the willingness of Labour's core vote to stay at home when not motivated, and perhaps, a sign of future trouble.

SCOTTISH NEW LABOUR: A NEW PARTY OR A CONTRADICTION?

The creation of New Labour challenged many assumptions in Scottish Labour. John McAllion articulated this: 'Old Labour was never unelectable in Scotland. Even at the high tide of Thatcherism in 1983, Michael

Foot's Labour won a majority of seats in Scotland'.[46] A belief in traditional social democracy and its electoral appeal has remained in
Scotland. New Labour thus caused some difficulties with Labour's
voters, as System Three focus groups pre-1997 made clear; they
showed that uncommitted voters perceived Labour and the Tories as
too similar, with Blair too middle-class and moving right, while a sense
of loss was still felt for John Smith: 'Tony Blair is perceived to be
English, and his identity or image is associated with that of a south-
erner.' [47]

The Scottish Parliament elections raised a number of issues about
New Labour in Scotland. First, the pre-candidate selection process saw
the party institute a central system of approval to get on a panel. This
caused controversy when Dennis Canavan and two other left-wing
MPs were prevented from getting on the panel, prompting allegations
of Blairite 'control freakery'.[48] Not surprisingly, widespread unease
was evident in the party, even in those successful in the process; 27 per
cent of candidates thought the panel process was undemocratic, as did
24 per cent of panel non-candidates; while three quarters of both felt
the list candidate selection was undemocratic; and whereas only 22 per
cent of candidates thought the leadership had too much influence on
constituency selection, this rose to 74 per cent on list selection.[49]

Second, the 1999 election saw a centralist attempt to brand the party
as 'Scottish New Labour', with corporate colours and key phrases: all
recognised elements in Mandelsonian marketing. However, at the level
of local candidates another election campaign was fought, which
avoided the agenda, symbols and priorities of New Labour. A survey
of 52 of Labour's 73 constituency candidates found that 17 per cent
(n=9) used the phrase 'New Labour' and 10 per cent (n=5) 'Scottish
New Labour' in their election materials, while 86 per cent (n=45) used
the more traditional 'Labour' and 58 per cent (n=30) 'Scottish
Labour'.[50] Thus, most local Labour candidates avoided the language
and codes of New Labour when the party was trying to enforce a standard modernising message; whether this was a deliberate attempt to
resist Blairite modernisation or merely local parties retaining a historic
degree of discretion against the centre can only be guessed at, but it still
reveals significant centre-regional tensions in Labour's appeal.

TOMORROW'S LABOUR
Scottish Labour is a unique and distinctive party in Scottish politics
and within the British Labour Party. It is differentiated by a number of
factors: historical, cultural and political, and while, formally, its autonomy has often been restricted, informally it has developed its own
Scottish identity. It is not surprising that Scottish Labour sees itself as

the best advocate and champion of Scottish interests north and south of the border, and has called itself 'the national party of Scotland'. However, Scottish Labour also sees itself as a unionist party, and a defender of a Union which is flexible and responsive to Scotland. Managing these sometimes opposing tendencies has often been a difficult task. It has also been a party shaped by the politics and culture of labourism, of working-class politics, trade unionism and a defensive, insular approach; this still shapes the Scottish party to this day, albeit less than it used to.

This is a party of many paradoxes. First, it has long prided itself on its radical traditions and romantic view of itself, from its earliest leader Keir Hardie, but it has increasingly become a conservative party, and the political establishment. Second, during the 18 years of opposition it became more and more Scotland's leading party, controlling every level of Scottish government with the exception of the Scottish Office. It became, in effect, a quasi-establishment party, whereby the lines were blurred between the state and civil society. In this it reflected what happens in one-party dominant systems the world over, where the dominant party's values and priorities become those of the state and civil service, and the party becomes bureaucratised and atrophied: a transmission belt more for career politicians than ideologues. This has happened to the PRI in Mexico, LDP in Japan, DC in Italy and SAP in Sweden.

The third paradox is that Scottish devolution has been advanced by many in Scottish Labour in order to maintain its leading role, but the processes thereby unleashed contain within them the potential of sweeping away and dismantling this one party dominant model of politics. Scottish Labour politicians seem to be unaware that all one-party dominant systems end at some point, as they are the creation of certain historic, social and economic events. All the dominant-party models listed above came to an end at some point. It is clear that the old Scottish Labour model, founded on the primacy of one party and labourist culture, has been severely weakened and is under threat from different directions.

Scottish Labour will have to confront these paradoxes as the Scottish political system evolves over the next decade from an asymmetrical party system to a more pluralist, multi-party politics. This will witness the dilution of an institutionally focused labourist culture and the development of a more open, democratic politics. Labour's dominance as a quasi-establishment party where its values and ethos have shaped state and civil society will be weakened, allowing independence between these terrains of Scottish public life and party. Over the next decade it is highly likely in the Scottish Parliament that the anti-Labour majority will coalesce at some point around the SNP and form an administration. This could take many forms, with the SNP on its own challenging Labour's hegemony and trying to run a single party, probably minority administration, or in formal or informal alliance with the Lib Dems, or by trying to strike a deal with an expanded Scottish Socialist-Scottish Green group. New alliances and understandings will emerge, but the arrival of an SNP administration would transform Scottish politics, giving the Nationalists a serious opportunity to build a strategy for independence and prove its credibility as a governing party. Scottish Labour would find this a unique opportunity and challenge – being in opposition in a way it has not been for a long time.

New relationships are developing across the United Kingdom as a result of devolution. One of the central pillars of the British constitution has been the British Labour Party, and devolution will pose new questions about the priorities between Scottish Labour as the national party of Scotland and a centralising force in the United Kingdom. Gordon Brown wrote about these difficulties describing Scottish Labour in the 1920s:

> No theorist attempted in sufficient depth to reconcile the conflicting aspirations for home rule and a British socialist advance. In particular, no-one was able to show how capturing power in Britain and legislating for minimum levels of welfare, for example, could be combined with a policy of devolution for Scotland.[51]

The Scottish Labour Party had a relatively comfortable period during UK Labour's first term. Devolution was achieved, the Conservatives had been in disarray since the fall of Thatcher, and economic prosperity provided falling unemployment and increasing public expenditure. Scottish Labour was able to govern without any real governing strategy or sense of statecraft, beyond redistributing the largesse of Gordon Brown's Comprehensive Spending Review. Individual reforming ministers at Holyrood established their reputations, but had little time to think strategically beyond their remits.

The future pattern of Scottish and UK politics is unlikely to be so benign. For all Gordon Brown's rhetoric of ending 'boom and bust', a slowdown in the global economy is widely predicted in the next few years, whilst New Labour's dominance in the UK is unlikely to continue at the levels of popularity of the first term. These factors will affect Scottish Labour; but more crucial will be the changing nature of the Scottish political environment, with a more competitive, possibly fragmented, politics. This could involve the development of a political climate where it becomes more difficult for any party to assemble a governing coalition, particularly if it involved more than two parties, and where the anti-Labour majority in votes and seats at Holyrood may eventually coalesce into a Scottish administration.

How Scottish Labour reacts to the coming to power of a non-Labour administration will be a defining point for the party. Some will want to see it as an affront to their very narrow idea of democracy, but it will provide both a challenge and opportunity to pluralists and radicals in the party. The Scottish party has not lost an election since 1959, whereas the UK party lost four elections from 1979 onward, producing very different internal psychologies. The former has seen a majoritarian, labourist culture validated in places in the party, while the latter has developed a more outward-looking strategy based on the pursuit of 'Middle England'. This is not to argue one is better than the other; there are strengths and weaknesses in both. But the coming decade will see whether Scottish Labour can develop a politics that takes the best from its past, while embarking on a road of renewal and redefinition which does not replicate the failings of the UK New Labour project.

Many thanks to the following people for comments on an earlier draft of this paper: Alice Brown, Gordon Guthrie, Stephen Low, Jim McCormick, Tom Nairn and Lindsay Paterson; thanks also for the time and advice of numerous Labour officials, advisers and elected representatives.

NOTES

1. G. Hassan, 'Blair and the Making of New Scotland', in M. Perryman (ed), The Blair Agenda, London: Lawrence and Wishart 1996, pp170-97; G. Hassan, 'Caledonian Dreaming: The Challenge to Scottish Labour', in A. Coddington and M. Perryman (eds), *The Moderniser's Dilemma: Radical Politics in the Age of Blair*, London: Lawrence and Wishart 1998, pp111-42; G. Hassan, 'A Case Study of Scottish Labour: Devolution and the Politics of Multi-Level Governance', *Political Quarterly*, Vol. 73 No. 2, forth, 2002.

2. On Scottish Labour see: I. Donnachie, C. Harvie and I. S. Wood (eds), *Forward!: Labour Politics in Scotland 1888-1988*, Edinburgh: Polygon 1989. On the Welsh Labour Party see the highly recommended: D. Tanner, C. Williams and D. Hopkins (eds), *The Labour Party in Wales 1900-2000*, Cardiff: University of Wales Press 2000. This combines both historical and contemporary political analysis within one volume.

3. Scottish voting averages for 1945-70 were: Labour 47.3 per cent, Conservatives 43.5 per cent, Liberals 5.0 per cent, SNP 2.8 per cent, Others 1.3 per cent. For the period 1974-2001 they were: Labour 40.0 per

cent, Conservatives 25.0 per cent, SNP 19.9 per cent, Lib Dems 13.9 per cent, Others 1.2 per cent.

4. Labour returned 56 MPs in 1997 and retained all these in 2001, although, technically, the election of Michael Martin as Speaker of the House of Commons and MP for Glasgow Springburn meant that only 55 Labour MPs were actually returned.

5. The Welsh Labour Party has won over 50 per cent of the vote in eight out of sixteen elections since 1945, but its popularity has declined: from 1945-70, it won over half the vote in seven out of eight contexts, whereas from 1974 onwards it has done so only once – 1997.

6. Donnachie et al, op. cit.; .A. McKinlay and R. J. Morris (eds), *The ILP on Clydeside 1893-1922: From Foundation to Disintegration*, Manchester: Manchester University Press 1991.

7. K. Aitken, *The Bairns O' Adam: The Story of the STUC*, Edinburgh: Polygon 1997, p34.

8. M. Keating and D. Bleiman, *Labour and Scottish Nationalism*, London: Macmillan 1979, p56.

9. H. Drucker, *Doctrine and Ethos in the Labour Party*, London: Allen and Unwin 1979.

10. H. Drucker, 'The Influence of the Trade Unions in the Ethos of the Labour Party', in B. Pimlott and C. Cook (eds), *Trade Unions in British Politics: The First 250 Years*, London: Longman 2nd edn. 1991, p244.

11. Hassan, 'Caledonian Dreaming', op. cit., pp113-14.

12. Keating and Bleiman, op. cit., pp27-29.

13. F. Wood, 'Scottish Labour in Government and Opposition 1964-1979', in Donnachie et al, op. cit., pp109-10.

14. J. Mitchell, 'The Evolution of Devolution: Labour's Home Rule Strategy in Opposition', *Government and Opposition*, Autumn 1998, Vol. 33 No. 4, pp479-496.

15. L. Quinn, 'It's conference Jim, but not as we know it', *Scottish Labour Party Conference Guide*, Glasgow: Scottish Labour Party 2000, p4.

16. Ibid, p4.

17. Ibid, p5.

18. Scottish Labour Party, *Annual Report*, Glasgow: Scottish Labour Party 1993; Scottish Labour Party, *Annual Report*, Glasgow: Scottish Labour Party 1997; Labour Party, *Annual Conference Report*, London: Labour Party 1994; Labour Party, *Annual Conference Report*, London: Labour Party 1997.

19. *Tribune*, 29.6.01.

20. *Observer*, 16.12.01.

21. Scottish Labour membership as a proportion of Labour voters fell marginally between 1997 and 2001, from 2.4 per cent to 2.1 per cent. British membership fell significantly over the same period from 3.1 per cent in

1997 to 2.1 per cent in 2001.

22. P. Whiteley and P. Seyd, 'New Labour – New Grass Roots party?', paper to Political Studies Association, April 1998.

23. I. Crewe, 'Elections and Public Opinion', in A. Seldon (ed), *The Blair Effect: The Blair Government 1997-2001*, London: Little Brown 2001, pp67-94.

24. D. Butler and G. Butler, *Twentieth Century Political Facts 1900-2000*, London: Macmillan 2000, p153.

25. M. Keating, 'The Role of the Scottish MP in the Scottish Political System in the UK Political System and in the Relationship Between the Two', unpublished Ph.D., Council for National Academic Awards 1975.

26. Butler and Butler, op. cit., pp154-55.

27. *PMS Parliamentary Companion: United Kingdom and European Union*, July 1997, London: PMS Publications 1997, p1.

28. In Blair's post-election reshuffle after the election of 7.6.01, the number of Scots MPs in the cabinet still stood at five: Gordon Brown, Robin Cook, John Reid, Helen Liddell and Alastair Darling.

29. *Labour Party Handbook: Facts and Figures for Socialists*, London: Labour Party 1951, p340.

30. B. McLean, *Labour and Scottish Home Rule Part One and Two*, Broxburn: Scottish Labour Action n.d. 1990.

31. Scottish Office, *Scotland's Parliament*, Edinburgh: HMSO 1997 Cmnd. 3658, para. 4.5.

32. *Sunday Herald*, 22.10.00; *The Scotsman*, 23.10.00.

33. *Sunday Herald*, 18.11.01.

34. A. Brown, 'Taking Their Place in the New House: Women and the Scottish Parliament', *Scottish Affairs*, Summer 1999, No. 28, pp44-50. The Labour Group had 6 MPs all of whom had 'dual mandates': excluding these, the 50 new MSPs split 28 women, 22 men: an indication of the gender revolution that Labour had undertaken.

35. G. Hassan and C. Warhurst, 'A New Politics?', in G. Hassan and C. Warhurst (eds), *The New Scottish Politics: The First Year of the Scottish Parliament and Beyond*, Edinburgh: The Stationery Office 2000, p4.

36. M. Cavanagh, N. McGarvey and M. Shephard, 'New Scottish Parliament, New Scottish Parliamentarians?', paper to the Political Studies Association, April 2000.

37. M. Watson, *Year Zero: An Inside View of the Scottish Parliament*, Edinburgh: Polygon 2001, pp3-10.

38. *Sunday Herald*, 18.11.01; G. Hassan, 'Social Democracy in a Cold Climate: The Strange Case of Scottish Devolution', *Renewal: The Journal of Labour Politics*, Vol. 10, No. 1, 2002, pp91-8.

39. *The Herald*, 14.11.01. This contains a list of Jack McConnell's 33 Labour MSP nominations from which this analysis is taken.

40. T. Brown, 'Responsibility without Power', *New Statesman*, 12.6.00.
41. *The Scotsman*, 6.2.01. The last Boundary Commission changes saw the kind of problems on a smaller scale Labour will have to encounter – with the Glasgow area seeing a reduction from 11 to 10 seats, and an acrimonious and public contest between Mike Watson and Mohammed Sarwar for the Glasgow Govan seat.
42. P. Crompton, 'The Lothian Affair: A Battle of Principles?', in D. McCrone (ed), *The Scottish Government Yearbook 1983*, Edinburgh: Unit for the Study of Government in Scotland 1983, pp33-48.
43. The water privatisation saw, on a 72 per cent turnout, 97 per cent of voters opposing the government's plans: this was a highly innovative and unusual action by a Labour council and its success took everyone – Labour and Tory – by surprise.
44. G. Hassan and P. Lynch, *The Almanac of Scottish Politics*, London: Politico's Publishing 2001; D. Denver and H. Bochel, 'The Forgotten Elections: The Scottish Council Elections of 1999', *Scottish Affairs*, Winter 2000, No. 30, p122.
45. Kerley Committee, *Report of the Renewing Local Democracy Working Group*, Edinburgh: Scottish Executive 2000.
46. J. McAllion, 'Blair's modernisers want a party of the people. But up here, the people want a party of the left', *The Observer*, 22.3.98.
47. 'The Views of Scottish Floating Voters', System Three unpublished paper, October 1996, p8.
48. G. Hassan and P. Lynch, 'The Changing Politics of Scottish Labour: Culture and Values, Political Strategy and Devolution 1979-1999', paper to the Political Studies Association Annual Conference 1999.
49. J. Bradbury, J. Mitchell, L. Bennie and D. Denver, 'Candidate Selection, Devolution and Modernisation: The Selection of Labour Party Candidates for the 1999 Scottish Parliament and Welsh Assembly Elections', in P. Cowley, D. Denver, A. Russell and L. Harrison (eds), *British Elections and Parties Review*, Vol. 10, London: Frank Cass 2000, pp151-72.
50. M. Shephard, 'Is it Really Devolution?: Scottish Devolution and Blair's Clones', paper to the American Political Science Association, Atlanta, September 1999.
51. G. Brown, 'The Labour Party and Political Change in Scotland 1918-1929: The Politics of Five Elections', unpublished Ph.D., Edinburgh University 1981.

The Scottish National Party after devolution: progress and prospects

NICOLA McEWEN

Scottish politics has undergone dramatic changes since the 1997 general election, and in particular, since the establishment of the Scottish Parliament in 1999. The changes in the Scottish National Party have been no less dramatic. The party has gone from being a small party on the fringes of the Westminster political debate to the official opposition in the Scottish Parliament and the alternative party of Scottish government. The party has also witnessed significant internal transformation provoked by the resignation of Alex Salmond as leader and the subsequent election of John Swinney as his successor.

This chapter will examine the SNP's progress since the 1997 general election and consider its prospects in the coming years. In reflecting on the party's progress and development, the discussion focuses upon three areas. Firstly, it examines the recent electoral performance of the SNP in elections to Westminster and to the Scottish Parliament. Secondly, it considers the nature of the party in light of the leadership election of September 2000, and questions the extent to which the new leadership signifies a period of continuity or change. Thirdly, it examines the role of the SNP in the home rule movement and argues that devolution has strengthened the SNP and engendered new challenges that the party must address.

Towards the end of the chapter, consideration is given to the challenges facing the SNP in advance of the 2003 Scottish Parliament election and beyond. A number of obstacles must be overcome if the SNP is to progress from being a party of opposition to a party of government. The SNP competes in elections not only for the opportunity to serve. The objective of Scottish independence is its *raison d'être* and the party is committed to holding a referendum on independence if elected to government. The chapter considers the difficulties that might be faced in such a referendum, and proposes that a multi-option referendum may be a better mechanism to ascertain the views of the Scottish electorate and achieve progress in the development of the Scottish Parliament.

ELECTORAL PERFORMANCE

Although founded in 1934,[1] the SNP did not become an electoral force until the late 1960s, overturning one of Labour's largest Scottish majorities in the Hamilton by-election of 1967, and winning its first parliamentary seat in a general election in 1970.[2] The breakthrough came in the two general elections of 1974. In February, the SNP won 7 seats on 21.9 per cent of the vote. This was surpassed in the October election eight months later, when the party won 11 seats and 30.4 per cent of the Scottish vote, its best performance to date (see Table 2.1).

Most of these gains were lost in the subsequent general election, following a difficult period in a Parliament dominated by debates over devolution which led ultimately to the failure of the 1979 devolution referendum and the defeat of the Labour government soon after.[3] For the SNP, the Thatcher years were dominated, first by a period of bitter internal division and disillusionment, and later by a period of consolidation and recovery. By the end of the Thatcher decade, the SNP had re-established itself as a significant voice in Scottish politics.[4] It exploited Scottish antipathy to Conservative government and, in capitalising on the repeated failure of the Labour Party to win in England, sought to challenge Labour's dominance of Scottish politics. Although gains were made in its share of the popular vote, the first-past-the-post electoral system ensured that this was never enough to make a breakthrough in parliamentary representation. In 1992, for example, the SNP's share of the vote jumped from 14 per cent to 21.5 per cent while its share of seats remained static, winning only 3 of Scotland's 72 seats, i.e. 4.2 per cent of Scottish seats. This disparity between the popular vote and constituency representation, evident in Table 2.1, contributed to reinforcing the view that the SNP remained a minority party on the fringes of electoral politics.

Table 2.1: SNP Electoral Performance at Westminster 1945-2001

	Candidates	No. of Votes	% of Votes	Seats
1945	8	30, 595	1.2	-
1950	3	9,708	0.4	-
1951	2	7,299	0.3	-
1955	2	12,112	0.5	-
1959	5	21,738	0.8	-

1964	15	64,044	2.4	-
1966	23	128,474	5.0	-
1970	65	306,802	11.4	1
1974 (F)	70	633,180	21.9	7
1974 (O)	71	839,617	30.4	11
1979	71	504,259	17.3	2
1983	72	331,975	11.8	2
1987	72	416,873	11.0	3
1992	72	629,564	21.5	3
1997	72	622,260	22.1	6
2001	72	464,305	20.1	5

Source: Kellas, *The Scottish Political System*, 4th edn. 1989; Hassan and Lynch, *The Almanac of Scottish Politics*, 2001; House of Commons Research Paper 01/54.

Modest gains were made in the 1997 general election. The party secured only a 0.6 per cent increase in its share of the vote but doubled its parliamentary representation from the three seats won in 1992, and for the first time retained a seat won in a by-election (the Perth and Kinross by-election of 1995, won by Roseanna Cunningham).

These were small but significant gains on a night that belonged to the Labour Party. Two factors bear mention. Firstly, in securing Tayside North and Galloway and Upper Nithsdale, and in retaining the Perth and Kinross seat, the SNP benefited from the anti-Conservative coalition that wiped out that party's parliamentary representation in Scotland. Secondly, the 1997 election established the SNP as the second party in Scotland in terms of the popular vote, although the Liberal Democrats had more Scottish MPs.[5]

Whereas general elections tend to be dominated by the battle for UK government between Labour and the Conservatives, the first election to the Scottish Parliament in 1999 centred upon the contest for power in Scotland. The SNP were not expected to win the election, but they represented the main alternative to a Labour-led Executive. As such, the party enjoyed more exposure and endured more scrutiny than in any previous election. It was ill-prepared for both. The campaign was dominated by two problematic issues of the SNP's own making. Salmond's criticism of the NATO bombing campaign in Serbia as 'unpardonable folly' and of 'dubious legality' proved deeply damaging. Survey evidence suggested that his intervention had little added effect on the already evident decline in the SNP's support,[6] but the issue dominated press conferences and coverage and made it much more difficult for the party to convey its message. The second problematic area was the 'Penny for Scotland', the pledge to use the

Parliament's taxation powers to reverse the one penny cut in the basic rate of income tax announced in Gordon Brown's budget in March 1999.

Table 2.2: Attitudes to Taxation and Spending by Party List Vote (per cent)

	SNP	Labour	Lib Dem	Cons	SSP	Green	Didn't vote	All
Cut tax & spend	2.5	1.4	0.7	3.4	–	–	4.6	**2.6**
Keep same levels	31.4	37.0	34.6	56.4	27.3	23.4	40.4	**38.2**
Increase	63.0	58.1	62.9	38.4	72.7	76.6	48.1	**55.3**
Dk/na/none of these	3.1	3.5	1.8	1.9	–	–	6.9	**3.9**
Total (N)	297	364	163	153	13	25	408	**1482**

Source: Scottish Parliament Election Survey, 1999

As Table 2.2 indicates, a clear majority of respondents to the 1999 Scottish Parliament election survey were inclined to support an increase in taxation where it implied an increase in social expenditure, and were least favourable to taxation cuts which would have a knock-on effect on the delivery of social services. Only Conservative voters preferred to maintain current levels of taxation and spending, rather than support an increase in both. The difficulty for the SNP was that Brown's budget promised a tax cut *and* increased social expenditure. Moreover, it forced the SNP to make what appeared to be a hasty policy U-turn just two months before the election. As one commentator noted, 'the weakness of the SNP strategy was forced on them by the speed of the decision', creating uncertainty and leaving the party vulnerable to charges of economic incompetence.[7] In addition, by seeking to present itself as an alternative Scottish government, the focus of the SNP campaign was on issues devolved to the Scottish Parliament, with the independence issue relegated to the sidelines. It was thus ill-equipped to defend its platform of independence in the face of fierce and highly effective Labour attacks on the costs and consequences of 'divorce' from the rest of the United Kingdom. In spite of these difficulties, the Scottish Parliament election marked a significant step for the SNP. Aided by the system of proportional representation, the Additional Member System, the party secured 35 seats, and a 28.7 per cent and 27.3 per cent share of the constituency and regional list vote, respectively. Only 7 of its 35 seats were constituency victories; the rest were drawn from regional party lists. Notably, the SNP's share of the party vote from which list MSP allocations are drawn was slightly lower than its share of the constituency vote. This suggests that, whereas Labour voters were evidently willing to switch their allegiance in the second vote, it was the smaller parties and not the SNP that stood to benefit.[8] The result elevated the SNP to the status of official opposition in the Scottish Parliament.[9]

Surveys of opinion have consistently demonstrated that a significant proportion of the Scottish electorate holds contrasting voting preferences for Westminster and Scottish Parliament elections. More people express a preference for the SNP in a Scottish election than in a UK election.[10] Hence, the results of the 2001 general election more closely resembled the 1997 UK election than the Scottish election of 1999. For the SNP, the result was disappointing. Its percentage share of the vote decreased by 2 per cent to 20 per cent, it lost Galloway and Upper Nithsdale, and it came within 48 votes of losing Perth. Although the loss of Galloway and Upper Nithsdale may in part be explained by the constituency's problems with Foot and Mouth Disease, the near loss of Perth and the general swing away from the party demand further explanation.

A number of inter-related factors help us to interpret the result. Firstly, with the exception of Alex Salmond in Banff and Buchan, the SNP candidates were largely unknown to the public and the press, and were mostly inexperienced in the field of politics. The one exception was Annabelle Ewing in Perth. In addition to the renown attached to the Ewing name, she had acquired experience and a political profile by contesting the Hamilton South by-election in 1999. Secondly, with the exception of Banff and Buchan and Tayside North, the party organisation in constituencies remains weak. Constituency associations lack the technological sophistication of their competitors and, as a consequence, rely upon outmoded canvassing techniques. Thirdly, while Labour and the Liberal Democrats were largely successful in maintaining the anti-Tory coalition of 1997, this proved more difficult for the SNP.

The post-devolution context may also have engendered the view that the SNP was less relevant to Westminster. Since 1999, the party had itself focused most of its attentions on the Scottish Parliament, evident in the initial decision that all six sitting MPs step down from Westminster to become full-time MSPs. Moreover, the establishment of the Scottish Parliament effectively removed the constitutional question from the election campaign and for the first time in many years, the campaign issues in Scotland mirrored those in the rest of the United Kingdom. This made it difficult for the SNP to articulate its distinctiveness and reinforced the British nature of the campaign. However, given the low profile of the candidates, a new and relatively unknown leader, and a political climate in which the party and the constitutional issue were marginalised, the SNP's election was not the disaster that post-election commentary might suggest. The central campaign was polished and effective, albeit without the degree of scrutiny that may be expected in a Scottish election contest, and the campaign achieved one of its core aims of raising the public profile of its new leader, John Swinney.

NEW LEADERSHIP, NEW DIRECTION?
When Alex Salmond announced his resignation in the summer of 2000, it concluded one of the most successful periods of leadership in the party's history. The ultimate objective of independence eluded him, but over his ten years of leadership, the SNP had become the second party of Scottish politics and, effectively, the government-in-waiting in the Scottish Parliament. Perhaps his most significant contribution was to give the SNP an ideological and policy profile it previously lacked. Although the SNP had described itself as social democratic as far back as 1974, in the 1970s, the party and especially the parliamentary group remained ideological weak.[11] In the context of Conservative dominance of UK government and Conservative decline in Scotland, the SNP came to position itself on the centre-left of Scottish politics. Policy development and political practice during the Salmond leadership provided an ideological coherence to the party and reinforced its credibility as an alternative to Labour in Scotland. Salmond was less successful in overcoming one of the most significant and persistent tensions within the SNP: the split between gradualism and fundamentalism. As Mitchell observed, this reflects a tension over strategy rather than policy.[12] For 'fundamentalists', independence must always take precedence in SNP strategy and, as such, they have been suspicious of co-operating with other parties in support of devolutionary measures. For 'gradualists', such measures should be supported as a means of enhancing Scottish self-government and as a positive step towards independence. Alex Salmond's election as the Convenor of the party marked a victory for gradualism. However, these tensions remained and, exacerbated by personality clashes and mutual suspicion, occasionally resurfaced to cause considerable difficulty during his leadership.

The leadership election of September 2000 once again brought the gradualist-fundamentalist tensions to the fore. The result exposed the strength of those advocating the gradualist route to independence. John Swinney won a convincing victory, taking 67 per cent of the vote, some 10 per cent more than that secured by Tony Blair or Charles Kennedy in their respective leadership contests. Moreover, his supporters secured a clean sweep of senior positions within the party. As Table 2.3 illustrates, all those identified as supporters of the fundamentalist leadership contender, Alex Neil, were defeated in contested elections for vice-convenorships. Of the 10 additional members elected to the National Executive Committee, only Neil himself was elected from the fundamentalist wing of the party. The renewal of the party's leadership has quietened internal disputes over strategy and Swinney may be better placed to prevent their re-emergence. The fundamentalist critique of a step-by-step approach to independence was somewhat muted by the election of many of its leading exponents to the devolved Scottish Parliament.[13] In addition, Swinney's leadership style may avoid the personality conflicts that affected his predecessor's reign, and may be more conducive to accommodating and overcoming internal division. The appointment of Alex Neil, the defeated leadership candidate, to the prestigious position of Convenor of the Scottish Parliament Committee on Enterprise and Lifelong Learning may reflect this accommodative approach.

Table 2.3: Contested Elections of SNP Vice Convenors, September 2000

		1st count	Only/Final Count
National Convenor	**John Swinney**		547
	Alex Neil*		268
Senior Vice Convenor	**Roseanna Cunningham**	391	457
	Kenny MacAskill	312	323
	Peter Kearney*	108	–
Organisation[a]	**Kate Higgins**	256	372
	Stewart Gibb*	230	273
Policy	**Fiona Hyslop**		523
	Tom Chalmers		285
Publicity	**Anne Dana**		550
	George Adam*		133
	Brian Goodall		113

Youth Affairs	Shirley-Anne Somerville	389	469
	Heather Williams*	203	243
	Richard Thompson	201	–
National Secretary	Stewart Hosie		509
	Gerry Fisher		241
	Alex Orr		61
National Treasurer	Jim Mather		632
	Ian Blackford*		143
	Jim Wright		26

Note: Winning candidates emboldened. Candidates with an asterix* were identified supporters of Alex Neil's leadership bid.
(a) Five candidates stood for election as Vice Convenor for Organisation. Only the first and second-placed candidates have been shown here.

Source: SNP, Results of Elections at Annual Conference, 2000.

Measured against his predecessor, does Swinney's leadership reflect continuity or change? It remains early days - at the time of writing, Swinney has been leader for only for one year - but there are signs of some changes. The most notable is in leadership style. In contrast to the dominating style of Salmond, Swinney is more of a team player. His approach with colleagues is more consultative and persuasive. He has also engaged in consultation with the party, evident in a series of post-general election consultations with party members and constituency associations. Indeed, this consultative approach may represent a return to a more traditional style of SNP leadership, from which Salmond marked a departure. The numbers of women elected to senior positions is also noteworthy (see Table 2.3). The SNP has always had a few women in prominent positions, but female representation in the higher echelons of the party is more marked within the new regime. One can identify a further change in the style of campaigning. Notwithstanding the difficulties identified above, the nationally-run campaign in the 2001 general election was more focused and better organised than any that had preceded.

There are also signs of continuity, particularly with respect to the party's ideological and policy profile. Independence remains the party's raison d'être, and the policy of holding an independence referendum 'to complete the powers of the Scottish Parliament' is an unswerving commitment of the new leadership. In the aftermath of the SNP's 2001 manifesto launch, some commentators noted a drift to the centre in party policy.[14] Some former commitments had been abandoned, such as the commitment to lift the ceiling on National Insurance contributions and the restoration of benefits for 16 and 17-year-olds. The manifesto also presented a new criminal justice policy, including a proposal to increase parental responsibility for young offenders and impose a financial penalty, in the form of a compensation order, on parents whose children had caused 'physical damage to property or tangible upset to a victim'.[15] Tackling crime was tied to the promotion of good citizenship. In a passage reminiscent of New Labour discourse, the manifesto hailed the virtues of 'good citizenship' and the need to match citizens' rights with greater responsibilities. However, these policies sat alongside social democratic commitments, such as the restoration of the link between pensions and average earnings, the complete abolition of tuition fees, free fruit for school children, and free personal care for the elderly. In his first speech to the party's annual conference as National Convenor, Swinney also reaffirmed the party's commitment to publicly-funded public services and defined his over-riding ambition as the eradication of child poverty. In so doing, he indicated a willingness to use the Parliament's tax-raising powers, if necessary.[16]

Thus, while Swinney's leadership style is a significant departure from that of his predecessor, the party's policies have been marked more by continuity than change.[17] There is little evidence of a general swing to the right. However, the Swinney agenda does appear to signal a shift towards a more populist policy programme and political rhetoric, evident in the manifesto commitments on criminal justice discussed above. Populism is not the preserve of the right. The challenge for the SNP ahead of the 2003 election will be to identify and articulate populist policies within the party's social democratic tradition, policies which will be sufficiently distinctive to capture the imagination of disaffected Labour/ Liberal Democrat voters, or to entice non-voters to participate in the democratic process.

THE SNP AND DEVOLUTION

The SNP's role in the history of the campaign for a devolved Scottish Parliament has been an uneven one. Its electoral strength in the 1970s was the prime factor motivating Labour's reversion to a commitment to devolution. In Parliament, the SNP co-operated fully with the Labour government in support of its devolution legislation and played a key role in the 1979 referendum. The referendum's subsequent failure fostered suspicion of cross-party co-operation and mistrust of Labour's commitment to Scottish home rule. Although its 1984 conference passed a resolution in support of an elected constitutional convention and co-operation with the Campaign for a Scottish Assembly (CSA), the SNP chose to boycott the CSA-inspired Constitutional Convention in 1989. The devolution debate went to the heart of the gradualist-fundamentalist conflict over strategy, making it difficult for the party to develop a consistent and coherent approach. Notwithstanding this chequered history, the SNP's involvement in the 1997 devolution campaign may have proved crucial to the referendum's success.

Under Salmond's leadership, the SNP's position on devolution became more coherent, reflected in Salmond's insistence that while independence remained his first choice, devolution would be his second choice preference over the then status quo. This position became more difficult to maintain after the Labour Party, in advance of its 1997 general election victory, adopted the policy of holding a pre-legislative, two-question referendum for a devolved Scottish Parliament with tax-raising powers. SNP support for this policy would have effectively meant conceding the argument for independence in the election campaign. Criticising it risked fuelling the perception that the SNP, along with the Conservative Party, was hostile to devolution.

Thus, before giving its endorsement, the SNP waited until after the election and after the publication of the devolution proposals in the government White Paper, *Scotland's Parliament*. A central concern was whether the government's proposals would include mechanisms designed to block further constitutional change. Denver et al suggested that there was evidence within the White Paper of an attempt to allay those fears.[19] Some assurance had been given prior to this when, during the second reading of the Referendum Bill, the then Secretary of State for Scotland, Donald Dewar, noted that he 'should be the last to challenge the sovereignty of the people or to deny them the right to opt for any solution to the constitutional question which they wished'.[20] An additional assurance was secured in a parliamentary exchange between Dewar and Salmond on the day of the White Paper's presentation to Parliament. Responding to a question by Salmond asking him to confirm that the documents contained nothing that would 'interfere in any way with the sovereign right of the people of Scotland to determine their own constitutional future, whatever that may be', Dewar replied: 'If I did try to build such barriers, they would be futile and without effect. At the end of the day, in practical politics, what matters is what people want. If the hon. Gentleman is able to carry the people of Scotland, no doubt he will be able to advance his cause'.[21] Shortly afterwards, the decision to support the proposed Scottish Parliament and participate fully in the referendum campaign was passed overwhelmingly at the Party's National Council.

As well as organising its own campaign, the SNP participated in the cross-party Scotland Forward campaign and co-operated behind the scenes with the Labour Party and the Liberal Democrats, directly and indirectly through Scotland Forward. The local campaign reflected the co-operative spirit of the national campaign, with survey evidence

suggesting that 75 per cent of SNP constituency associations participated in some form of cross-party campaign.[22] Since the devolution
referendum, political claims have often been made on Labour's behalf
to suggest that the Labour Party delivered devolution to Scotland.
There is some truth in this assertion. The election of a Labour government was a pre-requisite to the legislative proposals being devised and
later implemented, and to the devolution referendum being held.
However, the home rule campaign stretched beyond the confines of the
Labour Party, incorporating the SNP, the Liberal Democrats and a
broad consensus within Scottish civil society. It is questionable
whether a parliament, especially one with tax-raising powers, would
have secured as comfortable a majority without this support.

An analysis of the referendum results revealed that, other things
being equal, the Yes, Yes vote was greater where Labour had been
stronger in the general election *and* where the SNP vote was higher.
The evidence further suggested that while support for the proposals
was very high among Labour voters (81 per cent), it was higher still
among SNP voters (88 per cent), with the latter recording the highest
rates of turnout.[23] Thus, the success of the 1997 referendum campaign
must in large part be attributed to the cross-party and co-operative
nature of the campaign, as well as the consensus of support for devolution throughout much of Scottish civil society.

If the SNP contributed to securing devolution, devolution has in
turn contributed to strengthening the SNP. Its status as official opposition in the Scottish Parliament has enhanced the credibility of the
party and reinforced the idea of the SNP as a potential Scottish government. Two further beneficial consequences may be identified. Prior to
the establishment of the Scottish Parliament, the SNP had been seen as
a one-man band in the image of Alex Salmond. Even before Salmond's
resignation as leader, this was no longer the case. The SNP's status
within the Scottish Parliament has raised the profile of the party and of
individuals within it. Party spokespeople are commonly referred to as
shadow ministers, and their opinions sought and reported on a daily
basis. Secondly, the election of 35 MSPs has strengthened the party's
resources, with consequential benefits for its research and policy
output. Moreover, as full-time politicians, the MSPs have been afforded
the opportunity to develop political experience and expertise, enhancing their campaigning and debating skills.

Devolution has brought challenges as well as opportunities. In elections to the Scottish Parliament, the SNP must present a manifesto for
devolved government while simultaneously promoting its ultimate goal
of independence. The leadership must seek to establish and maintain the
view within the party and among the electorate that governing a devolved

parliament and seeking independence are complementary objectives. As long as support for independence remains static, electoral success is unlikely unless the SNP can broaden its appeal beyond its core voters to those seeking a change of government irrespective of their attitude towards independence. At the same time, the party must be prepared to promote and defend its independence policy against the inevitable attacks of political opponents. Promoting a programme for devolved government while advocating independence is a delicate balance and one that the party clearly had difficulty maintaining in the 1999 election.

PROSPECTS FOR GOVERNMENT AND INDEPENDENCE: THE NEXT TEN YEARS

There are a number of challenges facing the SNP if it is to progress from its status as official opposition to a party of government. In particular, the party must address the organisational weakness evident in previous elections and find a coherent approach to promoting a policy programme for devolved government alongside a vision that can nurture support for independence. In the immediate aftermath of the 2001 election, the National Executive Committee set in train three working groups aimed at addressing some of these issues in advance of the Scottish Parliament election. The first examined the role of the party's Headquarters, with a view to enhancing its efficiency and effectiveness, and improving links between the central and local organisations. The second, Project 2003, was charged with devising a campaign plan and identifying the most effective means of communicating the party's message. The third, Platform 2003, was geared towards developing the message and strategy to be employed in the run-up to the Scottish Parliament election of 2003. These working groups reflect an awareness of the need to significantly reform the party's management, organisation and communication. The extent to which this is achieved will represent a test of the Swinney leadership, as well as being crucial to the prospects for electoral success.

In considering the prospects for government and independence, this chapter assumes that an SNP-led government in the Scottish Parliament is a distinct possibility in a future Scottish election. An immediate challenge facing the SNP as the largest party would be whether to form a coalition and with whom. While minority government is an option, it would not be a wise one. Minority government provokes instability and creates enormous difficulties for any administration hoping to make progress in delivering its programme for government. The architects of the devolution settlement clearly had coalition government in mind when they designed the Scottish Parliament's electoral system. The SNP has in the past refused to consider forming a coalition with the

Conservatives and there is little prospect of a change of heart in this respect. While the pro-independence position of the Scottish Socialist Party and the Scottish Green Party make them natural allies for the SNP, their parliamentary representation is unlikely in the near future to increase to the extent that they hold the balance of power. That leaves the Liberal Democrats. In 1999, the Liberal Democrats insisted that they would not enter into a coalition with the SNP if doing so meant agreeing to hold an independence referendum. This was always a difficult policy to sustain for a party whose name reflects a commitment to democracy. It implied a refusal to permit the Scottish electorate to decide their constitutional and political future. Although coalition politics necessitates that all parties be prepared to negotiate and compromise, for the SNP, holding an independence referendum would be non-negotiable. It seems unlikely that the Liberal Democrats would risk a constitutional crisis by refusing to negotiate with the SNP on these terms.

A further challenge facing the SNP concerns its independence objective. Although devolution has strengthened the SNP, opinion poll evidence thus far suggests it has contained support for independence. In seeking to build support for independence, the SNP might look to the devolution campaign to learn the lessons of its success. There are two key lessons to be drawn here. The first is that support for the establishment of a Scottish Parliament was greater when it was viewed as a vehicle for social change. Those who supported a Scottish Parliament with tax-varying powers saw it as the best arena in which Scottish priorities on health, education and social welfare could be addressed.[24] This reflected a change within the campaign for a Scottish Parliament. Responding to the dominance of the Conservatives at Westminster, the home rule movement of the 1980s explicitly tied the demand for constitutional change to a defence of the welfare state and Scottish manufacturing jobs. A Scottish Parliament came to be presented as a pre-requisite to progressive social and economic change. During Salmond's leadership, arguments for independence had emphasised the economic case, suggesting that Scotland might be more prosperous were it an independent nation-state. To some extent, this was necessary to counter, if not to neutralise, claims by opponents regarding the economic costs to Scotland of 'separating' from the United Kingdom. There are some signs of a willingness within the new leadership to engage more explicitly in advocating a social case for independence. Shortly after his election as SNP leader, Swinney asserted the need to focus on 'the key issues of concern to the public', including health, education, pensions and poverty, in order to 'demonstrate how independence will make a real difference'.[25]

The second lesson that can be learned from the success of the home rule campaign is that support for devolution was ultimately carried by a broad coalition. This coalition encompassed three of the four main political parties in Scotland and much of Scottish civil society. Moreover, it isolated the Conservative Party as the one identifiable political organisation which was overtly hostile to the setting up of a Scottish Parliament. Notwithstanding the pro-independence position of the SSP and the Greens, there is little sign of a broad coalition in favour of independence. Three of the four main political parties are overtly hostile and much of Scottish civil society remains committed to devolution. In theory, independence can be secured without the support of the Scottish elite; all that is required is majority support from the Scottish electorate expressed in a referendum. However, without a broader coalition in support of independence than currently exists, the SNP would surely find itself isolated in any referendum campaign. As the Conservatives found to their cost in the 1997 referendum, such isolation would make it considerably more difficult for the SNP to build support for independence beyond its own electoral base.

In addition to promoting independence, Swinney has advocated increased powers for the Scottish Parliament, with a particular emphasis on support for fiscal autonomy. This reflects the prevalence of a gradualist strategy within the new leadership. There may be more scope in building a broad coalition in support of an extension to the Parliament's existing powers. The Liberal Democrats and the Conservative Party have not ruled out supporting a change to the current settlement, particularly to enhance the Parliament's fiscal powers. It might be expected that such a change would also find sympathy within the home rule wing of the Labour Party. Scottish civil society may also be more inclined to favour strengthening the Scottish Parliament while remaining within the UK. Swinney has made some efforts to generate a consensus in favour of change, most evident in his first St Andrew's Day speech as leader. Addressing an invited audience of representatives of Scottish civil society, he appealed to 'those of you who built the consensus which delivered the Scottish Parliament' to renew the consensus in arguing for additional powers for the Parliament, and 'to be partners in this process of continuing Scotland's journey'.[26] Since the referendum, surveys have also indicated that there would be majority support among the Scottish electorate for additional powers for the Parliament, short of independence.[27]

While there may be scope for building a consensus in favour of enhancing the powers of the Scottish Parliament, the mechanism for doing so remains unclear. Any change to the existing devolution settlement would require a change to the Scotland Act (1998). As an act of the Westminster Parliament, all amendments require the approval of a majority of Westminster MPs. Increasing the powers of the Scottish Parliament implies a weakening of the powers that the Westminster Parliament exercises over Scotland, and the approval of Westminster MPs may therefore be difficult to attain. Moreover, the current devolution settlement was given popular endorsement in the referendum. Although Labour's decision to hold a pre-legislative referendum was at the time a controversial one, the referendum majority gave the Scottish Parliament a democratic legitimacy that it might otherwise have lacked. To retain this legitimacy, any significant change to the current settlement might require a further referendum. A popular endorsement would have the added advantage of lending amendments a degree of democratic legitimacy sufficient to carry them through the legislative process at Westminster, and would certainly make it more difficult for Westminster to resist the change.

There is a way that an SNP-led administration could facilitate this process. The SNP is already committed to holding an independence referendum. Instead of restricting such a referendum to a simple Yes/No choice in favour of or against independence, a third option could be available for those wishing to endorse a proposal to extend the Parliament's powers. Voters would then be asked to express their first and second preferences. The SNP has supported a multi-option referendum in the past, when it advocated a referendum which would have allowed voters to choose between independence, devolution and the status quo. Such a referendum also won the approval of the Labour Party when in opposition in the wake of the 1992 general election, and was the founding objective of the home rule pressure group, Scotland United. In facilitating the expression of a broader range of views, a multi-option referendum may also better reflect the opinion of the electorate. Indeed, one of the drawbacks of straightforward Yes/No referenda is that they often try to over-simplify something complex, dividing an issue into black and white while ignoring the grey mass of opinion in the middle. A multi-option referendum on Scotland's constitutional future would, in the spirit of upholding the principle of self-determination, facilitate a more accurate expression and reflection of the complex preferences of the people of Scotland.

CONCLUSION

Devolution has changed the SNP. Its representation within the Scottish Parliament and its status as the official opposition signalled its transformation from a minor party on the margins to a party at the centre of the new Scottish politics and a potential party of government. The establishment of the Scottish Parliament has also contributed to enhancing the visibility and experience of a greater number of its leading figures, helping the party move away from the one-man band image that dogged previous campaigns. The renewal of the party's leadership appears to have resolved some of the internal disputes over strategy, for the time being at least. Gradualism underpinned the party's support of devolution and a step-by-step approach to independence remains the predominant strategy of the new leadership. While devolution has evidently presented new opportunities to the SNP, it has also given rise to new challenges. Becoming a party of devolved government is now a realistic possibility. However, whether this brings the party closer to achieving its ultimate goal of independence is open to debate. The SNP must develop a strategy to ensure that competing for government and campaigning for independence are logically consistent. It must also seek to emphasise the social and economic rationale for independence and build a broad coalition of support for independence beyond the party's electoral base. The degree of support for independence will not be dependent upon the SNP's efforts alone. To some extent, support for independence will be predicated on the degree of dissatisfaction with the United Kingdom. Perhaps this is the final lesson to be drawn from the success of the home rule movement. Support for devolution rose with the belief that UK government could no longer reflect Scottish priorities and preferences. The challenge for the SNP is whether it can channel any dissatisfaction with the new constitutional status quo, or dissatisfaction with UK governance, into a demand for Scottish independence.

Many thanks to Fiona Mackay and James Mitchell for helpful comments on an early draft. I am also very grateful to those who provided useful documentation or gave up valuable time to speak with me.

NOTES

1. R. J. Finlay, *Independent and Free: Scottish Politics and the Origins of the Scottish National Party*, Edinburgh: John Donald, 1994.
2. J. Brand, *The Nationalist Movement in Scotland*, London: Routledge and Kegan Paul, 1978, pp19-34.
3. The 1979 referendum produced a slim majority in favour of the establishment of a Scottish Assembly, but this fell short of meeting the requirement written into the Scotland Act (1978) that majority approval for the proposed Assembly include at least 40 per cent of those eligible to vote.
4. See for example the essays in the collection: P. Gallacher (ed.), *Nationalism in the Nineties*, Edinburgh: Polygon, 1991.
5. The Liberal Democrats secured 13.0 per cent of the popular vote in 1997, behind Labour (45.6 per cent), the SNP (22.1 per cent) and the Conservatives (17.5 per cent). Because their vote is geographically concentrated, Scottish Liberal Democrats benefit from the first-the-past-post electoral system,

though the party is disadvantaged by the system in England.

6. D. McCrone, 'Opinion Polls in Scotland: July 1998-June 1999', *Scottish Affairs*, Summer 1999, No. 28, pp37-38.

7. P. Jones, 'The 1999 Scottish Parliament Elections: From Anti-Tory to Anti-Nationalist Politics', *Scottish Affairs*, No. 28, Summer 1999, p4.

8. L. G. Bennie, 'Small Parties in a Devolved Scotland', in A. Wright (ed), *Scotland: The Challenge of Devolution*, Aldershot: Ashgate, 2000, pp68-82.

9. The distribution of seats is as follows: Labour 56, SNP 35, Conservatives 18, Liberal Democrats 17, Scottish Socialist Party 1. Scottish Green Party 1, Independent (Dennis Canavan) 1.

10. J. Curtice, 'The New Electoral Politics', in G. Hassan and C. Warhurst (eds), *The New Scottish Politics: The First Year of the Scottish Parliament and Beyond*, Edinburgh: The Stationery Office, 2000, pp35-37.

11. J. Mitchell, *Strategies for Self-Government*, Edinburgh: Polygon, 1996, pp207-9

12. *Ibid*, p173.

13. P. Lynch, *Scottish Government and Politics: An Introduction*, Edinburgh: Edinburgh University Press, 2001, p173.

14. *The Herald*, 19.5.01.

15. Scottish National Party, *General Election Manifesto*, Edinburgh: Scottish National Party, 2001, p10.

16. J. Swinney, Speech to the SNP Annual Conference, Scottish National Party Annual Conference, Dundee, September 21 2001.

17. See for a different view: I. Macwhirter, 'Swinney seeks a Radical Future', *Sunday Herald*, 23.9.01.

18. Mitchell, *op. cit.*, pp212-19; 237-43.

19. D. Denver, J. Mitchell, C. Pattie and H. Bochel, *Scotland Decides: The Devolution Issue and the Scottish Referendum*, London: Frank Cass, 2000, pp60-63.

20. House of Commons Debates, May 21 1997, col. 725.

21. House of Commons Debates, July 24 1997, col. 1019.

22. Denver et al, *Scotland Decides*, *op. cit.*, pp107-8.

23. *Ibid*, pp148-59.

24. P. Surridge and D. McCrone, 'The 1997 Scottish Referendum Vote', in B. Taylor and K. Thompson (eds), *Scotland and Wales: Nations Again?*, University of Wales Press, Cardiff, pp41-64; N. McEwen, 'State Welfare Nationalism: The Territorial Impact of Welfare State Development in Scotland', *Regional and Federal Studies*, Vol. 12 No. 1.

25. J. Swinney, The Policy Challenge for Scotland, speech delivered at the Holyrood Hotel, Edinburgh 2000.

26. J. Swinney, St Andrew's Day Speech, 2000.

27. See for example, the annual State of the Nation poll in the *Sunday Herald*, March 11 2001.

The Scottish Conservative and Unionist Party: 'the lesser spotted Tory'?

DAVID SEAWRIGHT

On the Sunday following the 2001 General Election a national newspaper included an amusing piece which compared the election of Peter Duncan, the successful Conservative candidate in Galloway and Upper Nithsdale, with the reintroduction into Scotland of other 'extinct' species, such as beaver, red kites and wild boar. 'The very reappearance of this species [the lesser spotted Tory] has shocked naturalists and political observers alike, who thought the Scottish Tory was gone and forgotten – a victim of political climate change and a failure on its part to adjust to the new habitat'.[1] Unfortunately, this humour merely emphasises the egregious electoral position of the Scottish Tories. The 2001 election may have witnessed the return of one MP out of a possible seventy-two but such 'success' must be set against another decline in their overall share of the vote for a Westminster contest. As Table 3.1 shows it fell around another 2 per cent from an already post-war historical low of 17.5 per cent in 1997, when this 'species' of MP was totally wiped out in Scotland. In the intervening period we have seen a successful by-election gain in Ayr for the Scottish Parliament but the other 18 list MSPs were elected in 1999 on 16 per cent of the vote and by virtue of an AMS proportional electoral system that the Party officially objects to.

Table 3.1: Percentage Share of Conservative Vote in Scotland and England at Westminster Elections 1945-2001

	1945	1950	1951	1955	1959	1964	1966	1970
Scotland	41.1	44.8	48.6	50.1	47.2	40.6	37.7	38.0
England	40.2	43.8	48.8	50.4	49.9	44.1	42.7	48.3

	1974F	1974O	1979	1983	1987	1992	1997	2001
Scotland	32.9	24.7	31.4	28.4	24.0	25.6	17.5	15.6
England	40.2	38.9	47.2	46.0	46.2	45.5	33.7	35.2

Source: Kellas, *The Scottish Political System*, 4th edn. 1989; Hassan and Lynch, *The Almanac of Scottish Politics*, 2001; House of Commons Research Paper 01/54.

Similarly the Party has two Members of the European Parliament, again by virtue of a proportional list system, when it gained around 20 per cent of the overall share of the vote at the 1999 European Election in Scotland. However, when this result is set against the Party in England winning nearly 39 per cent of the vote at this election then one is reminded of the fact that Scottish Tories have usually performed about half as well as their English counterparts, particularly throughout the 1980s and early 1990s when the Scottish Conservatives held office by virtue of this 'English success'. It is only in the 1950s and early 1960s, in the post war era, that the Scottish Tories performed on a par with the Party south of the border. This begs the crucial question of why it was a victim of political climate change and of why it failed to adjust? Thus, this chapter first sets out to explain *why* the Party finds itself in such a lamentable electoral position and then examines the Party's future prospects for recovery as it struggles to re-create itself. In so doing it also analyses the problems and issues to be faced by a Scottish 'cartel party', within a multi-level polity.

A GOLDEN ERA AND AN ISSUE OF VALENCE

There is no doubt that the Party in Scotland achieved considerable success in the 1950s (see Table 3.1). Indeed in this 'golden era' the Scottish Unionist Party – as it was known then – gained 50.1 per cent of the vote and 36 of the 71 seats at Westminster for the 1955 Election. But a considerable element of doubt is raised by the competing theories and explanations for this success; and even more by the contested reasons posited for the subsequent precipitous fall in Party support.[2] The orthodox explanations, inclusive of class differences north and south of the border and of the decline in the Protestant Orange vote, have been shown to be flawed and to fall far short of any comprehensive account of this success and decline. Of far greater import is the dual premise that considers the 'Scottish consciousness' of the Party, in conjunction with both the Party's and Scots electorates' contrasting ideological shifts on the left-right spectrum. Thus, one component of the received orthodoxy which needed to be seriously challenged was the idea that the Scots were always more left-wing than their neighbours south of the border and had continually expressed values consistent with a social democratic culture. In a previous work, then, statistical techniques were utilised in order to analyse certain relevant socio-economic issues and the results clearly showed that the Scots were in fact relatively more right-wing in the 1950s and did not take the 'substantive' move to the left – that is now manifestly found in the ideological values of contemporary Scottish society – until the 1970s.[3]

But, unfortunately for the Party in Scotland it simultaneously decided on its own substantive move towards what was hitherto regarded as neo-liberal extremism, culminating in the eponymous title of Thatcherism. The laissez-faire discourse gained ground in the Party at the very time when the Scottish indigenous industrial base was facing an acute crisis of survival and it is not surprising that the Scots should have developed a taste for economic intervention. One piece of Thatcherite legislation epitomised the extent to which the Party had moved in the opposite direction to that of the Scots electorate. The Community Charge had little resonance of 'community' for Scots and its pernicious electoral effects for the party, as the 'Poll Tax' issue, were felt in the Election of 1987, even before its introduction.

Conversely, the Scottish Unionist Party in the 1950s used to great effect rhetoric which purported to reconcile the two themes of individualism and collectivism, enhancing an image of flexibility and pragmatism for itself:

> There are two fundamental instincts in human nature - Individuality and Social Service. Regard is paid to both of these in the Unionist Party's view of the object of politics and in its framing of policy. It is therefore wrong to describe the Unionist Party as being upon the Right in the political scale. It is not 'reactionary'. It is not out to 'exploit'. Rather it is on the Middle Road, between two extremes - the extremes of laissez-faire and Socialism. The Unionist Party realises the need for a synthesis of these two fundamental ideas of human individuality and of service to others and to the community. Remember that the Unionist Party initiated or supported most of the social reforms and the social services.[4]

This was the Party's public ethos and approach throughout the postwar period until at least the mid-1960s. A crucial aspect to this ethos and imagery in the 1950s was the Party's ability to concomitantly impose an alien identity upon Labour for a much longer period than that found in England. Thus the Party was successfully using the 'alien' term of Socialist to describe the Labour Party into the early 1960s. After all there was a historical precedent to justify such an approach. Keir Hardie had triumphed over his rivals, such as Hyndman, in having the socialist term expurgated from the infant Labour

Representation Committee for the very same reason, that in Hardie's eyes the term socialist was foreign and its use would alienate the British worker. The Scottish Unionist Association's Yearbook of 1955 neatly illustrates the strategy adopted:

> Nothing could be a greater misnomer than the name 'Labour' for Socialist policies. It is a name which attracts support; but let those who are misled by it ask themselves: what can the foreign doctrine of Socialism, with its denial of freedom of choice and of individual opportunity, profit the British people ...[5]

It is significant that Unionism's distinctive symbolism and imagery was jealously guarded by the party in the 1950s, to the extent that the term Conservative was expurgated from all official Unionist literature until the Party re-incorporated the term Conservative into its title in 1965, a term it had not used since before 1912. This was to have serious implications for the Party's Scottish identity. Crucially, we find that the Party's opponents were able to invert this alien notion in Scottish consciousness terms. As early as 1964 we see how this order of imagery was reversed to Labour's advantage. When the *Daily Record* was a Tory supporting paper it readily used the idea of 'alien' socialism but by the 1964 Election the *Record* was now equating Labour with 'Scottishness', a vote for 'Labour was a vote for Scotland'. More importantly, the *Record* may well have been the source that first gave public portrayal to the negative image of the Tory Party in Scotland as the 'Hooray Henrys' of the grouse moor. In the same eve of poll edition in 1964, the *Record* ran a double page spread which compared page 12 – with the headline of 'Jobless boys, meagre pensions' – with that of a facing page, page 13, with the headline 'gunfire on empty grouse moors'. The article then went on to starkly contrast unemployed teenagers and destitute pensioners with Tories shooting grouse.

> This chappie is following a well-known Tory sport: shooting grouse over the yawning, gaping, barren (except for grouse) land of some rich landowner somewhere in Scotland.
>
> This is the sport of the few, although the acres of space are great. Acres that a young couple might cry out for room to build a house; acres that might be utilised.
>
> Mark you, some other chaps do get employment through this sport; a handful of beaters, gamekeepers.
>
> But a few million other Scots (you and us), who have never seen a butt and shoot grouse, might have one.
>
> A grouse that, in Britain, 1964, while Sir Alec enjoys a day's shootin'

on the empty moors, old folks go hungry and young folk seek vainly for a job.

    This is life - or death - under the Tories.[6]

    Whatever the source, the extremely successful application of this negative connotation of the grouse moor image was matched in Scotland, from the mid-1970s, by a similar anti-Conservative style and tone from the four main Scottish national newspapers. A tone and style which confirmed the sea change of opinion that had taken place in Scotland in the mid-1970s. The Unionist ethos was no longer rooted in Scottish consciousness, the Conservative Party in Scotland would now be the party perceived as having an 'alien' identity; an 'anglicised' one. And we should keep in mind that it is by no means clear that the Conservative Party's electoral success had varied according to its position on devolution. For example, Mr Heath's 'declaration of Perth', where he advocated devolution for Scotland, was 'declared' in 1968 but there was no subsequent electoral benefit at the 1970 election, as the Scottish mandate remained firmly with Labour. However, it may be far more useful to view such position issues in Scotland as devolution, and others of a more traditionally left-right nature, as undergoing a metamorphosis into one of a valence framework.[7] This would fit comfortably with the idea of an increasingly vivid portrayal of the Scottish Tories – by a left-wing Scottish party consensus and a left wing 'Scottish establishment' – as being alien to the Scottish body politic.

    Stokes differentiates *position issues* that are on our left/right ordered dimension with *valence issues* that are more to do with the degree to which parties are linked in the public's mind with conditions or goals or symbols of which almost everyone approves or disapproves.[8] Adapting Stokes' work for Scottish politics has us, in this case, viewing Scotland itself as the valence issue. Such a valence issue acquires its power from the fact that rival parties are linked with the universally approved symbol of Scottishness and the universally disapproved symbol of non-Scottishness. The valence framework also facilitates the venal exploitation of negative campaigning. A valence issue will deliver maximum support for a party if its symbolic content is of high importance to the electorate and there is complete identification of the party with the positive symbol and of the rival party with the negative symbol.[9] Throughout the last two decades of the twentieth century, the left-wing parties, Labour, the Liberal Democrats in all their guises and the SNP, successfully portrayed the Tories in Scotland with the negative universally disapproved symbol of 'un-Scottish'. One has only to review the Scottish press at the time of Hague's speech on the need for a solution to the West Lothian Question, for a good contemporary example of the use of this negative symbolism. The argument for English MPs having similar rights to Scottish MSPs was viewed by the other three main Scottish parties as inherently divisive, typical of Tory anti-Scottishness and 'the small minded attempt to seek revenge on the voters who rejected them'.[10]

After the 1997 general election disaster which saw the Scottish Tory MP added to our Scottish extinct species category, the Party in Scotland, as in England, ran an internal enquiry which resulted in what was termed the 'Made in Scotland' Strathclyde Commission organisational reforms. However, the question is, did these reforms result in a fundamental rethink and was this 'new party' now a mass party or was its typology better categorised as a Scottish 'cartel party'? The section below sets out to explore such questions.

TARTAN TORY DISTINCTIVENESS AND THE IDEA OF A SCOTTISH CARTEL PARTY

In the wake of such a disaster as 1997, it was no surprise to find that the Party had embarked upon the customary period of reflection and two-stage recovery process that a defeated party usually undertakes. The first stage of this exercise of renewal was the re-building of the organisational base (Strathclyde reforms) on which the Party could re-create itself and develop a new policy agenda (Rifkind Policy Commission). Unfortunately, neither was perceived as having any great impact or any great success. Examining the second stage first, the Rifkind Commission (known thus as it was chaired by the defeated Edinburgh Pentlands MP and President of the Party in Scotland, Sir Malcolm Rifkind) admirably convened over 400 informative meetings throughout Scotland where an exchange of ideas could take place. The policy document the Commission produced, *Scotland's Future*, clearly delineated the principled acceptance of the essence of devolution, viz., the ability of the Party in Scotland to differentiate from the approach taken on policy south of the border. With our 'valence problem' clearly in mind, the Commission believed that policy should be crafted in line with Tory principles but designed to deal with Scottish circumstances, problems and aspirations.[11] Although the proposals from the Commission were portrayed in the Scottish media as anything but different, opportunities would quickly arise in the field of education and social policy which would allow for a manifest 'tartan' distinctiveness to policy making. Of course, this also raises problems for governance, as well as opportunities, for a 'unionist' party. We shall return to this issue in greater detail in the section below on multi-level governance, but for now we shall stay with the symbolism and imagery attached to these different policy agendas.

The goal of 'tartan distinctiveness' in policy, as set out by the Rifkind Commission, immediately fed itself into Scottish policy documents. In stark contrast to prospective policy for England and Wales, the Scottish manifesto for the 1999 Holyrood Election gave a commitment to abolishing Labour's university tuition fees. This distinctiveness continued through the policy document voted on by the membership in Scotland, *Believing in Britain, Believing in Scotland*, and on into the Scottish manifesto for the 2001 Westminster Election. In this 2001 manifesto, not only did we see different priorities flagged up under different subheadings in the Scotland and England editions, but more importantly, the Scottish edition was still advocating the abolition of tuition fees. Moreover, it was also stressing the need to implement the Sutherland recommendation on free long-term personal care for the elderly. This divergence from policy proposed for England and Wales has been bitterly criticised as departing from sound Conservative economic orthodoxy. Bill Jamieson was of the opinion that it 'flies in the face of fundamental Conservative values about thrift, personal responsibility and proper guardianship and care of the public finances'.[12]

But, this concern over the adoption of a policy of universality in social policy is not echoed amongst Scottish MSPs, who challenge such an interpretation. David McLetchie, the Tory leader in the Scottish Parliament, thought it was a superficial way of examining such policy and was proud of what the Party in Scotland had accomplished in the way of policy. Phil Gallie disagreed with the view that it was merely about outspending Labour, as the policy was carefully costed and it would be, after all, money well spent. Ben Wallace also agreed with the view that it was certainly not a case of trying to 'outleft the left'; he stressed that it was right that the party was proactive on tuition fees and the Sutherland proposals. He believed it was surely the Conservative way to protect citizens who had worked hard and saved all their lives, especially in the case of 'Sutherland'.[13] However, this policy divergence may merely reflect the view expressed by the Rifkind Policy Commission that the 'notion of the common good is deeply embedded in the Scottish consciousness' and that 'Scottish Conservatives must harness it to create a better future'.[14] Of course, as a unionist party the Tories in Scotland will also be judged on the overall performance of the Party in the UK, in short, on how it has performed at Westminster. The 2001 manifesto acknowledged this fact when the jointly signed introduction from Malcolm Rifkind and David McLetchie referred to the Scottish voters giving a verdict not only on the Labour government at Westminster but also on the record to date of the Labour and Liberal Democrat Scottish Executive.[15]

Unfortunately for the Scottish Tories, that verdict was very positive, which undermines the English nationalist claim that the Tories in Scotland 'were hated, above all, because they were the Government of England'.[16] Labour does not seem to suffer from any similar adverse reaction. Little wonder then at the election outcome when Tory policy made in Westminster would chop and change almost overnight, as in the case of pensions policy. Tax guarantees were very quickly no longer guarantees. And of course the flagship policy on the euro was ridiculed for its ambiguity; it should not have been beyond the brightest in an 'electoral professional' party to present a policy which was in tune with the majority of UK voters. But because of perceived problems on the backbenches at Westminster, the Party could not simply rule out the euro in principle, on constitutional as well as on economic grounds, while simply adding the caveat that parties can never say never in politics. This problem of policy formulation for the Scottish Tories was starkly portrayed in the 1999 Holyrood manifesto when the party in Scotland seemed to be against Bank of England independence – a stance that Michael Portillo would quickly change. This problem rather undermined the claim made in that manifesto of the Party being cognisant of the problem that policies looked as if they 'had London stamped all over them'.[17] Importantly, the 1999 Holyrood manifesto also went on to declare that 'this is a new party'.[18] We shall now examine the first stage of renewal, that of organisational reform, to examine the extent to which we can accept such a claim.

The Strathclyde reforms transformed the Party, from a three-legged structure that had incorporated a voluntary wing, a professional wing and a parliamentary party, into one structural body. In this sense it was a new party. But it is taking the image to exaggerated lengths to suggest, as the Rifkind Commission document did, that from being the oldest party in Scotland the Party had now become the youngest and newest party as well, reformed and invigorated as a result of the fundamental changes inherent in the Strathclyde reforms. The Strathclyde document stressed the new role of the Convenor, who would be elected by the Scottish membership and would play a pivotal role in the Party organisation, reflecting the new participatory role of the membership. However, ultimately this seemed to amount to the position of a Deputy Chairman, the reality of which, in the first year or two, was a continuation of the bickering and backbiting that the party seems to excel at in Scotland, as the Deputy Chairman's clique were faced down by the Chairman's clique.[19] Thus, we must ask whether the party really had been fundamentally transformed from a hierarchical elite model of a clique of notables to a participatory mass level party.[20]

The reality was more prosaic: the Chairman, who was the appointee of the UK leader, had control of the day to day running of the Party in

Scotland through the control of a Management Committee. Intuitively one would expect there to be tension if the Chairman was also an office-seeking politician. Daphne Sleigh, the Conservative leader of Edinburgh City Council, made this very point when she suggested that a Chief Executive should be appointed to run the day to day administration of the Party allowing the politicians to concentrate on policy and tactics.[21] Moreover, although there was now one bodily structure there appeared to be three separate figureheads of the Party in Scotland. It cannot be the easiest task for the average voter to differentiate between Malcolm Rifkind as President, Raymond Robertson as Chairman and David McLetchie as Leader in the Scottish Parliament. An analysis of this position is long overdue and the Party should take heed of the Mitchell analysis on this one. 'The only question that should be asked about David McLetchie's leadership is why did the Tories not give him the job much earlier'.[22] The obvious corollary to this observation is that there should be one unequivocal leadership position and there is a candidate already *in situ*. If the party does not conform to a model of a vibrant mass level party, then what typology would best describe it?

Katz and Mair argue that these models of party – the elite, the catch-all party, and in particular the mass party model – are attached to a now dated ideal of social structure and a dated ideal of their relationship to civil society.[23] They introduce a new model into this dialectical process of party transmutation, the 'cartel party', which challenges the party's relationship to civil society. The typology of the cartel party is characterised by the ever increasing symbiosis between parties and the state. Parties still compete but rather than a mobilising role in a civil society the major parties now have a mutual interest in collective organisational survival. An interpenetration of party and state leads to a pattern of inter-party collusion over patronage and the spoils of the state.[24] This cartel model can be detected in the formation of the institutional processes for the Scottish Parliament, for example when one considers the draft Order 'Assistance for registered political parties', which extends, for the Scottish Parliament, the role of 'Short money' in use at Westminster. In Scotland, like 'Short', the money will enable *opposition* parties in the Parliament to effectively hold the government to account. But, unlike 'Short', it will also enable *all parties* in the Parliament to carry out their parliamentary activities.[25] None of the major parties in Scotland seemed to be against the principle of state subventions, but David McLetchie was appalled at the 'hand out' for the Liberal Democrats, as they are a full part of the new Scottish Government.[26] And it is not only with subventions that we see evidence of this 'collusion'. Fully two years before David Steel, as Presiding Officer of the Scottish Parliament, has to vacate his chair we have had reports of a secret deal between Labour and the Tories to install Annabel Goldie as his replacement. Although it is recognised that she is an ideal candidate for the position, we should be aware that, with the idea of collective organisational survival in mind, 'the driving force behind many Labour backbenchers' support for Miss Goldie is their determination to stop George Reid, the Nationalist deputy presiding officer, stepping up to the job after 2003'.[27]

However, because of the 'valence problem' identified earlier, the Scottish Tories probably have even more of an acute concern than the other unionist parties over the perception of which part or parts of the structures of government they are seen to have a greater commitment to. In short, at what levels of a multi-level polity will this symbiotic relationship take place for the Scottish Tories?

A MULTI-LEVEL PARTY FOR A MULTI-LEVEL POLITY?

Of course, the acute concern over perception arises due to the Party's past robust critique of devolution itself. However, it is no exaggeration now to suggest that as 'a party, the Tories seem more at ease with devolution than does New Labour.[28] Indeed, this reconciled and even contented attitude with devolution is reflected in the comments from Tory MSPs themselves. David McLetchie stresses that the UK leadership is at ease with the flexibility the Party in Scotland has, adding for good measure that the Party in Scotland, or the people in Scotland for that matter, would not accept otherwise. Ben Wallace concurred with this view and intimated that the Party in England was not only at ease as well but was very supportive of what the Party in Scotland actually wanted.[29] Many of the MSPs spoke of the excellent liaison within the Party between Westminster, Edinburgh and Cardiff.[30] But for McLetchie and Wallace, liaison, balance and, of course, fairness between England and Scotland are the desiderata in the present arrangements of the multi-level polity that is now the modern United Kingdom. In that sense they were perfectly relaxed with Mr Hague's idea of English votes for English laws and believed the Scots as a fair minded people would accept that. However, the West Lothian question will no doubt remain the same for some time yet, while the English response to regional devolution appears to be 'a polite but firm no thanks'.[31] Simply not asking the Question then is no solution, as resentment in England may build to an unmanageable level. Some form of English votes for English laws is one answer but there are other inextricably linked questions which also need to be addressed by a Unionist party if it is to make the union work.

The Rifkind Commission acknowledged that with devolution there would be obvious constitutional implications for the governance of England as well, but thought it outside the remit of the Commission to consider them. The sensitivity to the 'valence problem' appears to have led the Party to a bout of amnesia on the dire predictions they gave for post-devolution UK politics at the 1997 Westminster election. But it may have been a salutary exercise for the Commission to consider these in detail. English votes for English laws may address the West Lothian question, but the 1997 warning that 'financial tensions would be created between a Scottish Parliament and Westminster'[32] has the potential in the near future to severely damage the devolution settlement and by extension the Union itself. And it is not the rabid right wingers of English nationalism that are now vociferously lambasting the Barnett settlement on funding. It is the very Labour politicians who backed devolution who are now challenging the Scottish block funding. Prescott, Mandelson and many backbench English Labour MPs have joined the chorus against it. We get a flavour of such sentiments from the columnist and New Labour MP for Birmingham Edrington, Sion Simon: 'English MPs are angry about how much core government money their regions don't receive compared, in particular with Scotland. "If my constituents knew", one disgruntled northerner told me, "how many more pounds per head they would be getting if the town were transplanted to Scotland, they'd go crazy"'.[33]

It is no use simply saying smugly 'we told you so'; it is the duty of a party who wants to protect the union to offer ameliorative solutions to such tensions in our new multi-level polity. But in the policy documents the term Barnett was conspicuous by its absence, while ambiguous reports appeared in the press. In November 2000 Malcolm Rifkind appeared to accept a regional needs-based formula which would replace Barnett.[34] However, by April the following year, in the prelude to the General Election, he appeared to suggest that the Party's policy of retaining the Secretary of State for Scotland was the only sure way of protecting the Barnett arrangement.[35] The political equivalent of ambulance chasing is no way to protect the Union; as the anguished cries of discontent from English Labour grow louder, the Tory Party in Scotland should avoid jumping on any tartan-clad bandwagons. Thus, principled policy, which offers long term solutions for stability, in and between the different layers of UK government, is the best and right way forward. One way to avoid the Nationalists, on both sides of the border, continually sniping at and exploiting funding arrangements would be to adopt 'Full Fiscal Freedom' for the Scottish Parliament. 'The Tuesday Club', who as a group have no formal affiliation with the Party, were led to offer such a solution.[36]

The group sketched out 'three good reasons', along with concomitant political benefits, for accepting this policy. Firstly, as the Party had lost heavily in the devolution referendum it should unequivocally accept the result, but it should also emphasise that those primary legislative powers for Scotland must carry financial consequences. Secondly, paradoxically, it would act as a bulwark against separation. Nationalists could no longer exploit this 'likeliest source of conflict'. Lastly, as there seemed to be no indication that the clarion complaints from England would diminish with time, the policy would effect the stable constitutional settlement needed, perceived on all sides to be fair and reasonable; strengthening the union rather than weakening it.

Moreover, such a strategy should break the social democratic mind-set of the Scottish people, and introduce the alternative values – thrift, personal responsibility, self-reliance and proper guardianship and care of the public finances – that Jamieson stressed were crucial Conservative tenets.[37] A recent poll for the *Scotland on Sunday* newspaper suggested that the Scottish people would indeed accept this as fair and reasonable. Two thirds believed that Holyrood should be their tax collector while 73 per cent did not want any truck with independence. Interestingly, the newspaper called for the creation of the fiscal equivalent of a Constitutional Convention to debate the need for a new concordat and settlement.[38] This could be the very opportunity the Scots Tories need: participating within a new Convention would no doubt have a beneficial impact on their 'valence problem'. That is, their perceived alien identification vis-à-vis the Scottish body politic could be to some considerable length addressed. In short, the degree to which they were linked in the public's mind with the conditions and goals of almost everyone in the unionist parties on this issue could only be of benefit to them in a Scottish consciousness context.

It is extremely important that such governance problems are solved for the long term because it is certainly not beyond the limits of our imagination to see different parties simultaneously controlling the different levers of governance, and exacerbating such issues. However, David McLetchie is still cautious about full 'fiscal powers', although he readily admits that anyone starting with a blank sheet of paper would not devise the present arrangement. And he further states: 'I don't set my face against it but if it was to come about then there must be a much broader consensus for it amongst the political parties and the business community. And there is the argument that you couldn't significantly expand tax raising powers of the Scottish Parliament without putting that matter to the people first in a referendum. After all it was put to them before'.[39]

Of course, there is the possibility that the SNP could exploit such powers if they were the administration in Holyrood with, let us say, a Tory one in Westminster. But McLetchie was remarkably relaxed about the scenario in our counterfactual crystal ball gazing exercise. He believes that there are lots of issues vis-à-vis the SNP and devolution which are unresolved. For him, even in the highly unlikely and unrealistic scenario that the SNP could form a majority government, under the present system that would immediately trigger a referendum. If they won it that would be the end of the show, and if they lost it then independence would be off the agenda for some considerable time. On the greater likelihood that the SNP could participate in a coalition, the unresolved issues would come to the fore. Thus, he states: 'If the SNP want to be in government in Scotland, it has to accept devolution. It doesn't necessarily have to accept the present distribution of powers – between Westminster and Scotland – but it has to acknowledge that there is a role for the British state. It has to come to an accommodation with the British state, at the very least in a single market and monetary union context'.[40] In short, the Scottish Conservatives now believe that there are now potentially more problems over the issue of devolution to be found within the ranks of the SNP than within their own party.

Indeed, returning to the issue of 'fiscal freedom', the Party has not set its face against local government raising its own revenue and envisages councils thus having greater self-reliance. To establish this greater autonomy and independence the Party believes that it is essential that these councils move in a direction which would allow them to raise more of their own revenue and decide the levels of their spending. This no doubt reflects one of the other dire warnings against the ills of devolution issued at the 1997 Westminster Election, that 'tensions between a Scottish Parliament and local government would be created'.[41] Two years on, in devolution terms, and Daphne Sleigh could still reiterate these concerns: 'it [devolution] has not done local government any good at all, local government has simply died. The scrutiny of the press is needed yet the press has simply ignored it. But that means that many areas have got away with murder'.[42] She goes on to suggest that one reason for this marginalisation of local government is that it is in danger of becoming practically a department of the Scottish Parliament. 'I would like to see it far more independent. It is in great danger of being a complete and utter cipher of Labour in power in Holyrood'. The answer for the Conservatives, according to Sleigh, is to devolve greater powers to local authorities reinforcing their separate identities and importance.

The Party's commitment to devolution per se, and commitment to greater devolution to local government, was witnessed by the its participation in the Renewing Local Democracy Working Group (the Kerley Committee). The Tories participated even though their preferred electoral system for local government (Single Member Plurality) was not even to be considered by the Committee's terms of reference. Moreover, for the Scottish Tories the discourse of Kerley was more suggestive of

'Millbank insincerity', with its 'modernisation', 'renewal', 'stakeholding' and 'parity of esteem', than any real empowerment of local democracy. Daphne Sleigh argued that, although there were a lot of warm words on the Single Transferable Vote system, it seemed that the issue of PR in local electoral reform had become rather a sticking point for the Scottish Executive. The Tories see local government as a useful measure of counter balance to Holyrood, in our new multi-level body politic.

At the opposite end of the multi-level governance framework, the Scottish Tories would like to seek consensus on lasting reform in the House of Lords, incorporating a substantial level of directly elected members. The Rifkind Commission suggested that this should include direct representation from the countries of the United Kingdom in the manner of the US Senate or German Bundesrat. On the question that never seems to go away for the Tories – Europe – the Party in Scotland seems to be at ease with a policy of challenging the elitist one size fits all model of federalist integration. The party appears to be moving in a 'hyper-globalist' direction, in that it wants the flexibility to gain from a more internationalist open seas policy, which it believes the present European Union, with its high levels of tax, regulations and directives, militates against.[43] Whatever the appropriate model should be for the EU, the Party in Scotland advocated that the Secretary of State for Scotland would, on issues of particular concern to Scotland, lead UK delegations to the Council of Ministers.[44]

With the above short examination of our multi-level governance framework in mind, it is clear that the Tories in Scotland have accepted devolution and are working for its success in order to save the union. After all, to paraphrase the Burkean tradition of Conservatism, change is inevitable if not always desirable but the party without the means of some change is without the means of its conservation. Burke also said that it is circumstances which give to every political principle its distinguishing colour and discriminating effect. The principle of devolution has complex circumstances creating a dynamic of demands for greater powers at different levels.

CONCLUSION: A FUTURE FOR TARTAN TORYISM?

The immediate to medium term future for the Scottish Conservative and Unionist Party is not one that readily conjures up a rosy image however much we keep in mind Harold Wilson's dictum of a week being a long time in politics. The Party may now be very much at ease with the devolution idea and be a willing, if not an overly enthusiastic, partner in the present Scottish post-devolution environment. But as this chapter has demonstrated, the Party must address the twin issues of a 'cartel party' having a severe 'valence problem' in today's UK multi-level body politic.

A change of name would not immediately re-root the Party firmly in 'Scottish consciousness'. But there may be an opportunity for the Party to revive the local government label of the 1950s, the Progressives, to use in local councils, particularly if these councils do have the greater autonomy and independence projected for them post Kerley. Although there would not be an immediate beneficial impact on the 'valence problem' over identity, it is of course sensible to start at ground level to re-root in the Scottish consciousness. This is, after all, where the necessary people are to be found who can rejuvenate the organisation. But if the Party were to utilise the Progressive Conservatives label advantageously it would still also have to address its position as a cartel party at different levels of government and this, counter-intuitively, may offer a greater opportunity to tackle the valence problem.

The SNP do not have a divine right to be considered the 'Scottish party' and, as outlined above, devolution may hold greater longer term pitfalls for the Nationalists than for the Scottish Tories. If the SNP were to hold power in Holyrood but fail to convince on independence, it could be the SNP who tear themselves apart – or even develop a 'valence' problem – if they refuse the necessary accommodation with Westminster. But more importantly, with the West Lothian and Barnett questions to mind, the Party may help its Scottish identity problem by being proactive in the development of a Scottish Convention on seeking the 'definitive' long-term solution to these issues. The three major unionist parties in Scotland have, as cartel parties, mutual interest in Scottish devolutionary collective organisational survival. The three unionist parties working along with the corporate and academic elites in a Scottish Convention could only be of benefit to the Party in a Scottish consciousness context.

Moreover, consideration of greater fiscal autonomy for Scotland is not the only question of autonomy that is long overdue for analysis. Further Scottish autonomous reform is needed in the Party's organisation. Making the leader of the Party in Holyrood the leader of the Party in Scotland would address the equivocal structural problem of the Party. If the Chairman or Chief Executive were not to be elected by the membership, along with other vital posts in Scotland, then the posts could be in the gift of the leader in Scotland to appoint. We have heard of the excellent liaison between Westminster, Edinburgh and Cardiff, so in theory such appointments should create no difficulty. After all, to paraphrase the leader of the Scottish Tories at Holyrood, the Party in Scotland, or for that matter the Scottish people, would not accept otherwise. However, with a new leader who has a reputation of being an 'arch Unionist', and once contemplated a future challenge to Labour's devolution settlement, policy on Scotland and on the Scottish Party may be far from settled in the years ahead.

NOTES:

1. *Scotland on Sunday*, 10.6.01.
2. For example see J. Kellas, *The Scottish Political System*, Cambridge University Press, 4th edn. 1989; J. Mitchell, *Conservatives and the Union*, Edinburgh University Press 1990; S. Kendrick and D. McCrone, 'Politics in a Cold Climate: The Conservative Decline in Scotland', *Political Studies*, 1989, Vol. 37; D. Seawright, *An Important Matter of Principle: The Decline of the Scottish Conservative and Unionist Party*, Aldershot: Ashgate 1999.
3. Seawright, *op. cit.*
4. Scottish Unionist Association, *The Year Book for Scotland and Scottish Parliamentary Election Manual*, Edinburgh/Glasgow: Scottish Unionist Association 1955, p13.
5. *Ibid.*, pp18-19.
6. *Daily Record*, 14.10.64.
7. D. Stokes, 'Valence Politics' in D. Kavanagh (ed) *Electoral Politics*, Oxford: Clarendon Press 1992.
8. *Ibid.*, p143.
9. *Ibid.*, p144-47.
10. *The Scotsman*, 14.11.00.
11. Scottish Conservative and Unionist Party, *Scotland's Future: The Policy Commission*, Edinburgh: Scottish Conservative and Unionist Party 1998.
12. *The Scotsman*, 29.1.01.
13. David McLetchie, Phil Gallie and Ben Wallace were interviewed as part of a series of interviews carried out at the Scottish Parliament March 27-29 2001.
14. *Scotland's Future*, *op. cit.*
15. Scottish Conservative and Unionist Party, *Time for Common Sense in Scotland: Manifesto for the 2001 General Election*, Edinburgh: Scottish Conservative and Unionist Party 2001.
16. S. Heffer, *Nor Shall My Sword: The Reinvention of England*, London: Weidenfeld and Nicholson 1999, p27.
17. Scottish Conservative and Unionist Party, *Scotland First: Manifesto for the 1999 Scottish Parliament Election*, Edinburgh: Scottish Conservative and Unionist Party 1999.
18. *Ibid.*
19. For example see *Scotland on Sunday*, 28.11.99.
20. M. Duverger, *Political Parties*, London: Methuen 1954.
21. Interview with Daphne Sleigh, Edinburgh, March 18.3.01.
22. J. Mitchell, 'The Challenge to the Parties: Institutions, Ideas and Strategies', in G. Hassan and C. Warhurst (eds), *The New Scottish Politics: The First Year of the Scottish Parliament and Beyond*, Edinburgh: The Stationery Office 2000, p27.

23. R. S. Katz and P. Mair, 'Party Organisation, Party Democracy, and the Emergence of the Cartel Party', *Party Politics,* 1995, Vol. 1, No. 1.

24. P. Mair, *Party System Change: Approaches and Interpretations,* Oxford: Clarendon Press 1998.

25. Scottish Parliament, Financial Assistance for Registered Parties, Research Paper 99/4, Edinburgh: Scottish Parliament Information Centre 1999.

26. *Ibid.,* p15.

27. *The Scotsman,* 8.5.01.

28. Mitchell, *The Challenge to the Parties, op. cit.,* p27.

29. It should be noted that with regard to the post of Presiding Officer, David McLetchie strongly emphasised that there was no deal between Labour and the Tories on this and thought there was too much reliance placed on a highly speculative newspaper report. Correspondence from David McLetchie, 25.7.01.

30. Interviewed at the Scottish Parliament, March 27-29 2001.

31. J. Curtice, 'The National Interest', *The Guardian,* 4.12.00.

32. Scottish Conservative and Unionist Party, *Fighting for Scotland: Manifesto for the 1997 General Election,* Edinburgh: Scottish Conservative and Unionist Party 1997.

33. *Daily Telegraph,* 30.4.01. Also see *Scotland on Sunday* 29.4.01.

34. *Scotland on Sunday,* 5.11.00.

35. *The Times,* April 25.4.01.

36. M. Fraser, M. Fry and P. Smaill, 'Full Fiscal Freedom: For the Scottish Parliament', The Tuesday Club, Occasional Paper No. 1, 1998.

37. B. Jamieson, 'Scottish Conservatives have lost the plot', *The Scotsman,* 29.1.01.

38. *Scotland on Sunday,* 18.2.01.

39. Interview with David McLetchie at the Scottish Parliament, March 27 2001.

40. *Ibid.*

41. Scottish Conservative and Unionist Party, Fighting for Scotland, op. cit..

42. Interview with Daphne Sleigh, 27 March 2001.

43. D. Baker, A. Gamble and D. Seawright, 'The British Conservative and Labour Parties and Europe: Euro-positive, Euro-sceptic or Euro-exit', paper presented to the British Council, The UK and Europe Conference, University of Orléans, November 2000.

44. Scottish Conservative and Unionist Party, *Time for Common Sense in Scotland: Manifesto for the 2001 General Election,* Edinburgh: Scottish Conservative and Unionist Party 2001.

Partnership, pluralism and party identity: The Liberal Democrats after devolution

PETER LYNCH

The Scottish Liberal Democrats can easily be considered as the great winners of devolution. Not only did the party participate heavily in the design of the Scottish Parliament through the Scottish Constitutional Convention – producing the additional members electoral system for example – but devolution has brought the Liberal Democrats into government in Scotland. The party has gained a good deal of political relevance in Scotland as the 'swing' party with clear coalition potential for both Labour and the SNP.[1] Whilst the combined impact of the electoral and party systems was always likely to involve a Lib-Lab coalition after 1999, the dramatically changed circumstances of the Liberal Democrats is striking. Out of government for decades, a static level of electoral support, plus the position of Scotland's fourth party, all made government status unlikely.[2] And yet, the party has been co-governor of the Scottish Executive since 1999, joined a coalition with Labour in the National Assembly for Wales in 2000 and enjoyed increased electoral support at the 2001 Westminster election. All seems rosy in the Liberal Democrat garden and devolution – rather than electoral reform at Westminster – has given the party the pivotal position formerly held by the liberal Federal Democratic Party in Germany: a status the Lib Dems coveted for many years.[3]

The question for the Liberal Democrats is whether this positive situation becomes a permanent one, with sustainable levels of electoral support and governmental participation as the norm. If so, this situation will have ramifications for the party's development, which will be explored below, not all of which are positive. Indeed, there is a clear need for the party at Holyrood and in the country at large to adjust to its new status as a party of government, whether its coalition partners are Labour or the SNP. Organisationally, the federal nature of the Lib Dems, plus the entrenched autonomy of the Scottish Lib Dems, prepared the party for devolution many years in advance of the advent of a Scottish Parliament. Similar to the Scottish Liberal Party before them, the Scottish Liberal Democrats are recognisable as a party within a party, with their own Scottish office, executive powers, policy-making capacity, staff, membership and manifestos.[4]

The only change is that the constitutional and political reality of devolution has finally caught up with the organisational reality of life within the federal Liberal Democrats. However, organisational auton-omy is one thing, successful participation in coalition government another. Coalition brings the opportunity to implement long-held Liberal Democrat policies but also the dangers of becoming subsumed in office by the larger coalition partner, with a loss of political identity and defections of voters from the Lib Dems. As the Lib Dems are likely to achieve a level of permanency as the smaller partner in coali-tions, then they will always face some challenges to their image, independence and identity. Political purity and a clear party identity on issues is always easier outside of government than in, with no need for messy compromises such as over student tuition fees, or loss of clear policy goals through negotiations with coalition partners.

THE ELECTORAL PERFORMANCE OF THE LIBERAL DEMOCRATS

The 2001 general election found the Scottish Lib Dems in a unique position – fighting an election on their record in government – even though the party was not in government at Westminster. Indeed, to some extent the 2001 election can be seen as 'judgement day' in relation to the performance of the coalition government and the Lib Dems' participation in it. Had the Lib Dems suffered badly at the 2001 elec-tion, losing seats and electoral support, it would have placed the party's coalition role under threat. However, as the Lib Dems held all their seats and saw their level of support increase by 3.4 per cent compared to 1997, and 2.2 per cent compared to 1999, the party could regard its coalition role as a success. Voters certainly did not punish the party for its two years of governing Scotland in alliance with Labour, and that was a substantial achievement in itself. Future elections will indicate whether this remains the case, as there is a sense in which all elections are a test of the Lib Dems' role in coalition, with electoral losses capa-ble of destabilising the party's role in the Scottish Executive. However, at the 2001 election the Lib Dems passed the coalition's first electoral test convincingly.

Moreover, the increased level of support in 2001 indicated a consid-erable turnaround in Lib Dem electoral fortunes in Scotland. In historical perspective, the Lib Dems' electoral performance in 2001 was impressive given its post-war experience. The old Scottish Liberal Party never gained more than 9 per cent at Westminster elections from 1945 to 1979. Indeed, despite occasional Liberal revivals in England, the party only made progress in Scotland with the emergence of the Liberal/SDP Alliance in 1983-7, with impressive levels of support of 24.5 per cent in 1983 and 19.4 per cent in 1987. At subsequent elections, however, the newly merged Liberal Democrats became the 13 per cent party at successive elections in 1992 and 1997. Paradoxically, though the level of votes for the Alliance and then the Lib Dems fell from 1987 onwards, the party was able to increase its number of seats marginally: an impressive achievement. The Scottish election of 1999 saw a slight increase in support to 14.2 per cent in the FPTP vote, which reversed the previous downward pattern and this upward trend continued fairly clearly with 16.4 per cent in the 2001 Westminster election (see Table 4.1).

Table 4.1: Liberal Democrat Vote in Scotland and England at Westminster Elections 1945-2001

| | Scotland | | | England | |
	Candidates	% Votes	Seats	% Votes	Seats
1945	22	5.0	0	9.4	5
1950	41	6.6	2	9.4	2
1951	9	2.7	1	2.3	2
1955	5	1.9	1	2.6	2
1959	16	4.1	1	6.3	3
1964	26	7.6	4	12.1	3
1966	24	6.8	5	9.0	6
1970	27	5.5	3	7.9	2
1974 (F)	34	7.9	3	21.3	9
1974 (O)	68	8.3	3	20.2	8
1979	43	9.0	3	14.9	7
1983	71	24.5	8	26.4	13
1987	71	19.4	9	23.8	10
1992	72	13.1	9	19.3	9
1997	72	13.0	10	18.0	34
2001	72	16.4	10	19.4	40

Note: Two Independent Liberal MPs were elected in 1945 and one in 1950, but none are included in the table above.
Source: Kellas, *The Scottish Political System*, 4th edn. 1989; Hassan and Lynch, *The Almanac of Scottish Politics*, 2001; House of Commons Research Paper 01/54.

What the 2001 result did not provide was any electoral gains for the Lib Dems, nor any additional seats for party to target in future. The party's most likely target in 2001 was Aberdeen South, which Labour held at Westminster and the Lib Dems at Edinburgh. However, the party fell back in this seat and Labour held it easily. This fact means that the most likely electoral gains for the Lib Dems are through the regional lists for additional members in 2003. Beyond that gains are unlikely unless the party makes some dramatic advances in support in other constituencies (Edinburgh South and Inverness East, Nairn and Lochaber were the most likely in 2001). The party therefore seems to have achieved something of a plateau in terms of its level of electoral representation, even though its share of the vote has increased. How the party responds to this situation and builds support in new areas of Scotland is a major challenge.

The party has remained astonishingly weak in the Central Belt throughout the 1999 and 2001 elections, holding only one constituency, Edinburgh West. In Glasgow it competes with the Scottish Socialist Party for fourth place in votes, while both elect one list MSP. Post-1999, as a party of government, the Lib Dems had to endure an embarrassing run of by-election humiliations, where in four out of five contests they were beaten by the Scottish Socialists. The worst result by far was Hamilton South in September 1999 where they managed to finish sixth – behind the Save Hamilton Accies candidate – a one-issue campaign in support of the local football team!

The Lib Dems focus on their 10 MPs and 12 FPTP MSP seats means that in many ways they are not a national party. Party organisation, electoral politics and political priorities are geared towards these seats, which contain, on some estimates, up to half the national Lib Dem membership. Thus, in non-Lib Dem areas, the party is often in no fit state to mount a challenge. This pattern not only prevents the Lib Dems from being a national party, but inhibits the development of a coherent overall identity. Instead, a provincial politics of patchwork priorities dominates, which has significant similarities to nineteenth century party politics. The politics which thus saved the Liberals in the 1950s and 1960s may now contribute to preventing the Lib Dems gaining wider support.

Electoral reform of local government, as discussed in more detail below, would provide a means for the party to gain local representation in areas from which it is currently excluded. Given the party's evident capacity to grow local roots into Holyrood and Westminster representation in a number of constituencies, the opportunities brought by PR at council elections will be considerable. However, until electoral reform is implemented, Lib Dem electoral prospects remain severely constrained, though it was ever so for the party, and represents a European-style reality the party adjusted to many years ago. The party only held a handful of seats in Scotland from 1945-79, and was so used to losing deposits that party activists used to have a song about it. Such days are long gone, as the party has gained a place in government as opposed to being simply concerned with electoral survival.

THE LIBERAL DEMOCRATS AND MULTI-LEVEL GOVERNANCE

> The greatest political revolution of our times in Britain has been the establishment of the Scottish Parliament, and the assemblies in Northern Ireland and Wales. Having entered the nineties as one of the most centralist states in Europe, we have begun the new century as a country well on the way to giving its excluded nations and regions a clear voice.
>
> Charles Kennedy, *The Future of Politics*, 2000[5]

Devolution has enabled Liberal Democrat participation in multi-level governance in Scotland, Wales and London, with elected members and Ministers able to insert themselves into their domestic, UK and EU networks of policy-making and discussion. In Scotland, the most obvious role for the Liberal Democrats in multi-level governance has revolved around the party's status as the coalition partners of Labour in the Scottish Executive, with two Cabinet Ministers and two junior Ministers within the Executive. Despite coming fourth at the 1999 Scottish election, the Lib Dems were able to participate in government office for the first time in decades. This development had a number of aspects to it.

First, it meant that the Lib Dems became a party of government after decades of opposition. Given the years of opposition the party endured – and distant opposition at that – to find themselves in government was clearly a transformation in the party's fortunes. And government meant a transformation in status for the party and its MSPs and MPs, party activists and the party conference. Of course, since the merger of the Liberals and Social Democrats in 1988 and during the Ashdown years, the party had taken on a more sober and serious image – with much less of the beard and sandals image of the old Liberals. But preparing for government is actually rather different from becoming one. Indeed, the current situation is significant as the Lib Dems and Liberals before then were a minority party which struggled to field candidates, win seats and have any great political impact in Scotland in the post-war period: until the late 1980s that is. Somewhere along the line, the party changed from being a radical, oppositionalist, agenda-setting pressure party – seeking to promote issues and ideas – to one which could anticipate its policies actually being implemented by its own Ministers rather than derided by its opponents. Such opponents laughed at David Steel's 'go back to your constituencies and prepare for government' speech in 1981, but probably are not laughing now.

Second, government office has given the Lib Dems the opportunity to present itself as a policy party rather than simply a PR party. The Lib Dems, like the Liberals before, were primarily known as a party which favoured electoral reform and the use of PR for national elections. This remark is not intended to suggest that the party lacked policies, but that its identity amongst the public largely revolved around electoral reform. Devolution changed that situation by giving scope to the party's broader policies in health, education and law and order, not just electoral reform. It also allowed some of the more recognisable Lib Dem policy areas to be implemented, such as land reform, freedom of information and more liberal social policies. Of course there is probably some public confusion about the 'ownership' of Executive policies, due to the presence of Labour Ministers in dealing with health and education. But this situation may change in future. Government status has allowed the party to implement policies and also campaign on its record in office.

Third, there is the fact that the role of the Lib Dems in government has brought rural Scotland into government. The party is very much the representative of rural and small town Scotland, especially the Borders, Highlands and Islands and North East. Indeed, for a brief period, half of the party's ministerial contingent in the Scottish Executive came from Orkney and Shetland. Coalition as well as Lib Dem electoral success has facilitated new patterns of geographic representation in Scotland, which have brought new issues to the fore in the work of the Parliament.

THE SCOTTISH EXECUTIVE COALITION
The Liberal Democrats' role in the Scottish Executive coalition with Labour was predictable though not definite. For example, Lib Dem partnership with Labour in the Scottish Constitutional Convention from 1989-95 made them likely to join a coalition with Labour as its partners. The two parties had developed a long-standing political relationship during the Convention years, particularly between party leaders Donald Dewar and Jim Wallace. Lib-Lab co-operation at Westminster was also a precursor to coalition, with Paddy Ashdown's policy of co-operation with Labour over constitutional issues and electoral reform, and Tony Blair's 'big tent' politics that sought links

between the parties of the centre-left.[6] The Lib Dems had nothing like this type of relationship with any other political party. And the 1999 election result itself made the Lib-Lab coalition the most likely outcome of the first Scottish election. This coalition was the only numerically and politically possible coalition. The SNP did not win enough seats to provide a parliamentary majority with the Lib Dems, though this may change in the future.

The Lib Dems, pre-election, had to maintain the pretence that they would enter into coalition with any political party that could construct a working majority. In answer, to the 'What happens?' question put many times by journalists at press conferences, the Lib Dems' public position was that they would open talks with the leading party in the Parliament – namely Labour.[7] If this were not enough, during the election campaign Jim Wallace made it clear they would not enter into any discussion with a party committed to a referendum on independence – the SNP.[8] Thus the Lib Dems professed a detached neutrality in these positions, but favoured Labour and expressly excluded the SNP.

The party entered coalition negotiations better prepared than Labour, as Jim Wallace, prior to the election, had had a draft negotiating paper drawn up by David Laws, researcher to Malcolm Bruce, MP for Gordon, which formed the basis of discussions with Labour.[9] The final agreement between the two parties was then put to the Lib Dem Scottish Parliamentary Group, which voted 13-3 to accept the agreement. The three dissenters were Donald Gorrie, John Farquhar Munro and Keith Raffan, all independently minded Lib Dem MSPs who were to go on to establish reputations as rebels.[10]

What made the Lib-Lab coalition a less than guaranteed outcome of the 1999 election was the policy distance between the two parties on key issues, as well as the potential for dissatisfaction over the substance of coalition negotiations. For example, whilst there is a considerable degree of policy convergence between the Lib Dems and Labour over a large number of policy areas – for example health and education – there were significant differences that made coalition problematic. Such differences were about the means of implementing policy as well as the substance of policy. Most notably, Labour was opposed to using the Parliament's tax-raising power to fund increased public spending in health and education whilst the Lib Dems were in favour of using the power if necessary after a budget review in 2000.[11] However, areas of policy convergence were also important, such as freedom of information, land reform, abolition of feudal tenure, and electoral reform of local government, as well as more liberal social policy and a more coherent rural affairs policy. When it came to negotiating the coalition deal, there was a great deal of common policy on which to base agree-

ment, and areas of contention such as student tuition fees were successfully dealt with through the establishment of an independent inquiry
into the issue. Finnie, an accountant and one of the key participants in
negotiations, reflected on the frantic talks and successful conclusion: 'It
had been an unbelievable experience. I had often negotiated complex
commercial transactions and no doubt that stood me in good stead but
this had been very different.'[12]

Two things are evident about the performance of the Lib-Lab coalition. First, there is the fact that the coalition largely achieved what it set
out to do: namely, implement the partnership agreement. This agreement was central to coalition performance and has formed a
fundamental plank of the Executive's legislative programme and activities since 1999. Legislation such as the Abolition of Feudal Tenure Act,
Land Reform Bill, National Parks Act, Standards in Schools Act and
Transport Act all had their origins in the initial partnership agreement
in 1999, as did increases in spending in education and health, greater
recruitment of doctors, nurses, teachers, and the principles of what
became the McCrone Report on teachers' pay and conditions.[13]
Though appearing defensive on occasions, the Lib Dems have also
promoted their policy effectiveness within the coalition, through
publicising the number of 1999 manifesto commitments implemented
by the Executive. In May 2001 the party declared that it had implemented 185 different policy commitments from its 1999 manifesto,
ranging from modernising the General Teaching Council to abolishing
tuition fees to the dispersal of government agencies across Scotland.[14]
Many of these commitments are fairly minor, but they do allow the
party to demonstrate that it has not been pushed aside as the junior
partner in the coalition, and will help convince party members that
participation in the coalition has brought positive policy benefits.

Second, strains which have developed within the coalition have not
been fundamental, though it is obvious that the coalition has a limited
depth within the Parliament. For example, Lib Dem MSPs did not
accept that the principle of collective responsibility that acted to bind
Ministers within the Executive applied to backbenchers. A number of
Lib Dem MSPs have therefore acted independently within the
Parliament on a number of issues in plenary and in committee, in defi-
ance of the Executive. This situation infuriated Labour backbenchers,
who frequently supported the Executive's position in the Parliament,
but it was a product of the disparate and independent-minded nature
of the Lib Dem Parliamentary Group (though it should also be pointed
out that Labour also has independent-minded MSPs who dissent from
Executive policy in the Parliament). However, it would be erroneous
to expect that Lib Dem MSPs would behave in the same way as Labour

members. Not only is the culture of the two parties very different, but the Lib Dems have nothing of Labour's experience of splits, divisions and extremism from the 1980s, which have been fundamental to Labour's adoption of strict discipline within the parliamentary groups at Holyrood and Westminster.

Despite the occasional dissension and media coverage of splits over coalition policy, most Executive legislation and policy has been accepted by the Lib Dem and Labour backbenchers. To take some examples, the most prominent issue of student finance was successfully negotiated between the two parties in the winter of 2000-1, with freedom of information also accepted despite pressures for policy convergence with similar legislation at Westminster. The Clause 28 debate did not divide the two coalition partners, though it did seriously divide Labour ministers and MSPs. Land reform legislation was implemented in 2000, further reform was in progress in 2001 and the Sutherland report on financing care for the elderly was agreed by both parties in the Executive. Where the coalition did come to grief was over the support package for fishermen in March 2001, when Lib Dem backbenchers combined with the opposition parties to defeat the Executive position. This event brought the subsequent resignation of Shetland MSP Tavish Scott as Deputy Minister for Parliament over the Executive's position. Though this event brought major difficulties for the coalition partners and pressure on the Lib Dem MSPs for failing to support the Executive position, the main reason for the Executive's defeat was the absence of Labour MSPs to attend the party conference in Inverness. Had those MSPs been present, the Executive would not have been defeated. Despite the disquiet over this affair, the Executive parties reversed the vote and the fishing vote was very much the exception rather than the norm for coalition voting patterns.

Local government and multi-level governance
Future reform of the electoral system for local government elections in Scotland also offers opportunities for the Liberal Democrats in the arena of multi-level governance. Though this issue is a difficult one for the coalition partners to agree – and has coalition-splitting potential – the issue is central to the Lib Dems' participation in the coalition, and therefore likely to be implemented in the future. Currently, Liberal Democrats are not a substantial force in local government. Indeed, in many local authorities the party has no representation and has even struggled to field candidates at local elections. Liberal Democrats have no council seats in 14 of Scotland's 32 local authorities and only two of these councils – Orkney and the Western Isles – are non-partisan councils. Across Central Scotland in particular, Liberal Democrat council

involvement is extremely limited. The party has shares of the vote as low as 1.93 per cent in East Ayrshire, 5.73 per cent in Dundee, 3.66 per cent in Falkirk, 6.13 per cent in Glasgow, 1.78 per cent in North Lanarkshire and 0 per cent in North Ayrshire, South Ayrshire and West Dunbartonshire.[15] Whilst electoral reform is most likely to produce a more 'SNP world' in local government, it will also bring benefits to the Liberal Democrats in some areas. First, in areas of strength such as Aberdeen, Edinburgh, Fife and Inverclyde, the new electoral system will likely propel the Liberal Democrats into government in the locality. Second, in areas of weakness, there is the prospect of greater Liberal Democrat representation from existing shares of the vote, as well as increased shares of the vote. The electoral system will give local parties something to aim at in contrast to the current FPTP system.

Of course, the pattern of coalitions in local government offers interesting and permanent facets to the Scottish Executive coalition. Locally, coalitions will become the norm in most councils, but the exact political colouring of local coalitions will differ markedly and complement or conflict with arrangements at Holyrood.[16] This level of complex governance is common in other European countries, but rare in Britain. It will likely produce a situation in which Liberal Democrats enjoy coalition governance with all possible configurations of parties and independents locally, whilst acting in alliance with Labour and, in time, the SNP at Holyrood. The dynamics of these coalition arrangements in terms of policies, local finance, Executive-council relations, etc, should prove challenging. Furthermore, as the Association of Liberal Democrat councillors has proven an important grouping within the Liberal Democrats, the elevation of councillors and council groups will increase their level of influence within the party as a whole. It might also create a situation in which the council and group leaders form a counterweight to the MSPs within the Scottish party – a development that would be particularly interesting in relation to local government finance and autonomy, as the two sets of interests come into conflict. The different coalition priorities of Lib Dems in Edinburgh and in local authorities would provide a substantial area of conflict for the party to manage.

Multi-level governance in the UK and EU
The participation of Liberal Democrats within the institutions of multi-level governance is not solely limited to the Scottish Executive and local authorities. Devolution has seen the development of multi-level governance across the UK, with the involvement of Scottish Ministers in Joint Ministerial Committees with UK ministers, in EU

working groups and Council of Ministers as well as institutions such as the British-Irish Council. Links with Wales and Northern Ireland, as well as other European regions and organisations such as the Committee of the Regions, all offer extended opportunities for Liberal Democrat participation in multi-level governance and opportunities for alliances and influence outwith Scotland itself. The party has not exploited such opportunities so far, but there are clearly opportunities for the party in the broader multi-level governance arena.[17] Finally, despite the Labour government's tepid commitment to regional government in England, the prospect of elected regional assemblies in England offers substantial additional opportunities to the Lib Dems.

PARTY IDENTITY AND INDEPENDENCE

Organisationally, the Lib Dems in Scotland have coped well with devolution. The constitutional independence of the Scottish party within the federal British party pre-devolution has enabled a considerable level of Scottish policy autonomy to be practised and, indeed, the party has made a virtue out of allowing the Scottish party to do its own thing. The history of independence within the old Scottish Liberal Party has fed its way into the organisational culture and activism of the Scottish Liberal Democrats.[18] Westminster meddling does not happen within the Liberal Democrats as it does with Labour. It has no strong centre like Millbank seeking to impose its will, and no need for Scottish policy consistencies with Westminster, because the Lib Dems are not in government in the UK Parliament; and there is no-one like Gordon Brown who sees Scotland as a sphere of influence and control. The future of the Scottish Lib Dems is therefore very much in their own hands and related very closely to the party's role in coalition in the Scottish Executive.

The patterns of coalition established from 1999-2003 are not necessarily a guide to future coalitions, though the experience might well provide some precedents. The potential for alternative coalitions may continue to be negligible, for the same reasons as in the first elections. But future coalitions might not follow this simple formula: fragmentation of the party system might lead to alternative coalition partners emerging, as well as a move away from minimum winning coalitions of two parties to three-party coalitions or more.

It is likely, however, that the Liberal Democrats will find a semi-permanent role in coalition arrangements beyond the 1999-2003 government. Their position as the 'swing party' gives them a built-in advantage as a coalition partner – they could easily operate in coalition with the SNP as well as Labour. In future elections the Lib Dems may decide to indicate their preferred coalition partner in advance of the election campaign. In Germany, it is common for the parties to make such pre-election statements, which can assist voters in their voting decisions.[19]

However, a permanent position in government could bring problems. The party could become tainted through permanent government status and perceived policy failures, or from policy compromises with its coalition partner. It may become too closely associated with Labour and begin to lose its own party identity. Equally, its permanent government status could mean it runs out of ideas for new policies and innovations; the party is not well-connected to the Scottish policy community in terms of academia, think-tanks or policy networks, and its own internal organisation is not especially attuned to innovative policy debate. The party at large as opposed to just the Ministers and MSPs will have to adapt to coalition politics.

The advantage the Liberal Democrats will have in future coalitions will be through their experience of coalition and government itself. This situation will be particularly advantageous should the Lib Dems form a coalition with the SNP. Under that scenario, it would be the Lib Dems who had experience of the government machinery as well as the practice of coalition partnership. However, producing potential ministers may in the future offer a difficult challenge for the party at Holyrood, especially given the maverick nature of a number of Liberal MSPs, and the fact that David Steel resigned from the parliamentary group to become Presiding Officer. Furthermore, the Lib Dem group in the Scottish Parliament is predominantly middle-aged and male, which creates problems for the party's renewal and image in Scotland. Only two female MSPs were elected in 1999 and the average age of the Lib Dem MSPs was 49 – a higher average than Labour or the SNP.[20] This leads to questions about the development of a group of MSPs who will have some longevity within the Parliament and provide a future leadership. However three younger Lib Dem MSPs – Iain Smith, Tavish Scott and Nicol Stephen – have held ministerial office in the Parliament's first two years (though with mixed consequences).

Given the age profile of the Lib Dem Parliamentary Group, there are clear possibilities for the party to experience an age and gender shift in its parliamentary group through retirement rather than deselection. For a small party, with limited personnel and public offices, continually recruiting new elites to both Holyrood and Westminster is an important task, especially at Holyrood where those elites play prominent roles as Ministers, frontbench spokespersons and committee convenors. However, the party does have its councillors as a base from which to recruit future parliamentarians and future electoral reform in local government should expand this grassroots base even further.

THE FUTURE'S BRIGHT, THE FUTURE'S LIB DEM?

Over the next ten years, the Scottish Liberal Democrats face three main challenges. First, there is the challenge of electoral expansion. Should the party seek to maintain its position as a rural representative with a limited geographical appeal, or should it aim to expand across urban Scotland to become more than a regional party? If it does seek to expand in urban Scotland, what does this do to its identity and policy agenda in rural Scotland? Will it undermine its support in the rural heartlands? In urban Scotland, both Aberdeen and Edinburgh stand out as areas to build on, with a mix of Scottish and Westminster seats and councillors all providing grounds for electoral optimism. Other areas of support to build upon are more difficult to see, though the use of PR for local elections will alter this bleak situation fairly radically for the party. However, steady growth in key areas of existing support rather than dramatic advances are the most likely electoral future for the Lib Dems.

Second, there is the challenge of operating as a party of government in Scotland. Key questions in this area revolve around whether the party will benefit or lose electorally from its role as a government party. Will it suffer from its identification with Labour in current and future coalitions? Some opponents have tried to label it 'rural Labour' in an effort to associate the party with Labour.[21] It has previously, for example in the 1992 general election, suffered electorally for its close co-operation with Labour in the Scottish Constitutional Convention and would be vulnerable to any future electoral recovery by the Conservatives.[22] How will it fare if linked to the SNP in any future coalition? The electoral outcome of the Lib Dems' role in government has initially been positive, as the 2001 Westminster election demonstrated, though this scenario may not be repeated at future elections. Therefore, at some stage in the future it is likely the party will face a period of unpopularity as a consequence of its performance in government or even of the performance of its coalition partner.

Third, there is the challenge of playing a key role in policy making in Scotland either in or out of government. Since the election of New Labour in 1997, the Liberal Democrats have seen a number of their policies actually implemented. Constitutional policies such as devolution, the European Convention on Human Rights, reform of the House of Lords and freedom of information have been implemented. Electoral reform at Westminster was rebuffed, though implemented in Scotland, Wales and London. Land and rural policies for Scotland have been implemented through coalition involvement. Therefore, as discussed above, there are signs that the Lib Dems could suffer from programmatic fulfilment. The issue of the euro remains one area of policy independence, though, given limited public support for it, not a particularly positive one for the Lib Dems. However, at some stage in the future, it is possible that the Scottish Lib Dems will face a policy crisis, as it is the Executive, civil service machine and pressure groups that drive party policy rather than the party itself. A period of opposition in the future – which seems unlikely, given the Scottish electoral system – may be one mechanism for the party to recover some of its policy autonomy from domination by the Executive.

CONCLUSION

Scottish politics have changed dramatically since the 1997 election and the establishment of the Scottish Parliament in May 1999. Lib Dems have been at the centre of this process, and see it as a harbinger to wider constitutional and political change at a UK level. This was the substance of the Blair-Ashdown project of centre-left co-operation.[23] Charles Kennedy, Lib Dem leader since 1999, has reflected a more suspicious attitude in relation to Labour's motives: 'It is not yet clear what New Labour really means by devolution. One is reminded of the line from Orwell's *Animal Farm* ... In the new Britain, we celebrate diversity. But some are more diverse than others ...'[24] The added value of Lib Dem participation in government has had immense value to the UK Lib Dems after decades in the wilderness.

In spite of the ups and downs of participation in the Scottish Executive coalition and future uncertainties about the coalition's benefits, it is fairly clear that the Lib Dems have achieved both electoral and policy gains from the devolution process. Government office, policy success and an initial electoral test in 2001 all indicated that the years of coalition thus far were a positive experience. The party's placement in the Scottish political system would also seem to indicate its potential role as the pivotal party, central to coalition formation for years to come. The party is thus likely to achieve a considerable level of political realignment in Scottish politics. Rather than replacing another party in the electoral system, the Lib Dems have become part of the process of political realignment through policy implementation in the Scottish Executive. For Scotland's fourth party, with a very chequered electoral history from 1945 until 1983, this position is one to be savoured.

NOTES

1. G. Sartori, *Parties and Party Systems*, Cambridge: Cambridge University Press 1976.
2. P. Lynch, 'Third Party Politics in a Four Party System: The Liberal Democrats in Scotland', *Scottish Affairs*, Winter 1998, No. 22.

3. D. MacIver, 'Introduction', in D. MacIver (ed), *The Liberal Democrats*, Hemel Hempstead: Prentice Hall/Harvester Wheatsheaf 1996.

4. S. Ingle, 'Party Organisation', in D. MacIver (ed), *op. cit.*

5. C. Kennedy, *The Future of Politics*, London: Harper Collins 2000, p145.

6. See on Lib-Lab co-operation: P. Ashdown, *The Ashdown Diaries: Volume One 1988-1997*, London: Allen Lane 2000; and *Volume Two 1997-99*, London: Allen Lane 2001.

7. R. Finnie, 'The Negotiation Diaries', *Scottish Affairs*, No. 28, p51.

8. B. Taylor, *The Scottish Parliament*, Edinburgh: Polygon 1999, pp202-3.

9. Finnie, *The Negotiation Diaries*, *op. cit.*, p51. Also see *The Ashdown Diaries: Volume Two*, *op. cit.* Laws went on at the 2001 general election to inherit and win Paddy Ashdown's old seat of Yeovil.

10. M. Watson, *Year Zero: An Inside View of the Scottish Parliament*, Edinburgh: Polygon 200, pp7-8.

11. Scottish Liberal Democrats, *Raising the Standard – Scottish Election Manifesto 1999*, Edinburgh: Scottish Liberal Democrats 1999.

12. Finnie, *The Negotiation Diaries*, *op. cit.*, p56.

13. Scottish Executive, *Partnership for Scotland: An Agreement for the First Scottish Parliament*, Edinburgh: Scottish Executive 1999.

14. Scottish Liberal Democrats, *Making the Difference in Government*, Edinburgh: Scottish Liberal Democrats 2001.

15. G. Hassan and P. Lynch, *The Almanac of Scottish Politics*, London: Politico's Publishing 2001.

16. A. Adonis, *Voting in Proportion: Electoral Reform for Scotland's Councils*, Edinburgh: Scottish Council Foundation 1998.

17. Though David Steel now sits as a non-party member, as the Parliament's Presiding Officer he has played a significant role in promoting the Parliament both in the UK and internationally, thus bringing some degree of Liberal Democrat profile to the arena of multi-level governance.

18. Lynch, *op. cit.*

19. B. Gebauer, *Coalition Government in Germany: The Formation and Operation of Multi-Party Rule*, London: Constitution Unit 2000, p6.

20. P. Lynch, *Scottish Government and Politics: An Introduction*, Edinburgh: Edinburgh University Press 2001, p52.

21. *The Scotsman*, 30.10.00.

22. The Lib Dems suffered several setbacks in the 1992 general election with the Conservatives dramatically cutting into Lib Dem majorities in seats such as Gordon and Tweeddale, Ettrick and Lauderdale. This was widely perceived to have been aided by the preceding Lib-Lab co-operation over questions of devolution and a general sense of Lib-Lab closeness.

23. P. Ashdown, *The Ashdown Diaries: Volume Two*, *op. cit.*

24. Kennedy, *The Future of Politics*, *op. cit.*, pp148-49.

Exploiting new electoral opportunities: the small parties in Scotland

LYNN G. BENNIE

Small parties and independent candidates in Britain have, historically, existed on the 'political fringe'.[1] Under the single member plurality electoral system used in British general elections, small parties and their candidates expect to lose election deposits. The Scottish Greens, for example, have been taking part in elections since 1979, but saved a general election deposit for the first time in 2001.

Devolution, accompanied by the introduction of the principle of proportional representation to elections in Scotland, Wales, and European Elections, has presented small parties with new electoral opportunities, and in the process this has raised new questions about the importance of such parties. For example, where have they come from, what do they stand for, and how influential are they? This chapter focuses on the two small parties to enter the Scottish Parliament in 1999 – the Scottish Socialist Party (SSP) and the Scottish Green Party (SGP) – exploring the character of these parties, their electoral history, and their experiences since devolution.

THE ORIGINS AND IDENTITY OF THE SCOTTISH SOCIALIST PARTY

The roots of the Scottish Socialist Party can be traced back several decades to when the Militant Tendency was fighting for revolutionary socialism within the Labour Party. Militant was a radical caucus group that promoted an uncompromising, revolutionary socialist agenda, loosely based on the ideas of Leon Trotsky. Trotsky had argued that it was quite acceptable for revolutionaries to enter European social democratic parties with the objective of capturing the labour movement.

Militant did not regard parliamentary democracy as important. As Crick documents, electing members of parliament was viewed as a means of raising workers' consciousness in advance of revolution.[2] Similarly, Militant's public programme was transitional and 'designed solely as a method of increasing workers' consciousness'.[3] The real objective was for the working class to reject reformism and embrace revolution. Other campaigns of the left – CND, the feminist movement, and the gay rights movement – were seen as distractions by Militant in the 1970s and 1980s. Crick argued that Militant's approach was 'secretive' and 'disciplined' and completely incompatible with the democratic traditions of the Labour Party.

In the 1980s Militant in England enjoyed some success within the Labour Party. Militant members were selected as parliamentary candidates and elected as MPs. Organisationally, Militant was also strong, with large numbers of highly motivated activists, and almost as many permanent staff members as the Labour Party. In Scotland, Militant's base was in Glasgow where supporters came close to being selected as Labour Party Westminster candidates for the 1987 general election. In both Provan and Pollok the Militant candidates came very close to being selected.[4]

Scottish Militant Labour (SML) was formed as an independent electoral force in the autumn of 1992 when a group of Militant members formally abandoned entryism, largely in response to the Labour Party's concerted attempts to purge Militant from its organisation. Militant supporters in Springburn, Cumbernauld, Kilsyth, Provan and Pollok had all been ejected from the party in the late 1980s. Tommy Sheridan was one of the Militants to be expelled, widely reported by the media at the time.

However, Sheridan had come to prominence at the height of Scotland's protests against the Community Tax. Militant vehemently supported non-payment, providing a strong voice for those who opposed the tax, and in 1992, as President of the Anti-Poll Tax Federation, Sheridan was imprisoned for six months for protesting against a warrant sale. Sheridan's mother Alice ran his election campaign for Glasgow city council, and he was elected as a Militant Labour councillor for Pollok in 1992, taking his seat beside three other Militant councillors.[5] Militant Labour had a total of seven local government representatives by the end of 1992, including one from Aberdeen (elected in 1990) and two Strathclyde Regional councillors elected in 1992 (see Table 5.1. on the growth of SML/SSP support).

By the 1997 general election, the Scottish Socialist Alliance (SSA) had been formed. This was a relatively successful attempt to bring together Scottish Militant Labour and a wide collection of other left-wing groupings and parties, providing them with some unified focus. The Alliance fielded 16 candidates and performed relatively well in a number of Glasgow constituencies. The party's best result was in Glasgow Pollok where Tommy Sheridan came third, ahead of the Conservative and Liberal Democrat candidates.[6]

The Scottish Socialist Party was formed shortly after these elections, in 1998, merging Militant Labour supporters, ex-Communists and community and environmental activists. The party was launched by Sheridan, with the backing of the Euro MP Hugh Kerr who was expelled from the Labour Party for criticising the 'right-wing' approach of Tony Blair.

Table 5.1: Scottish Socialist Party and predecessor party votes

	Election	% Vote	Party
1992	Pollok Westminster constituency	19. 2	SML
1994	Glasgow, Euro elections	7.6	SML
1997	Pollok Westminster constituency	11.1	SSA
1999	Glasgow-wide, FPTP	6.3	SSP
1999	Scotland, Euro elections	4.0	SSP
2001	Scotland, Westminster elections	3.1	SSP

Within a short time the SSP was developing a full set of policy proposals. Standing for an independent Scottish socialist republic and projecting itself as a socialist alternative to New Labour, the party was attempting to appeal to disillusioned traditional Labour supporters. Manifestos included commitments to collective ownership of transport, oil, finance, electricity and gas; a minimum wage of 'at least' £7 an hour; progressive taxation; abolition of student fees and the reintroduction of grants; free TV licenses and heating vouchers for pensioners; rejection of the Private Finance Initiative; phasing out of private health care; and a nuclear free Scotland.[7]

The ideology of the Scottish Socialists remains Trotskyist, with commitments to democratic international socialism. Like its Militant predecessors it criticises the evils of capitalism, as well as the bureaucratic state centrism of the former Soviet Union, while advocating a democratically planned socialist economy and egalitarianism. However, the tone and strategy of the SSP is very different from that of the hardline 1980s Militants. It advocates a democratic and 'modern' socialism – decentralist, high-tech and environmentally responsible.

This is also tolerant, socially libertarian socialism. Party literature makes it quite clear that the SSP sees no place for discrimination – racism, sectarianism, sex discrimination, ageism, homophobia, or discrimination against disabled people.

Furthermore, the party takes a liberal position on the use of 'soft' drugs, promising to 'license the sale and production of cannabis for medical and personal use'.[8] Sheridan and McCombes argue: 'In all spheres of human activity, the emphasis of 21st century socialism will be on individual freedom on personal matters, combined with collective decision-making on the wider problems of society'.[9] This is very different to the picture of early Militant provided by Michael Crick, when sexism and homophobia were part of the organisational culture, and rigid democratic centralism was the order of the day.

Also gone is the Militant position of non-co-operation with other groups. The SSP makes concerted efforts to forge alliances with other campaigns and groups. Traditionally, the left in British politics has been bitterly divided. The SSP, however, has been quite successful at bringing together a number of radical left-wing groups, as indicated by the Socialist Workers Party's recent decision to join forces with the SSP. In the most recent, 2001, election manifesto, the SSP describes itself as a 'pluralist party which seeks to unite socialists from all traditions while allowing platforms and groupings the right to organise within the party'.

The SSP unequivocally stands for independence. This appears quite natural for a party that believes in the decentralisation of power. Members of Militant were much more ambivalent on the question of nationalism, many of them arguing that devolution was a 'slippery slope to separatism'.[10] The feeling at the time of Militant was that socialism could only be achieved at the UK level. For the SSP, the model is an independent Scottish Republic with links to anti-capitalist movements across the globe.

All in all, this is a less 'revolutionary' approach, which some may interpret as a dilution of principles. Sheridan and McCombes quite frankly admit that 'in a socialist Scotland, some sections of the economy would most likely remain in private hands'.[11] However, the party remains radical in its fundamental critique of capitalism and its demand for a reordering of society. Given the fragmentation of the political left, the SSP has done well to emerge as the principal left force in Scottish politics.

THE ORIGINS AND IDENTITY OF THE SCOTTISH GREEN PARTY

Green party activity in England began in 1973 with the creation of 'People', Europe's first green party.[12] The Ecology Party in Scotland emerged in the late 1970s from a group of environmentally concerned activists based in Edinburgh. While a handful of Scottish activists had been involved with People and the UK Ecology Party in the 1970s, the

Scottish arm of the Ecologists did not formally came into existence until November 1978. The 'formation' of the Scottish Ecologists took place in the house of Leslie Spoor, a retired teacher and former long-term member of the Labour Party, who had joined the UK Ecology Party in 1977 and served on its executive committee. The first Scottish Ecology candidate stood in the May 1979 general election, five years after Ecologists contested elections in England.

The ideology of the Ecologists had originally been inspired by the work of Edward Goldsmith.[13] Goldsmith's 'Blueprint for Survival', published in the *Ecologist* magazine, provided the basis for the party's first General Election manifesto. Goldsmith claimed that industrial society was threatening the survival of the planet and advocated an ecological society based on a complex mix of community decentralisation, traditional family structures and central planning. Policy recommendations included the rejection of equal rights for women, strengthening law and order and a more restrictive immigration policy.

However, this 'survivalist' tradition was criticised for its authoritarian undertones and by the end of the 1970s (by the time the Ecologists had mobilised in Scotland) the UK party had rejected many of these ideas. Instead, it developed a rather more gradualist, democratic agenda, and an increasingly professional approach to elections. Rüdig and Lowe describe the rising influence at the end of the 1970s of a new national leadership that included Jonathon Porritt. The new style of leadership involved a rejection of the survivalist ideology and the development of a more democratic and pragmatic ecological vision. As Rüdig and Lowe argue: 'Their conception was of structural reform initiated by an ecological government which had gained a foothold through the electoral process, leading to a steady-state economy with decentralised political institutions.'[14] Activists involved in the formation of the Scottish section of the party fully endorsed this democratic ecological view.

For most of the 1980s, the party failed to make an impression, with only a small number of candidates standing in national elections. However, against a background of increasing public concern for environmental issues, the Greens made a dramatic impact on the 1989 European elections. Green candidates stood in all seven European constituencies in Scotland, on a platform of traditional green issues – sustainable growth and the development of renewable energy sources – criticising the European Union for being centralised, bureaucratic and unresponsive. The Greens in Scotland received 115,000 votes, 7.2 per cent of the vote.

The Greens' performance in Scotland was undoubtedly less dramatic than in some parts of the UK. In the South East of England, for example, the Greens attracted 20 per cent of the vote, and the Greens averaged 14.5 per cent of the vote across the UK. However, this performance was considerably better than at any previous election. Furthermore, it coincided with a remarkable increase in party membership. From a base of only a couple of hundred members, membership of the Scottish Greens rose to a high of 1,250 and branch organisations peaked at 36. Party branch activities were concentrated in certain areas of Scotland, mainly in the big cities of Edinburgh and Glasgow and in the far North.

The Scottish Greens formally gained their independence from the UK party in September of 1990, then creating two Green parties in the UK: the Scottish Green Party and the Green Party of England, Wales and Northern Ireland. Throughout the 1990s the party struggled to stay afloat, as the public lost interest in green issues.

Membership declined just as dramatically as it had increased and many branches collapsed. Nevertheless, the party survived and played a role in the campaign for Scottish devolution. During and following the 1992 election the Greens participated in broad alliances to generate grassroots support for constitutional change through public demonstrations, vigils and petitions (Common Cause, Democracy for Scotland, and Scotland United). This contrasted with the elite-led Scottish Constitutional Convention's drafting of a constitutional package for change. The Greens left the Convention in 1990 because of a failure to agree on the principles of a multi-option referendum and a timetable for moving towards a system of proportional representation. The Greens returned to the negotiations in 1995 but they appear to have had little influence in the work of the Constitutional Convention.[15]

Overall, Scotland has proved a difficult battleground for the Scottish Greens, with its culture of materialism and general lack of political opportunities. Before the setting up of Scotland's Parliament, the Greens were a clear case of a struggling fringe party, with more lows than highs. In the 1997 general election, for example, the Scottish Greens stood in only five constituencies and attracted an average vote of 0.84 per cent.[16]

Despite the party's traditional 'fringe' status, the Greens in Scotland would argue that the issues they address are of central importance. The ecological principles of the party – sustainability, decentralisation, the redistribution of wealth – constitute a radical political programme, with some clear overlaps with the left. Indeed, the Scottish Green Party has always been keen to challenge any suggestions that it is a single-issue party. In fact, the policy programme deals with a wide range of environmental and social issues: pollution controls; a basic income scheme; a Scottish community bank to fund community businesses; local currency schemes; a housing investment scheme; the abolition of student tuition fees; the reintroduction of grants for the less well off; an integrated transport policy; and a ban on GM crops.

1999: A TURNING POINT FOR THE SMALL PARTIES

With the creation of the Scottish Parliament, the hopes of the small parties were raised. Prospects looked improved due to the regional party lists, which added a degree of proportionality to election outcomes. The rules governing the 1999 elections were also more encouraging for small parties than those in British general elections. For example, the £500 deposit required to stand in a regional list could include up to 12 named candidates, compared with a deposit of £500 for each general election candidate. More than 300 candidates from approximately 25 different small parties stood in the regions in May 1999 (not including independents), more than twice as many as in the 1997 general election. The Scottish Greens, the Scottish Socialist Party, the Socialist Labour Party and the Natural Law Party were the only small parties to stand in all the regions. The small parties, unsurprisingly, concentrated their efforts on these regional lists. Indeed, less than half of the constituencies – 35 – had a candidate from a small party or an independent. Apart from independents, only the Socialist Workers Party stood in the constituencies but not the regions, with five candidates.

Overall, the small parties and independents attracted 11.3 per cent of the regional vote, and 2.7 per cent of the constituency vote. The only parties to gain representation, however, were the Scottish Socialists and the Greens; Sheridan was elected in Glasgow with 7.25 per cent (18,581 votes) and Harper was successful in the Lothians region with 6.91 per cent of the vote (22,848 votes).

The SSP, standing in all regions in Scotland, with a total of 55 regional candidates, attracted 46,635 regional votes, or 1.99 per cent of all regional votes cast. The party also had candidates in 18 constituencies, attracting 23,654 of these votes (1.01 per cent). Of all the small parties in the constituencies, the SSP clearly dominated. Three SSP candidates finished third, ahead of the Conservative and Liberal Democrat candidates: in Glasgow Pollok Tommy Sheridan polled 5,611 votes (21.5 per cent); in Glasgow Shettleston Rosie Kane came third with 1,640 votes (7.99 per cent); and in Glasgow Ballieston James McVicar attracted 1,864 votes (7.86 per cent). In all, the SSP's performance greatly improved on that of the SSA in the 1997 general election. The party argued in 1999 that its support was not simply 'ghettoised' in the Glasgow area, but Glasgow was clearly its main battleground.[17]

Like the Socialists, the Greens were galvanised by the prospect of a fair voting system in 1999. The Greens took the decision to place candidates in all the regions (with a total of 41 candidates) but in no traditional constituencies, because of financial constraints and because they recognised that the proportional list system provided them with their best opportunity for election. A decision to concentrate grassroots campaigning on the city centre streets of Edinburgh was combined with simple media stunts and press releases. The party adopted the campaign slogan 'Vote Green 2' and used an enormous luminous Green '2' as an election prop, urging Labour supporters who were concerned about the environment to consider giving their second vote to the Greens. Overall, the Green campaign was inventive and well received by the media.

Robin Harper, an Edinburgh teacher, had been a party member since 1985 and had extensive experience of standing in elections. He had been a candidate in three European elections and the 1998 North East European by-election, two UK general elections, and in the Perth and Kinross Westminster by-election in 1995. He had lost every single deposit except in the 1989 European election, when he achieved 10.47 per cent of the vote in the Lothian region.

The Greens attracted 84,000 votes (3.6 per cent of regional votes). The Edinburgh area was the electoral core of Scottish Green support, the party being unable to surpass 4 per cent in any other region. The next best Green performance was in Glasgow, where the party attracted 3.96 per cent. (The worst result for the Greens was in Central Scotland, with only 1.79 per cent.) However, the Green vote did increase significantly across Scotland, and particularly in the Glasgow area. In the general election of 1997 the party had attracted less than 2000 votes. In 1999, the Greens claimed to be the fifth party in Scotland because they attracted more regional votes and more European election votes than any other small party.

Another non-main-party successful candidate in these elections was Dennis Canavan in Falkirk West, which was a considerable embarrassment to the Labour Party. The locally popular sitting Westminster MP, Canavan was rejected by Labour as a candidate for the Scottish election. This proved to be a very controversial decision, which prompted claims of Labour selectors acting like 'thought police'.[18] The result was a resounding personal vote for Canavan, amounting to 55 per cent of all votes cast.

The biggest 'other' party was the Socialist Labour Party (SLP). With 57 regional candidates (and 4 constituency candidates), it won over 50,000 regional votes (just over 2 per cent), more than the SSP. The Highlands and Islands Alliance was expected to do well in these elections, but to the surprise of many media observers it performed rather poorly. With a regional list of ten candidates, the Alliance attracted only 1.29 per cent (2,607 votes).

As well as the elections to the Scottish Parliament, there was an EU election in 1999, contested for the first time throughout Britain under a system of proportional representation in 1999. While the number of parties standing in these elections did not increase between 1994 and 1999, the number of votes cast for small parties increased considerably, from 3.22 per cent in 1994 to nearly 15 per cent of the total vote by 1999, again indicating the voters' willingness to turn to small parties in PR elections. The Greens finished in fifth place with 5.78 per cent, a rise of 4.18 per cent on their 1994 result.[19] The SSP also improved on Militant's 1994 performance, attracting just over 4 per cent, a gain of 3.22 per cent.

At this time, the SSP still looked very much like a regional party, with support concentrated in the Glasgow area, again doing particularly well in Pollok, with nearly 16 per cent of the vote. Other areas of strength were Glasgow Ballieston, Glasgow Maryhill, Glasgow Shettleston, and Glasgow Springburn, where the party was supported by more than 10 per cent of voters.

In the years following the first Holyrood elections, a number of by-elections provided a pointer to the strength of the small parties in Scotland (see Table 5.2). The SSP in particular had some memorable performances, with the Greens choosing not to compete in some of these contests. In the Hamilton South Westminster by-election, held in September 1999, the SSP's Shareen Blackall finished third behind Labour and the SNP, on 9.50 per cent of the vote. This was quite an achievement given the existence of the 'Hamilton Accies Home Watson Away' candidate, campaigning for reform of the local football club, who attracted just over 5 per cent of the vote and forced the Liberal Democrat Marilyne McLaren into sixth place.

Table 5.2: Scottish Socialist Party By-election Results 1999-2000

	Constituency	Votes	% Votes	Position
23.9.99	Hamilton South	1,847	9.50	3rd
16.3.00	Ayr	1,345	4.22	4th
23.11.00	Glasgow Anniesland	1,429	7.07	4th (SP)
23.11.00	Glasgow Anniesland	1,441	7.13	5th (W)
21.12.00	Falkirk West	989	5.07	4th

The first Holyrood by-election took place in Ayr, in March 2000, when the SSP's James Stewart, on 4.22 per cent, finished fourth, with the Liberal Democrats fifth, and the Greens in sixth position. In November 2000, by-elections were held in Glasgow Anniesland, following the death of First Minister Dewar. Rosie Kane delivered 7.07 per cent for the SSP in the Holyrood vote, again in fourth place ahead of the Liberal Democrats, while Charlie McGinty won 7.13 per cent in the Westminster count, just behind the Lib Dems. In December of the same year the Westminster by-election in Falkirk West was held to find a replacement for Canavan. The SSP candidate Iain Hunter attracted 5.07 per cent of the vote and once more forced the Liberal Democrats into fifth position.

The SSP's ability to overtake the Liberal Democrats in these by-elections boosted the profile of the new party, reinforcing its position as a credible electoral force. Indeed it is fair to say that of all the small parties the SSP attracted the most headlines in this period.

PARLIAMENTARY EXPERIENCES

Entering the Scottish Parliament, Sheridan, Harper and Canavan were given the opportunity to directly influence legislation, and there is little doubt that they did make an impact. For instance, they proved to have considerable 'nuisance value', free to ask pertinent and searching questions of the Executive.

The behaviour of the threesome within the chamber, particularly Sheridan, also received a considerable amount of media attention. Even though the small party representatives regularly complain that they do not receive their fair share of media coverage during elections, this did not appear to be the case in the reporting of parliamentary business. Events which sparked media interest in the first year included Sheridan's reluctance to swear allegiance to the Queen; attempts by the other parties (Liberal Democrats) to remove the three from their prominent seats in the Chamber; and a debate over whether the three would be allowed a seat on the committees.[20]

As individuals they had the opportunity to influence the work of the committees, and to introduce private members legislation. Harper, for example, focused attention on the issue of organic farming, with the introduction of the Organic Targets Bill. More famously, Sheridan introduced a bill to ban warrant sales for non-payment of debts, with the support of Labour and SNP MSPs. Sheridan's bill – the Abolition of Poindings and Warrant Sales Bill – had a major impact, particularly in creating divisions within the Labour Party. The bill aimed to end poindings and warrant sales as a means of recovering debt, and while the Executive agreed with this in principle, there was disagreement over alternative means of debt collection. The Executive opposed Sheridan's bill but was forced to back down in the face of overwhelming support from a large number of Labour MSPs. Watson argues that Labour MSPs had given their support to the bill in committee and were unwilling to renege on this commitment.[21] The Parliament voted by 79 votes to 15 in support of Sheridan's bill, with 30 abstentions. The 39 Labour MSPs who voted to support the principle of the bill were all backbenchers; the 15 Labour MSPs to abstain were all members of the Executive. Indeed this was one of a very small number of issues to cause any significant division in the Labour group during this period. The event was regarded as a 'victory for minority parties' and described by Watson as 'among the most significant events of the Parliament's first year'.

It is clear that, as well as enjoying powers as individual MSPs, Sheridan, Harper and Canavan can have influence working with others. When voting on legislation they have been able to form alliances with each other and with sympathetic rebels within other parties. As another clue to the ways in which the small parties relate to the main parties, we can examine how Sheridan and Harper, as well as Canavan, have voted in the Parliament. Cowley's assessment of voting on legislation in the first year of the Parliament provides some indication of informal coalitions that may exist, or may be in the process of forming, between the parties.[24] Cowley's analysis reveals how infrequently the three individual MSPs supported the executive parties in parliamentary votes. They were in fact most likely to vote with the SNP and/or with each other (Table 5.3). For example, Canavan voted with his former party in only 26 per cent of votes, whereas he voted with the SNP on 63 per cent of occasions, and with Harper and Sheridan around 50 per cent of the time. Sheridan was the least likely to support the executive, again having more in common with the SNP and the individual MSPs.

Table 5.3: Voting Coalitions and the Small Parties (% of votes in which the parties' MSPs vote together)

	Lab	Lib	SNP	Cons	Canavan	Harper	Sheridan
Canavan	26	25	63	38	-	54	49
Harper	30	30	45	27	54	-	39
Sheridan	15	15	43	18	49	39	-

Source: Adapted from Cowley, 2001, p98

These data provide some evidence of an informal party block forming between the SNP and the individual MSPs. What is not clear is whether this is pure opposition politics (when opposition parties vote against the governing block and therefore with each other) or whether there is a potential working relationship developing between these opposition parties. What is clear is that the SNP, Canavan, Harper and Sheridan have a tendency to vote together but the other opposition party – the Conservatives – is not part of this informal relationship.

THE 2001 GENERAL ELECTION
The experience of fighting in a British general election under first-past-the-post was characteristically unrewarding for the small parties. Only the SSP was able to challenge this general principle by making some advances in terms of party image and credibility.

The SSP put forward candidates in every constituency in Scotland, which was a considerable feat for such a small party. The party's self-imposed objective was to attract 100,000 votes across Scotland. In the event, they received 72,518 (3.13 per cent), well short of the stated aim. Nevertheless, this represented the major share of votes going to small, non-major parties.[25] Indeed the SSP was by far the most prominent of the smaller parties in these elections. The SSP complained about unfair media coverage, gatecrashing one BBC studio debate with a panel of representatives from the four main parties. However, to the neutral observer, the SSP attracted quite a bit of media attention, certainly more than any of the other small parties or independents. For example, the SSP's party political broadcast was widely reported.

The SSP performed considerably better than the SSA in 1997, and also built on its Scottish election vote in 1999. The party's strongest performances were again, unsurprisingly, in Glasgow – in Pollok, Keith Baldesarra attracted just below 10 per cent of votes, only a little down on Sheridan's 1997 performance, and in seven Glasgow constituencies the party attracted more than 6 per cent of the vote. However, with candidates in all constituencies the party could also argue that it was making more of an impression across Scotland, saving 15 per cent of election deposits. In areas like Dundee West, Edinburgh East and Musselburgh, and Orkney and Shetland, the party polled over 4 per cent; better than its average performance. The steady electoral improvement of the SSP was also reflected in its membership trends. The party claimed that membership rose significantly during the campaign, and reached over 2,000 by election day.

Other small parties were definitely less active in these elections than in the past. There was a real decline in the number of candidates belonging to non-major parties between 1997 and 2001, and even more of a decline between 1999 and 2001, the likely result of a calculation by small parties that they can make more of an impact in Scottish Parliamentary elections. This was certainly true of the Greens, whose participation in the election amounted to four candidates, in Glasgow Kelvin, Edinburgh Central, Stirling, and Ross, Skye and Inverness. The party attracted a total of only 4,551 votes (0.2 per cent). However, the party was cheered by the result in Edinburgh Central where, with 5.3 per cent of the votes, it retained its deposit for the first time in a British general election. It also came within 55 votes of retaining the deposit in the Glasgow constituency, and in Edinburgh Central and Ross, Skye and Inverness it finished ahead of the SSP.

Scargill's Socialist·Labour party had 11 candidates in these elections (over 100 UK wide) and gathered 3,184 votes. The UK Independence party also had 11 candidates (over 400 across the UK), and attracted 1,968 votes. The Pro-Life Alliance had four candidates, attracting less than 800 votes.

Of all the non-major parties only the SSP could claim to have made an impression on these elections, and to have noticeably improved on past performances. The party's claim that these elections were a 'dress rehearsal' for the Scottish elections in two years time, with the aim of raising its profile and membership, was perhaps justified.

FUTURE OPPORTUNITIES AND CHALLENGES

While the SSP and Greens have entered a national Parliament and enjoy some degree of influence, they do not currently enjoy 'coalition potential'. What are their prospects in this respect? The small parties' place in Scottish politics depends on whether they can build on and improve previous election performances. Under PR it is certainly possible that they will gain more MSPs, creating a critical mass of representatives that could potentially be called on to form part of a coalition. For instance, as the Labour MSP Mike Watson has acknowledged, an SNP-SSP coalition is not beyond the realms of possibility:

> An SNP-SSP coalition would not require a huge leap of the imagination, nor would it necessitate major policy concessions on either side, given the SSP's support for an independent (Socialist Republic of) Scotland. Such an eventuality could only emerge if the Labour Party is deserted by a core vote much wider than that which the SNP and SSP are currently contesting, which could never happen ... could it?[26]

Much depends on how the voters respond to the new electoral context, as well as how the parties respond to the challenge, including their strategic choices and ability to attract members and financial resources.

The voters so far have given limited support to the small parties, but the 1999 elections provide some evidence that voters are capable of adapting to different electoral contexts and may turn to these parties under certain conditions. In 1999 support for the smaller parties in Scotland was nearly 9 percentage points higher in the second, list, vote – it was 2.7 per cent in the constituency vote and 11.3 per cent in the list vote. In Wales the differences were much smaller (4.7 per cent and 5.1 per cent). However, these figures tell us little about how many voters supported different parties in the two ballots. In fact, one out of every five Scots voted differently in the two ballots, compared to one in four of Welsh voters, a statistic revealed by the Scottish Parliament and Welsh Assembly election studies.[27]

Future levels of support may depend on the extent to which Labour voters turn to the small parties, with the SNP, SSP and to some extent the Greens competing for the traditional Labour vote. Paterson et al argue that Scottish voters perceive a rightward shift in the Labour Party and that this is out of step with voter preferences. Moreover, they illustrate increasing disillusionment with Labour amongst its core supporters, and suggest that the SNP, the SSP and to a lesser extent the Greens all benefit from this trend. So, Labour may indeed lose some support to these parties.[28]

Furthermore, opinion polls continue to suggest that a significant number of voters are willing to vote for the small parties with their regional, list vote. The *Herald*'s System Three poll reveals that the small parties maintained support after the 1999 Scottish election, and that, after some fluctuations, support levelled out at around 4 per cent across Scotland, for both the SSP and Greens. With this level of support, both the SSP and Greens would return two MSPs at the next Holyrood election.

Nevertheless, the small parties still face real difficulties and it is possible they will not improve their position at the 2003 elections. The electoral system is by no means entirely proportional, with only 56 list MSPs, and the small parties are still discriminated against in the alloca- tion of seats. As Curtice and Steed argue, the allocation of seats regionally results in a high de facto threshold that makes it hard for small parties to win seats. In the Scottish elections in 1999, the thresh- old for most regions was just over 5 per cent. So, while over 11 per cent of voters supported small party or independent candidates in the list vote, only 2 per cent of all elected MSPs did not belong to a major party. Curtice and Steed argue that if seats had been allocated nation- ally in 1999, no less than nine 'other' representatives would have been elected, including four Greens, two from the SSP and two from the Socialist Labour Party.[29]

Future developments also depend on the strategies pursued by the small parties. The SSP's stated short-term objective is to achieve six to eight MSPs in 2003. While this a rather optimistic assessment, in the run up to the 2003 elections the SSP does appear to be the strongest of the small parties. Organisationally, it has an expanding membership and activist base. In its election literature, the SSP is keen to declare that it has over 50 local branches across Scotland (including the Highlands and Islands), that it is 'Scotland's fastest growing political party', and that membership has multiplied by three since Sheridan was elected as MSP in 1999.

An obvious challenge for the SSP is to counter claims that it is a 'one man band'. Sheridan is evidently a very charismatic individual and a popular figure, so much so that the party emphasises his leadership at every opportunity. On ballot papers and election literature, the party constantly emphasises the Sheridan factor. Putting too much emphasis on a party leader can be a risky strategy in that voters may be reluctant to vote for unknown candidates. However, so far the SSP has clearly benefited from Sheridan's profile and a number of SSP candidates can point to strong performances in recent elections. Moreover, many of these candidates are experienced politicians who have transferred their support from other parties, or who have a lengthy record of community activism and environmental campaigning. The party also has a number of high-profile 'stars' who attract publicity for the party, including the actor and film-maker Peter Mullan, and a number of prominent writers and academics.

The Greens meanwhile have a less impressive membership base; around 500 individual members. However, increasing the number of members is the party's number one priority, a very sensible electoral strategy since energetic foot soldiers are a necessity. However, the activist base is less well developed than in the SSP, with only half a dozen local green parties, meaning the party will find it difficult to campaign in all the Scottish regions. Furthermore, the financial challenge of standing in the elections remains a problem for them. Nevertheless, the Scottish Greens have a record of sensible strategic choices, and they enjoy the benefit of an experienced and energetic group of core activists. They have survived in Scottish politics for over two decades and will take advantage of any opportunities that come their way.

A long-term dilemma for these parties is whether to invest scarce resources in British general election campaigns. While the profile of the party is kept high, the drain on valuable financial resources can be crippling. For these reasons, the Greens have chosen to invest almost everything in the Holyrood elections. This is an understandable course of action for a party with limited funds. However, there is an immeasurable cost in terms of voter loyalty, in that green voters may get out of the 'habit' of voting for the party. Furthermore, one lesson of 1989 was that voters are quite prepared to turn to the Greens when conditions are right. If the party does not stand in elections it cannot benefit from protest votes or from any short-term increases in public sympathy for its cause. Indeed, an ICM poll published in *The Scotsman* in the run up to the 2001 election suggested that the public were indeed concerned about environmental issues and that the main parties were not representing these views.[30] However, in many areas in Scotland voters did not have the opportunity to voice these concerns by voting Green.

CONCLUSION

The underlying question in this chapter has been whether Scotland's party system is likely to be fractured significantly by the existence of the small parties. It is clear that devolution, and more importantly PR, has raised the stakes for the SSP and Scottish Greens. They are now able to contest elections with some hope of making an impact on the outcome. The evidence reviewed in this chapter does suggest that both of these parties are likely to build on past electoral performances.

It can also be argued that once representatives of the small parties are elected they enjoy disproportionate influence. Their behaviour at Holyrood has so far been well received and they have shown signs of forging political alliances that increase their strength. There can be no doubt that the Socialists and Greens are now relevant and credible in a way they were not prior to 1999. Furthermore, as Paterson et al have noted: 'Because of their presence in the Scottish Parliament, the Scottish Socialist Party and the Greens make an impact on public debate in Scotland that is greater than anything made by similar parties in England'.[31] The 1999 electoral breakthrough for the small parties, combined with their effective performance in the Parliament, is likely to have a positive effect on voter perceptions.

Nevertheless, the small parties still face substantial difficulties, not least the limited proportionality of the Additional Member electoral system. Furthermore, if the parties do grow in influence they could be faced with the dilemma of compromising principles in order to gain more power.

So far, the small parties in Scotland have remained true to their radical roots. The SSP and the Greens have performed important roles, offering the electorate something very different from the programmes of the 'mainstream' parties. As voters become increasingly disillusioned with the major parties, it can at least be said that the SSP and Greens are real alternatives.

NOTES

1. In this chapter, small parties are treated as those parties that have existed on the periphery of mainstream politics, never having achieved representation at Westminster, although they may have had electoral representation in local government. In practice, in Scotland this means parties other than the four major parties. See, for a wider definitional debate: F. Muller-Rommel and G. Pridham, *Small Parties in Western Europe: Comparative and National Perspectives*, London: Sage 1989.

2. M. Crick, *Militant*, London: Faber and Faber 1984.

3. *Ibid*, p71.

4. J. Allison, *Guilty by Suspicion: A Life and Labour*, Glendaruel: Argyll Publishing 1995, pp67-70. The Militant candidates were Jim Cameron in Provan, beaten by Jimmy Wray by only one vote, and David Churchley, who lost to Bob Gillespie.

5. T. Sheridan and J. McAlpine, *A Time to Rage*, Edinburgh: Polygon 1994.

6. Overall, the SSA attracted 9,508 votes.

7. T. Sheridan and A. McCombes, *Imagine: A Socialist Vision for the 21st Century*, Edinburgh: Rebel Inc. 2000.

8. Scottish Socialist Party 2001 General Election Manifesto (*http://www.scottishsocialistparty.org/manifesto.htm*).

9. Sheridan and McCombes, *Imagine*, op. cit., p221.

10. Allison, *Guilty by Suspicion*, op. cit., p158.

11. Sheridan and McCombes, *Imagine*, op. cit., p191.

12. W. Rüdig and P. Lowe, 'The withered "greening" of British politics: the case of the Ecology Party', *Political Studies*, 1986, Vol. 34. People became the Ecology Party in 1975, and changed their name to the Green Party in 1985.

13. E. Goldsmith (ed), *Can Britain Survive?*, London: Tom Stacey 1971; E. Goldsmith, *The Stable Society: Its Structure and Control*, Wadebridge: Wadebridge Press 1978.

14. Rüdig and Lowe, *op. cit.*

15. J. Mitchell, 'Constitutional Conventions and the Scottish National Movement: Origins, Agendas and Outcomes', Strathclyde Papers in Government and Politics, No. 78, Glasgow: University of Strathclyde 1991; P. Lynch, 'The Scottish Constitutional Convention 1992-5', *Scottish Affairs*, Spring 1996, No. 15.

16. C. Bennie, 'Small Parties in a Devolved Scotland', in A. Wright (ed), *Scotland: The Challenge of Devolution*, Aldershot: Ashgate.

17. T. Milligan, 'Left at the Polls: The Changing Far-Left Vote', *Scottish Affairs*, Autumn 1999, No. 29.

18. J. Bradbury, D. Denver, J. Mitchell and L.G. Bennie, 'Devolution and Party Change: candidate selection for the 1999 Scottish Parliament and Welsh Assembly elections', *Journal of Legislative Studies*, Vol. 6, No. 3, pp51-72.

19. Two Green MEPs were elected in England – Jean Lambert in London, and Caroline Lucas in the South East region – along with two UK Independence Party candidates in the Eastern and South West areas.

20 It was claimed that the three were not entitled to a seat on a committee under parliamentary rules, as the committees are supposed to represent the balance of power between the parties. However, the business bureau created spaces for them.

21. M. Watson, *Year Zero: An Insider's View of the Scottish Parliament*, Edinburgh: Polygon 2001, p101.

22. Iain Macwhirter, *Sunday Herald*, 30.4.00, quoted in Watson, *Year Zero, op. cit.*, p107.

23. Watson, *op. cit.*, p108.

24. P. Cowley, 'Voting in the Scottish Parliament: The First Year', in J. Tonge et al (eds), *British Elections and Parties Review*, Vol. 11, London: Frank Cass 2001.

25. The total number of votes won by small and independent candidates was 92,863.

26. Watson, *op. cit.*, pp77-8.

27. J. Curtice and M. Steed, 'And Now for the Commons?: Lessons From Britain's First Experience with Proportional Representation', in P. Cowley et al (eds), *British Elections and Parties Review* Vol. 10, London: Frank Cass 2000.

28. L. Paterson, A. Brown, J. Curtice, K. Hinds, D. McCrone, A. Park, K. Sproston and P. Surridge, *New Scotland, New Politics?*, Edinburgh: Polygon 2001.

29. Curtice and Steed, *op. cit.*, p115.

30. *The Scotsman*, 15.5.01.

31. Paterson et al, *New Scotland, New Politics?, op. cit.*, p130.

Scottish Social Democracy and Blairism: difference, diversity and community

LINDSAY PATERSON

It used to be easy under the Conservative government. There was Scottish social philosophy and there was laissez-faire Conservatism, and the one baulked at the other. Out of this conflict grew almost everything we now have politically – the Scottish Parliament, the strengthening sense of national identity, and the left-of-centre majority ensconced now in some form for a generation, whatever its party colours. Scottish communitarianism against English individualism was the bedrock on which Scottish politics grew into self-government.

Then it turned out not to be so simple. Tony Blair and his disciples and mentors discovered communitarianism too; some of them even through the writings of such impeccably Scottish philosophers as John Macmurray and Alasdair MacIntyre.[1] The rhetoric changed in Scotland and there was much reviling of Blairite authoritarianism. Simultaneously, the Scottish community began to appear rather problematic, with its apparent intolerance of free debate about sexuality, its persisting awkwardness in discussions of racism, and its quickly developing cynicism about its indigenous politicians, even though the Parliament as an institution is opposed by almost no-one.

So what is going on? Was Scottish communitarianism just a convenient myth after all, a combination of partisan resentment at the Tories and – as some would allege – a respectable front for complaining about England? Are Scots who dismiss Blair's moral authoritarianism ignoring (or ignorant of) its Scottish origins? And, when it comes to anti-communitarianism, are the Scottish non-Tory political parties really all occupying much the same ideological position?

SCOTTISH COMMUNITY

There was nothing bogus, ephemeral or incoherent about Scottish support for various notions of 'community' in the 1980s and 1990s.

Indeed, looking back, it is the sheer persistence of this support in the face of sometimes virulent denigration that stands out.

Most obvious, of course, were the voting patterns. It really was the case that the Conservative Party's share of the vote steadily declined between 1979 and 2001,[2] and that – more to the point – no attempt to rescue a right-of-centre sense of Scottish community seemed to make any difference at all. Scottish social attitudes may generally not have been much to the left of those England, but that was because English attitudes remained almost as social democratic as Scottish ones.[3] The achievement of the Scottish left, broadly defined, was to continue to be able to translate social democratic popular views into social democratic political action. The people of Scotland continued to appreciate that if you want a fairer and more equal society, you have to vote for parties that have fairness and equality among their fundamental principles.

That continued political awareness was a remarkable achievement. If it had not been for it, there might not have been a British Labour Party with a coherent ideology to revive. If Scotland had gone the way of England in 1983, when Labour beat the Social-Democrat-Liberal Alliance by just 0.6% of the vote,[4] the Alliance might have triumphed for long enough to destroy the credibility of a left-of-centre alternative, but not long enough to take over from Labour. The Labour Party of the early 1990s would then have lacked the experience and sense of its own reforming mission which was carried through the 1980s by such unexciting but indisputably radical politicians as John Smith, Donald Dewar, Gordon Brown and Robin Cook. If that still seems an odd claim for the last two of these, remember that Brown's budgets have been consistently redistributive (as is shown in successive analyses of them by the Institute for Fiscal Studies[5]), even though not enough to offset the continuing rapid growth in the levels of high incomes. Cook's re-positioning of himself on the question of Scottish self-government in 1983 was one of the key moments in the unification of the home rule movement, as important in its way and in its time as the unity achieved by Dewar and Alex Salmond in the 1997 referendum.

For the long run, too, the shift to the left by the SNP was of almost as much importance as the continuing strength of Labour.[6] Again, it is easy to take this shift for granted. It is especially easy for that party's opponents to pretend that the SNP's ideological position either does not matter or is a charade. The latter is easier to deal with, as any reasonably impartial reading of their policies and political actions in the last decade and a half will indicate, especially in contrast to the 1960s and 1970s. But the significance is not just for the partisan rivalry between it and the Labour Party. The absence of a right-wing nationalism in Scotland was of crucial importance in freezing the

Conservatives out. It ensured that Scottish national identity would come increasingly to be defined as being on the left, and would also be increasingly embarrassed by accusations of parochialism, racism or xenophobia. That does not mean, of course, that Scotland is free of these problems, but for progressive politics it does help that they are not part of the current national self-image. One example may illustrate this point. Ever since William McIlvanney famously celebrated Scotland's 'mongrel' character (at the democracy demonstration during the Edinburgh European Summit in December 1992[7]), that epithet has been embraced with enthusiasm by anti-racist politics in Scotland. It took the Conservative MP John Townend to introduce the word into English discourse in March 2001,[8] deploring it, and thus making it much more difficult for the English left to claim the mongrel description as its own.

However, the real, not illusory, tradition of Scottish communitarianism goes further than the party-political battle. Popular views and practices point in the same direction, and in this respect Scottish attitudes to education are fundamental. Throughout the 1980s and 1990s, Scots remained firmly attached to the principle of the non-selective comprehensive school while attitudes in England turned hostile: by the time of the 1997 general election, one half of people in England supported a return to selection, but only one quarter in Scotland.[9] Scottish parents used the school boards that were created by Michael Forsyth in 1989 to defend schools against what were regarded as inappropriate and politically motivated intrusion, most successfully by organising a boycott of the Conservatives' scheme of national testing of primary children, forcing the policy to be, in effect, withdrawn. Parents also nearly always resisted attempts to detach schools from the control of the local authority: only three small schools did so (one not in time to achieve self-governing status before the 1997 election), in contrast to one quarter of all secondary schools in England.

This support for a public education system is fundamental in the sense that education is not just another area of social policy: in important respects it underpins democracy.[10] That can plausibly be argued to have been the main Scottish tradition of education – the view that the purpose of education is to create a society of critical citizens, and to acquaint children with a sense of their mutual dependence in society. This educational philosophy extends back through the welfare state and nineteenth century philanthropy to the aftermath of the Protestant Reformation, with its aspiration to a school in every parish. The tradition was strengthened in the twentieth century by Catholic social thinking – the principle that education can create the social capital on which society depends. The persistence of public support for a public system to the end of the century shows that these traditions are not just rhetoric, or romanticism: they are real, politically relevant instances of Scottish attachment to ideas of community.

The same kinds of communitarian principles were generalised in the debates on the constitutional question from 1988 onwards. One of the striking features of these discussions, compared to the 1970s, was the interest in sovereignty and the emerging conclusion that Scottish ideas about legitimate government rested on the principle of popular sovereignty. Again the religious origins are unmistakable, and indeed Church of Scotland theologians in particular were eloquent in their contribution to the debate, modernising the Knoxian idea that the people have the right to overthrow unjust rulers. Sovereignty, they argued, is intrinsically limited. Federalism is not just a way of organising a constitution, but a principle based on human fallibility. Because we have a duty to respect our fellow human beings, government should seek to share power, not monopolise it. Once again, similar conclusions were reached by Catholic thinkers, drawing also on the European tradition of subsidiarity, which entered Scottish debates through discussions about the character of the European Union.

Beyond politics, public attitudes and the implicit philosophy of the Constitutional Convention, there was the diffuse spirit that has informed Scottish artistic creativity from the 1950s onwards. William McIlvanney may be the most well known exponent of this idea, but some form of communitarianism could be found in many writers and other artists. In the aftermath of 1979, the theatre provided a forum for national debate about society, Scotland and power. The social philosophy of Scottish novelists was in stark contrast to the increasingly private concerns of their counterparts in England (although semi-outsiders such as Salman Rushdie began to change that). Folksong has been inseparable from a socially committed politics since the CND days of the early 1960s.

So Scottish communitarianism was real. Without it, there would probably not now be a Scottish Parliament, there might not have been a Labour Government in 1997 and any distinctive Scottish Government at all would be facing a very uncertain future where the traditional rationale of the Scottish Office – to safeguard Scottish public services – would be rapidly declining since so many of these services would have been privatised. Keeping alive the ethic of social responsibility is a vital Scottish achievement that needs to be repeatedly stated – against claims on the political right that a sense of public responsibility for community services is backward-looking, and against claims in segments of the metropolitan left that Scottish radical commitment is no more than rhetoric.

SCOTTISH LIBERALISM

Nevertheless, there have always been paradoxes and contradictions. Misinterpretations of these are the source of some odd suggestions that Scots are really not social democrats after all, or that Scottish communitarianism is no more than superficial. From the start of the Thatcher period, Scots did seem to be keen on selective aspects of her reforms. Scots bought their council houses in as large proportions as people in England. Scots, including Donald Dewar, bought shares in privatised utilities. Scottish parents chose to send their children to non-local schools. Scots engaged in a massive increase in car buying, relishing personal mobility just as much as people elsewhere in the developed world. How are these individualising trends to be reconciled with the apparent communitarianism?

Scots also, even more puzzlingly, shared in the common, growing contempt for politicians, even while also campaigning for their own homegrown breed. Distrust of politics, doubts about the value of voting, and declining expectations of government are common phenomena across Europe, and Scots are no exception. This is one explanation of the abrupt lurch into cynicism following the Scottish Parliament elections in 1999. The Parliament seems to have been accepted as a permanent feature, but as soon as the prospect became reality, the 129 MSPs who occupy the Parliament were treated with as little respect as politicians in other countries can expect.[11]

Indeed, the paradox is all the more difficult to understand if we follow a common line of argument on decentralisation and devolution. Among constitutional reformers who are not motivated primarily by nationalism, the main argument for a Scottish Parliament and similar bodies is as one way of countering public criticism of the political process, one way of empowering people now that respect for old hierarchies of power has significantly declined. The entire recent movement for Scottish self-government can be attributed to an interpretation of 1960s radicalism – the challenge to the old Stalinist left, the rediscovery of community as a basis for a decentralised, ecological socialism, and the socialist-feminist attempt to re-engage public politics with the politics of everyday life. It was a rediscovery of the socialism of G. D. H. Cole[12] and Harold Laski,[13] with acknowledgement to a rejuvenated anarchism. This line of argument also appealed to left nationalists, to whom straightforward nationalism was problematic because of its potential for centralism, for the imposition of artificial homogeneity and – at worst – for fascism.

The main ideological carriers of this view in the 1980s and 1990s were Scottish Labour Action[14] and the left of the SNP[15] – both highly influential in their respective parties and more widely, and the only segment of Scottish politics where truly original thinking has taken place in the last two decades (as opposed to the derivative and trite 'modernisation' that emanates from the fashionable think tanks). The common forums for this radical thinking were the magazine *Radical Scotland*[16] and the John Wheatley Centre (now the Centre for Scottish Public Policy[17]). A Scottish Parliament, it was repeatedly asserted, was a means of renewing social democracy because it would recognise both community and individuality. It would be a participatory democracy, decentralised and empowering.

The main outcome of such thinking, however, now seems to be a parliament that is not that different from most other parliaments. It is more open, more consultative, and less stuffy than Westminster (although that is not a very difficult standard to be measured by) but it is still a body of the same kind as provokes criticism the world over.[18] Some of the victims of the resulting popular doubts are the very people who developed the decentralising socialist ideas of the preceding two decades – John McAllion, Susan Deacon, Malcolm Chisholm, Jack McConnell, Jackie Baillie and Wendy Alexander of the Labour Party, and Roseanna Cunningham, Alex Neil, Mike Russell and Fiona Hyslop of the SNP (however much these people may disagree with each other over details). Only really Robin Harper of the Green Party and Tommy Sheridan of the Scottish Socialist Party have, perhaps, managed to remain somewhat immune to the scepticism, because – as representatives of small parties – they can still be seen as critics of the new Scottish political establishment.

I think that a resolution of these paradoxes requires us to think more carefully about what the dominant Scottish social philosophy is. It is best characterised as social democratic communitarianism, with social democracy as important as community, because it brings with it an inescapable element of politicisation (unlike straightforward liberal-ism) and nationalism.

Communitarianism, like all political philosophies, comes in a variety of forms. They all share a principle that human identity is intrinsically social, and that personal fulfilment depends on our relations with others. The main aim of public policy should be to safeguard and develop the community conditions that can help individuals to be fulfilled. Modern versions of communitarianism also tend to define themselves mainly by contrast with classical liberalism, according to which the essence of humanity is freedom, and the purpose of public policy is to release people from collective constraints. Of course, at present, the most relevant instance of liberalism is the various New Right regimes of the 1980s, against which current communitarianism tends to define itself. A reaction against liberal individualism, however, has always been part of communitarian thinking, at least since the eighteenth century when liberalism in its modern form emerged.

Scotland has contributed to this tradition of communitarian debate with liberalism, not only in the twentieth century writing that was noted earlier – with philosophers such as John Macmurray, Alasdair MacIntyre and John Anderson – but also in the eighteenth century. Adam Smith's primary concern was to understand the social conditions that made human freedom possible, and so his writing contains the debate between liberalism and communitarianism. In anachronistic terminology, we can understand the whole sociological school of thought in eighteenth century Scotland as being about the tension between human individuality and social solidarity. That is what underlies Adam Ferguson's development of the concept of civil society, or Thomas Reid's and others' increasingly subtle analysis of the concept of human 'sympathy' or 'moral sense' or 'common sense'. Their thinking about individuals and society pervaded Scottish society in the nineteenth century through university teaching: it became the basis of Scottish practical theology and so of the training of thousands of ministers, and permeated also the philosophy classes which were taken by ministers and school teachers. It was then reinterpreted in the twentieth century as social democracy – not socialism, not liberalism, but an amalgam of community and individualism.

This tradition of social thought is worth bearing in mind, not to imply that ideas drive politics or social change, but to indicate that the ways in which Scottish thinkers have reacted to the apparent tension between individuality and community have a certain historical coherence. Being aware of a tension is neither new nor a sign of confusion. It is a source of political creativity. The situation we now face illustrates the paradoxes with particular clarity. Education is again an example here. Scottish attitudes to public education for the last half century seem to combine a belief in collective provision with an enthusiasm for personal liberation. The resulting freedom is often still of a very competitive sort: while educational policy has significantly widened opportunity since the 1960s, it has mostly done so by extending public examinations to a greater and greater proportion of young people, so that meritocratic selection is now even more firmly entrenched than it was in the much more structurally divided system of half a century ago.

This delicate balance between individualism and collective action is not only not new; it is also not unique. It can be found in most places where social democracy was strong and politically successful in the twentieth century. The pre-eminent instance is Sweden. As long ago as 1954, the social democratic prime minister, Tage Erlander, praised the liberatory purposes of collective action: 'it is a mistake to believe that people's freedom is diminished because they decide to carry out collectively what they are incapable of doing individually'.[19]

Tim Tilton, in his account of the philosophy of Swedish social democracy, comments that 'Erlander never tired of citing the increased security and freedom that modern social policy created for common people', and sums up the social democrats' programme thus: 'The drive for integrative democracy means that all citizens are to be embraced in the national community, to be treated there with equal consideration and to enjoy fully the freedoms of citizenship.' He adds that 'these freedoms cannot be limited to the political sphere' but include in particular the freedom of consumer choice.

Much the same kind of balance between individuality and community can be found in theories of liberal nationalism as developed by, for example, Neil MacCormick and Yael Tamir. Making this link is important in placing Scottish debates in context. As Tamir puts it, 'a liberal national entity ... will endorse liberal principles of distribution inwards and outwards; its political system will reflect a particular national culture, but its citizens will be free to practice different cultures and follow a variety of life-plans and conceptions of the good'.[20]

That freedom of choice over culture is what distinguishes liberal nationalism from other kinds of nationalism. It is still nationalist because there is an overlapping consensus about certain values essential to the functioning of the national community, and it is liberal because of the pluralism of cultural values.

SCOTTISH DOUBTS ABOUT BLAIRISM

Scotland is in the process of discovering all of this in its own way. We grew used to an assertion of Scottish communitarianism when the Conservatives were in power at Westminster, but now there is a different external reference – the new communitarianism of Tony Blair. On the face of it, we might expect Scots to like Blair's philosophy. There is not only the recognition that strong communities are necessary to freeing individuals; as he said in his pamphlet for the Fabian Society on the Third Way: 'we all depend on collective goods for our independence; and all our lives are enriched – or impoverished – by the communities to which we belong'.[21]

There are also the impeccably Scottish credentials of Blair's philosophical antecedents. He gets his sense of community not only from Scottish philosophers such as Macmurray, but also in his attachment to meritocracy. Take, for example, his speech near the beginning of the 2001 UK general election campaign in which he said that New Labour ideology 'is based on a notion of equality that is not about outcomes or incomes, but about equal worth'.[22] That kind of equality, he believed, was best achieved through 'genuine meritocracy', and he linked that to nineteenth century liberalism in preference to social democracy: 'in many ways, twentieth century politics was the aberration'. This belief is not very far from, say, Walter Elliot's highly influential essay of 1932 in which he coined the term 'democratic intellectualism', defining the Scottish heritage as one 'wherein intellect, speech and, above all, argument are the passports to the highest eminence in the land'.[23] Likewise, Blair would have agreed with Duncan MacGillivray, a president of the Educational Institute of Scotland, when he defended meritocracy in 1919, but added that democracy inclined people to ignore 'differences and inequalities ... of capacity, aptitude, temperament', and that it 'cannot wipe out distinctions laid down in the primordial cells ... No system of education can secure equality of capacity or product'.[24]

The similarity goes further. Blair's notion of community also contains a strong authoritarian streak. In 1995, for example, he argued that 'rights are not enough. You can't build a society that isn't based on duty and responsibility.'[25] That linking of meritocracy, community and strong moral duties is strongly redolent of Scottish nineteenth century Presbyterianism, however odd that may seem for the Anglo-Catholic Blair. As in that tradition, there is something curiously contradictory about Blair's enthusiasm for individual 'independence'. It is an independence only on the terms laid down by the community – not by the individual – and preferably a wholly apolitical independence confined to the home and the family. Neither in Blair's rhetoric nor in that Scottish Presbyterian tradition is there much encouragement to real political dissent. The depoliticising of community is intensified in New Labour ideology by the tendency to depoliticise everything: the stress on pragmatism, on measures of output, on indifference in principle between public and private ownership, on 'standards not structures' (as educational policy in England would have it[26]).

The key point about the reception of Blair's ideology in Scotland is that Scots have forgotten about the similar kind of rhetoric in their own traditions and seem to prefer the social democratic 'aberration'. If rhetorical obeisance to 'community' is now apparently secure, Scots seem to be choosing to emphasise the liberatory aspect of the ideology they developed in the 1980s. If 'community' had to be asserted in the face of Thatcher's rampant individualism, awkward dissent is the only way to react to Blair's amalgam of community and competition. That would make sense of a sort of curmudgeonliness that runs through Scottish politics at the moment, resentment at London Labour running Scottish Labour. It would explain, too, the Scottish doubts about the most authoritarian aspects of the New Labour programme, for exam-

ple concerning those features of the New Deal which withdraw benefits from people who do not want to take part in one of the approved
schemes.[27] It might explain the emerging difference between Scottish
and English policy on citizenship education. In England, that policy is
to be most concerned with community duties. In Scotland, it is also
about the right to dissent – 'to challenge established conventions and
the status quo'.[28]

One way of summarising the distinction between current Scottish
views and New Labour is in the extent to which individual differences
are seen as having political implications. Simplifying greatly, we could
say that the liberal view of individualism is apolitical, while the social
democratic view is highly political. Both Scottish and New Labour
views contain elements of both, of course, but the emphasis is different. Scotland inclines to the view that communities enable individuals
to achieve political freedom. The community must remain political
because it is through politics – through the state – that the community
is maintained and strengthened. That is, indeed, a legacy of Scottish
voting patterns in the 1980s: the persisting commitment that the only
way to achieve social democratic goals was by voting for (broadly
defined) social democratic parties. Blair, on the whole, seems to be
more interested in the capacity of communities to achieve the classical
liberal project of freeing individuals from politics.

Put that way, the Scottish view probably sounds quite attractive to
most of the politicised readers of this book. But there is more to the
matter than this, as debates about minority rights in Scotland illustrate.
On the whole, England and New Labour seem rather more comfortable with gay rights and multiculturalism than Scotland does.[29] Most
obviously, there was far more public anguish about the repeal of Clause
2a in Scotland than there was about similar proposals in England.
There is also a distinct uneasiness in Scotland about according rights to
cultural minorities as such. There is no evidence that Scots are less in
favour of equal individual opportunities for minorities, but Scottish
enthusiasm for political dissent does not seem to extend to the self-
organised collective action of minority groups. It is difficult to pin this
down, but evidence would include the clear doubts of the majority
about the public funding of separate Catholic schools (a view shared
now by a majority of Catholics themselves[30]) and the apparent reluctance to develop public schools for other faith communities. It would
include the doubts about the repeal of Clause 2a, which, because of the
campaign run by opponents of repeal, can be interpreted as fears that
individual children would not be free to choose their own sexuality.
Despite much commentary, there was no evidence that Scots were
more homophobic than people in England. There is survey evidence

that shows a clear willingness to tolerate diverse lifestyles[31] but the majority Scottish view seems to be that these should remain private.

So we may have to refine the tentative conclusion that Scots want a politicised dissent while Blair prefers an apolitical liberalism. Scots do want a politicised national community, as in classical social democracy – they want to use the power of an active state to maintain community – but they are not so happy with the politicisation of minorities within that community. The issue does not arise in Blair's philosophy because everything there is apolitical – national community as well as minority communities. Yael Tamir, once again, helps to make sense of this dilemma. She notes that membership of a liberal nationalist entity will be accessible to those individuals who are 'capable of identifying the political entity as their own', and she goes on to explain the importance of government in this context, 'even if governing institutions respect a wide range of rights and liberties and distribute goods and official positions fairly, members of minority groups will unavoidably feel alienated to some extent'. She concludes that the main problem affecting minorities in such a culture is 'alienation rather than deprivation of rights' – lack of political power rather than lack of individual opportunity.[32]

CONCLUSION: SCOTS SOCIAL DEMOCRACY AND WHO STANDS FOR SCOTLAND?

So we can sum up the emerging difference between Scottish social philosophy and Blair's. An apolitical community – such as Blair's liberal communitarianism seems to aspire to – can be much more relaxed about autonomous groups within it than a politicised community of the type that social democracy has classically sought to establish, and as Scotland seems to have been growing to prefer during the three decades of campaigning for home rule. Interpreted thus, there is no real contradiction, at least in a historical sense, between Scottish assertion of the thrawn political independence of the Scottish community and Scottish scepticism about the political organisation of minorities. Neither is there a contradiction between Scottish attachment to liberal rights and Scottish doubts about minority group rights. Rights are acceptable to the majority in Scotland if they are rights to join the majority – to become full members of the national community. The acceptable political rights are the classical social democratic rights to be political advocates of that same national community. It is a view that does not see the twentieth century as 'aberrant'. It is also a view that finds the very notion of apolitical group rights incomprehensible. In this view, group rights – as opposed to the individual rights of members of groups – are inevitably political and so are treated with suspicion because they clash with the political expression of the national community as a whole.

None of this tells us much about internal Scottish politics in a partisan sense, since only the Conservatives appear to dissent from these broad views. That party is so isolated and so far from achieving power on its own that its political impact is likely to remain muted for a long time. It could be that Scottish views could shift in the direction of Blairite apolitical communitarianism if Labour remains in power for a long time at the UK level and continues to share power beyond 2003 in Scotland. But the main obstacle to such a shift towards Blairism is the persisting sense that the rights of the Scottish community as a whole are an unavoidably political matter. For the foreseeable future, Scottish national elections will be about these rights – no longer about achieving or securing a parliament, but very much about protecting its interests. In that sense, Scottish elections continue to be about the constitution, however much Helen Liddell and John Reid might prefer otherwise. Furthermore, so long as the notion of the Scottish community is politicised in this way, so long will minority group rights in Scotland be regarded with some suspicion, as threatening to endanger the necessary political unity in the face of a hostile external world.

The Scottish Parliament election in 2003 may well partly turn on this issue, since the 1999 one did. The outcome of the primary battle between Labour and the SNP will continue to depend on which party best 'stands for Scotland' – which party is best able to articulate the rights of the Scottish community externally, increasingly perhaps in the European Union and not just within the UK. However, these parties do not differ in relevant ways in relation to the internal debate about the end-purpose of politics, and neither party differs fundamentally from the Liberal Democrats. All of these parties value the state and other forms of public action as a means of liberating individuals, and so dissent from the Conservatives. All of these parties are social democratic, and so dissent from Blair's liberalism (even the Liberal Democrats). All of these parties claim to speak for the political rights of the Scottish community, and so do not share Blair's apparent goal of an apolitical national community. But all of these parties, therefore, find the notion of minority group rights rather awkward, because – unlike Blair – they cannot conceive of these rights as anything other than an inevitably politicised threat to the coherence and very existence of the national political community.

NOTES

1. Tony Blair acknowledges John Macmurray as one of the major influences on his political philosophy in his formative years at Oxford University. J. Rentoul, *Tony Blair: Prime Minister*, London: Little Brown 2001, pp41-43; J. Naughtie, *The Rivals: The Intimate Story of a Political Marriage*,

London: Fourth Estate 2001, pp18-20.

2. D. Seawright, *An Important Matter of Principle: The Decline of the Scottish Conservative and Unionist Party*, Aldershot: Ashgate 1999; see also his contribution in this volume.

3. J. Curtice, 'One Nation?', in R. Jowell, S. Witherspoon and L. Brook (eds), *British Social Attitudes: The 5th Report*, Aldershot: Gower 1988.

4. D. Butler and P. Kavanagh, *The British General Election 1983*, London: Macmillan 1984, p301.

5. T. Clark and A. Goodman, *Living Standards under Labour*, London: Institute for Fiscal Studies 2001.

6. See on the changing nature of the SNP the contribution of Nicola McEwen in this volume.

7. Also see at the same time: W. McIlvanney, *Surviving the Shipwreck*, Edinburgh: Mainstream 1992.

8. *Daily Telegraph*, 31.3.01.

9. A. Brown, D. McCrone, L. Paterson and P. Surridge, *The Scottish Electorate: The 1997 General Election and Beyond*, London: Macmillan 1999, p96; L. Paterson, A. Brown, J. Curtice, K. Hinds, D. McCrone, A. Park, K. Sproston and P. Surridge, *New Scotland, New Politics?*, Edinburgh: Edinburgh University Press 2001, p151.

10. L. Paterson, *Education and the Scottish Parliament*, Edinburgh: Dunedin Academic Press 2000; L. Paterson, *Crisis in Classroom: The Exam Debacle and the Way Ahead for Scottish Education*, Edinburgh: Mainstream 2000.

11. Paterson et al, *op. cit.*, pp85 and 88.

12. G. D. H. Cole was one of the foremost socialist thinkers in the first half of the 20th century. See T. Wright, *G. D. H. Cole and Socialist Democracy*, Oxford: Clarendon Press 1979.

13. Harold Laski was a leading academic and Labour politician from the 1930s into the post-war era and was, famously, Chairman of the Labour Party in the 1945 general election. See I. Kramnick and B. Sheerman, *Harold Laski: A Life on the Left*, London: Hamish Hamilton 1993.

14. Scottish Labour Action were an internal campaigning ginger group formed in the aftermath of Labour's UK defeat in 1987 and return of 50 Scots Labour MPs. It always had a small membership, never rising above more than a couple of hundred, but several of its members went on to become members of the first Scottish Executive, including Wendy Alexander, Sarah Boyack, Susan Deacon and Jack McConnell.

15. The left wing of the SNP were initially organised around the '79 Group, which was set up in the aftermath of the SNP's reversal in the 1979 election. Its leading lights included Alex Salmond, Roseanna Cunningham, Stephen Maxwell, Jim Sillars and Margo MacDonald. Forced to disband by the party leadership in 1982, its influence went on to shape the future direction of the party.

16. *Radical Scotland* existed as a forum for cross-party discussions between 1983 and 1991, edited first by Kevin Dunion and then by Alan Lawson.

17. The John Wheatley Centre was formed in 1990 by a group of leading Labour figures including George Foulkes, David Martin and Anne McGuire. It changed its name to the Centre for Scottish Public Policy in 1997, and its most influential publications have been the Government of Scotland Working Party Groups which have covered a range of issues: law reform, transport, education, environmental policy, quangos and Europe.

18. L. Paterson, 'Scottish Democracy and Scottish Utopias: The First Year of the Scottish Parliament', *Scottish Affairs*, Autumn 2000, No. 33, pp45-61.

19. This quote and the others below are taken from T. Tilton, *The Political Economy of Swedish Social Democracy*, Oxford: Claredon Press 1990, pp268-69.

20. Y. Tamir, *Liberal Nationalism*, Princeton: Princeton University Press 1993, p163.

21. T. Blair, *The Third Way*, London: Fabian Society 1998, p4.

22. At a speech made in his Sedgefield constituency 13.5.01.

23. W. Elliot, 'The Scottish Heritage in Politics', in 8th Duke of Atholl and D. Y. Cameron et al (eds), *A Scotsman's Heritage*, London: Alexander MacLehose 1932, p63.

24. D. MacGillivray, 'Fifty Years of Scottish Education', in J. Clarke (ed), *Problems of National Education*, London: Macmillan 1919, p36.

25. J. Arthur, *Schools and Community: The Communitarian Agenda in Education*, London: Falmer 2000, p20.

26. A. Smithers, 'Education Policy', in A. Seldon (ed), *The Blair Effect: The Labour Government 1997-2001*, London: Little Brown 2001, pp405-26.

27. J. Fairley, 'Labour's New Deal in Scotland', *Scottish Affairs*, Autumn 1998, No. 25, pp90-109.

28. See *Learning and Teaching Scotland, Education and Citizenship in Scotland*, Dundee: Qualifications and Curriculum Authority 2000, p3; *Qualifications and Curriculum Authority, Education for Citizenship and the Teaching of Democracy in Schools: Final report of the Advisory Group on Citizenship* (chaired by Bernard Crick), London: Qualifications and Curriculum Authority 1998.

29. See on Section 28/Clause 2a debate in Scotland the contribution by Rowena Arshad in this volume.

30. Paterson et al, *op. cit.*, pp150-51.

31. T. Crichton and S. Braunholtz, 'The Truth: We're a Tolerant Nation', *Sunday Herald*, 23.1.00.

32. Tamir, *op. cit.*, p163.

Shifting from the 'old' to 'new' social democracy: ten propositions

JAMES MCCORMICK

In 1993, shortly before the New Labour project was named, the Institute for Public Policy Research (IPPR) published a collection of essays titled *Reinventing the Left*.[1] It was edited by David Miliband, a leading figure in Labour's intellectual revival and head of the Prime Minister's Policy Unit from 1997-2001. Produced some time before the Third Way, it was an impressive work: outward-looking, informed by progressive currents in European social democracy, long-termist and prepared to acknowledge some of the blind-spots in British centre-left thinking. Much of the agenda it outlined remains to be addressed. But taken together with the work of the Commission on Social Justice, published in 1994, the roots of Labour's recent policies on employment, family support and welfare reform can be seen.[2]

The book concluded with a short essay by James Cornford and Patricia Hewitt (then Director and Deputy Director of IPPR) titled 'Dos and Don'ts for Social Democrats',[3] highlighting what they called their 'ten commandments' arising from the other contributions. Almost ten years on, we return to their list and consider the implications for a devolved Scotland that has, arguably, a stronger social democratic tradition than New Labour's and an explicit commitment to social justice. Here we note that social democracy defines a much broader part of the landscape than that occupied by Scottish Labour. The political currents flowing towards a 'new' social democracy are not yet fully understood, and nor are they synonymous with what New Labour does in office.

FIRST: DON'T IMITATE, INNOVATE
'Don't imitate either your opponents or your past ... to reform is a sign of strength and not weakness'.
While Tony Blair's government may not be radical enough for some, its

main achievements look very unlike those of recent Conservative governments and its failures rather different from those of previous Labour governments. The Labour-Liberal Democrat coalition in Scotland has been willing to be different from Labour in Westminster in some areas of policy, notably tuition fees and paying for elderly care. While these areas of divergence have grabbed the headlines, it is not yet clear how the desire to be different (from England) will be expressed in future. Is it to become a matter of principle, or will the Scottish body politic be mature enough (and Westminster interested enough) to create a two-way trade of policy ideas? Will the brave talk of learning from smaller European nations encourage genuine innovation in Scottish government?

In its desire to do things differently, the Scottish Executive and Parliament must draw on a set of values as well as the best available evidence. Its chosen course of action on the Sutherland Commission proposals for funding long-term care is a case in point. A powerful cross-party consensus backed the universal option of meeting all personal care costs. Universal provision is better than means-testing in almost every way except cost. The substantial new investment required to meet this commitment will be targeted to the one-third of older people who currently contribute on a means-tested basis. The Scottish approach is considered more radical than England's use of targeting, where some new investment will be used to increase respite support to carers and standards of care services. Whatever solution works best in practice, it is notable that alternative ways of investing similar amounts of money were not considered openly by the Parliament. The assumption appears to be that the enduring social democratic value of equality means all should be treated the same, irrespective of their income or wealth. Another case can be made – that greater equality demands that we take account of the roots of difference (see Proposition Eight) and that each should contribute to the task of reducing inequality according to their means. Signing up to the Sutherland package was not the only generous or just approach for social democrats to take. The new politics will be in better shape when the full diversity of thinking on how to promote social justice is expressed more openly in Scotland.

SECOND: THINK BIG

'A social democratic programme must be universal not particular... there must be a view of the good society.'

Stung by Labour's failure to advance beyond its heartlands in the 1980s, Cornford and Hewitt cautioned against narrowly focused policies. In Scotland, centre-left parties have consistently won majority support in elections. The social democrat coalition has been broader, even if it has rarely acted together. But has this led to more ambitious policies, with a strong chance of securing continued support? Not yet. Scotland's own policy-making machinery is still young and the architects of it still cautious. Too little thought was given to what devolution was actually supposed to achieve in advance of the Parliament being established. Sooner or later, Scottish government must move out of its own comfort zone and articulate a vision of the good society and the values to underpin it, largely missing from the incrementalism of the Scottish Executive's Programme for Government.[4]

THIRD: DON'T BE FOOLED

'Don't believe the myth that prosperity has eliminated the problems which brought socialism into being in the first place. There is still poverty in the midst of abundance: class matters; inequality and exclusion are as strong as ever; anxiety and insecurity are growing.'

Despite our social democratic heritage, Scotland is a profoundly unequal country. Despite consistent improvements on average in incomes, housing, employment and health, the gap between the most and least advantaged continues to grow. And it is not clear that social democrats in government have managed to identify the roots of this problem effectively, let alone challenge it. That is not to take away from the Scottish Executive's solid programme of activity reported in the Social Justice Annual Reports,[5] nor the work of the Social Exclusion Unit (SEU)[6] and Performance and Innovation Unit (PIU) in London. But we should not be fooled into believing that the goal of reducing exclusion is the same as reducing inequality. Improving the life chances and incomes of the poorest is a fundamental aim – and Labour's Budget reforms have made steady progress in this direction in recent years. But it is possible to have less exclusion at the same time as greater inequality, when the forces that drive earning power and wealth accumulation are more powerful than tax-benefit improvements at the bottom of the ladder.

In all of this social democrats are divided: some have given up on greater equality, confusing it with the impossible (and undesirable) goal of equal outcomes; others stress the need to reduce *unjustified* inequalities, such as earnings growth among company directors that does not reflect risk (in the case of privatised utilities) or profits; while others believe the options for modern government are so restricted by international capital that inequality is the price to be paid for overall progress. If Scotland aspires to the greater prosperity and equality experienced by the Dutch and the Danes, it should say so, and ensure its own actions are aligned to that objective. Without a strategic vision, we can be certain that progress will remain modest.

FOURTH: DON'T RELY ON GROWTH

'Economic growth is a necessary but not sufficient condition of progress. Ecological constraints demand new ways of defining wealth. More wealth will not end poverty ... although it can help.'

Social democrats renounced the 'trickle-down' mythology of Conservative governments. Few believe, despite being more than three times wealthier than when the modern welfare state was created, that Scotland is three times happier, healthier or better equipped for the future. Yet the challenge to this way of thinking and acting remains unfocused. Scotland's debate on what kind of economic growth it wants has been dominated by inward investment versus home-grown business; knowledge-based versus labour intensive; and typically by the belief that any job is better than none.[7] Environmental concerns have been approached consistently as issues to be addressed once 'prior' objectives have been met or in conflict with those other objectives.[8]

Before long, social democrats who are impatient with this approach will have to make their views known by their actions. Taking environmental objectives seriously could begin to transform much of our economic activity, and create lasting opportunities for new types of growth. While the Scottish Executive's target on renewable energy is more demanding than the UK target, it looks like being too little, too late compared with Denmark's success in becoming Europe's leading manufacturer of wind energy turbines for example. Instead of Scotland striving to climb the productivity league by doing more of the same, it could seek better routes to sustainable growth. There is no advantage in waiting for the European Union to regulate changes in behaviour or for voters to start rewarding green politicians. Social democrats need to take the initiative and set Scotland's sights higher. On current trends, it would take a generation to match the level of product recycling and waste minimisation already achieved in other small European countries. Wherever we find ourselves in the economic growth cycle, a step change in approach to waste and energy will generate clear benefits.

FIFTH: DECIDE WHAT KIND OF CAPITALIST YOU ARE

'The idea of replacing the market with state ownership has breathed its last. But there are many kinds of market ... and the Left must construct markets which work by raising standards not driving them downwards.'

With the small but growing presence of the Scottish Socialist Party, the idea of state ownership has not quite breathed its last in Scotland. But elections in Scotland and the rest of Britain usually turn on what version of capitalism is on offer, or rather what version of spending the gains of the economic system is most convincing. That is not to say that the issue of how economic value is created is beyond debate or influence. The Irish approach is different from the Nordic; both are different from US or UK versions. While the language will jar with many Scots, if it really does come down to how the market is to serve your objectives, it makes it all the more important to be clear about what they are and how to achieve them.

SIXTH: REDISTRIBUTE WORK, NOT JUST INCOME

'Paid work is the main engine of distribution: the post-industrial welfare state must redistribute work (paid and unpaid) between men and women and across the life cycle.'

No one can accuse New Labour of neglecting employment. It has been single-minded in its work focus, leading to the New Deal programmes, integration of the Employment Service and Benefits Agency into a new Jobcentre Plus network, Employment Zones (including Glasgow) with significant powers to experiment, tougher responsibilities for Job Seekers Allowance claimants and greater support for other working age claimants such as lone parents and disabled people. In recent years Scotland has been faring almost as well as the UK average both in its rates of unemployment and proportion in employment. Some parts of Grampian and Lothian are as close to full employment as the best-performing areas in the UK. And the goal of full employment now encompasses women as well as men, part-time as well as full-time work, growing flexibility in working hours and the expectation of moving between jobs rather than jobs for life.

Yet, Scotland is as unequal in work as it is in income or health. Glasgow's resident employment rate is barely above 60 per cent, fully 12 per cent below the Scottish average, with some neighbourhoods registering under half of eligible adults in work.[9] Incapacity Benefit has served as a one-way ticket out of the labour market for many people who would still be working if they lived in reach of a more buoyant economy. There are three times as many people 'on the sick' as 'on the dole' in the city. Redistributing work must include a focus on those who would like to work but are not registered as jobseekers; much greater flexibility in working time; job rotation and sabbaticals to allow employees to trade-off more time for less money when they wish to; an assault on ageism in the labour market; and phased retirement options to challenge the potentially disastrous policy of promoting full-time early retirement. While the powers to act are mainly reserved to Westminster, much could be achieved outside of legislative means. The public sector is a large employer in Scotland. It has a responsibility to raise the quality of public services and it can help to do this through greater opportunities for employee learning and flexible use of time.

SEVENTH: BUILD TRAMPOLINES, NOT SAFETY NETS
'The aim of all welfare provision, with a few exceptions, should be to enable people to bounce back into health, work and active participation.'

The seventh proposition can be traced back to the time when modernisers were striving to find better ways of helping low-income households than simply increasing means-tested benefits. It is still too early to judge how effective government policies, combined with economic growth, have been in helping people living in poverty to secure higher incomes. Data from the British Household Panel Study in the 1990s showed very little 'trampoline' effect, with a considerable degree of short distance churning among the lowest income 10 per cent. The New Deal, national minimum wage, tax credits for working families and for children together offer brighter prospects than in the past, as long as employment levels are at least maintained. Yet, opportunities to earn cannot be the only route to higher incomes.

Trampolines are of course better than safety nets, but we still need safety nets for those who, at any given time, cannot work due to disability, illness, care responsibilities or because they have skills no longer valued or live in areas where labour demand is too weak (Proposition Six). It is better that safety nets are secure and catch people whose fortunes are in decline. Labour has announced significant improvements to Income Support for families with children, but that still leaves a sizeable proportion of working age adults with poverty level incomes. True, there are other ways of improving standards of living, such as reducing the cost of household basics like fuel, financial services and transport through government agencies acting as effective brokers with the private sector. But unless the issues of good enough support services for the most vulnerable (largely a devolved matter) and adequate incomes for the poorest are addressed with greater conviction, the safety nets will continue to look unfit for the times we live in.

EIGHTH: DON'T CONFUSE EQUALITY WITH SAMENESS
'Equality demands that people receive the same treatment when they are alike and different treatment when they are not. It is not equality to demand that women behave like men or children like adults.'

Children should have the right to be dependent. Young adults should have the right to be independent when they are ready. Men and women should expect greater equality in both the spheres of paid work (the labour market) and unpaid work (the home). Some members of minority ethnic communities will have greater support needs than others if they are to participate in society, but we must not assume that all do. These expectations demand that we take stock and review how well needs are being met. It is not hard to accept that people with disabilities will often need extra support to overcome barriers to work and learning. It is more challenging to recognise that the same applies to a recovering heroin addict or alcoholic, or an ex-offender, even if their predicament is believed by some to be self-inflicted. It is often said that prevention is better than cure – but cure is better than no cure. The goal of equality requires that we all experience human rights protection, but it does not mean we are all the same. Differences between groups of people must be respected, not denied or wished away. And differences *within* communities (whether based on geography, sex, ethnicity or age group) must also be better understood. Progress cannot be measured simply by how well the Scottish Executive or parliamentary committees address the worst forms of inequality, but also in the broader climate of opinion. Scotland needs to create a way of looking itself in the mirror and making sense of its reflection if these matters of culture as well as governance are to be influenced for the better.

NINTH: PAY ATTENTION TO MEANS

'Social democrats must remember that it is not (only) what you do but the way you do it that counts ... Power is a positional good: the more equally it is distributed the less there is at the top. Order must give way to persuasion and consultation must be for real.'

Since the devolution process began, government cannot be faulted for its work-rate. The Programme for Government is not short of ideas for action, each of them with a set of goals and a time-scale.[10] But the Executive has been so focused on doing (the 'what' issues), it has tended to neglect the delivery ('how to') issues. Even evidence-based policies don't translate into action without committed frontline staff, negotiated goodwill and a clear sense of purpose.[11] Westminster has been criticised for devolving the machinery of government but trying to cling to power. Those who wish devolution to succeed must ensure that the same criticism cannot be levelled at Holyrood. Power needs to be distributed in new ways to institutions with the capacity to use it wisely, to communities (including but not limited to the most excluded) and to individuals. Shoring up power in the Scottish Parliament should not be a badge of pride for social democrats. Moreover, if consultation is to be for real, governmental and parliamentary inquiry must dig deeper. Committees should look beyond the tier of representatives and organised interests – the usual suspects adept at capturing the attention of decision-makers – and also seek the deliberative views of citizens with no particular axe to grind.[12]

TENTH: THINK LOCALLY, ACT GLOBALLY

'Interdependence is now so great that many important problems can only be resolved at an international level. But social democrats should always have in mind the real effects of such decisions on individuals and communities.'

The familiar mantra of sustainable development turned round, this final proposition challenges us to look beyond our own patch, city or state, and make decisions with an eye on both the international context and local integrity. If negative consequences at the local level have international causes, they cannot be addressed only through action by the Council, Scottish Enterprise or the Scottish Parliament (although their combined efforts would help). This does not mean that internationalisation is a one-way street. It can be shaped by the sum of positive actions in nations and regions if the commitment exists. Where the consequences are truly global, the process for addressing them must be smarter. If the next G8 or Climate Change Summit were to be held in Scotland, what would social democrats do differently to secure commitment to action and stronger accountability?

CONCLUSION

The paradox of social democracy in Scotland is that the term is rarely used.[13] Memories are long: anything associated with the breakaway SDP of the 1980s, or the SNP's efforts to present itself as part of the European centre-left looks less than attractive to Labour Party loyalists. Yet it is clearly the defining feature of the first coalition government and offers the best way of building a bridge between the best of the past and a future where Scotland becomes a small, progressive European nation.[14] The 'old' social democracy can be proud of its achievements in raising standards of education, public health, housing, transport and ensuring that the benefits of progress were shared far more equitably than they would otherwise have been. More recently, the solidarity it offered during Thatcherism allowed a large part of the non-Conservative majority to seek common cause in achieving devolution.

But the old model came with too much baggage that frustrated further progress. The inherently conservative nature of the old social democracy has become increasingly clear: its majoritarian instincts, reflected in how the Labour Party disregarded electoral minorities, and how Glasgow and the west of Scotland often ignored other shades of opinion within the labour movement; its indifference to pluralism; and its belief that it should respond to the way things ought to be rather than current reality. The promise of the new politics of devolution cannot be realised by sticking to essentially the same model of social democracy. So what would the 'new' social democracy look like?

- Answering this question cannot be a task only for one party: the relationship between the new social democracy as a set of ideals/symbolic actions and the programme that New Labour politicians pursue in office is far from clear. There is a special responsibility on the SNP as the leading opposition party to do more than oppose. If it wishes to be part of social democracy's future, not just its traditions, it must contribute to finding coherent solutions fit for the next decade rather than the one we have left behind. If it cannot help Scotland decide what devolution is for, it is unlikely to put its own programme for government into practice let alone win greater support for its project of independence.
- Nor can the task of forging a new model for progressive action only involve those institutions who have shown that they too would prefer 'business as usual'. The limits to representative approaches must be clearly understood and effective use made of deliberative public involvement methods.
- The limits to evidence-based policy making should also be made explicit.[15] 'What matters is what works' is a fair basis for focusing the minds of civil servants, government agencies and frontline employees on the importance of better outcomes, but of limited value in the task of renewing a political philosophy. Decisions should emerge from the fusion of values as well as evidence. The new social democracy should not lose sight of the fact that values and actions thrive together.
- It should be willing to test its own assumptions and learn from its own mistakes. Notions of choice, responsibility and freedom, often neglected by social democrats on the grounds that the conservative version of them was alien, should be revisited.
- Perhaps most importantly, the new social democracy will manage to honour the past without clinging to it. Healthy societies will increasingly be defined by their relationship with the future.[16] Those in a position to look ahead with a core level of optimism, security and respect are more likely to thrive. Insecure societies cannot embrace change, fearful of being defeated by it. One of the most fundamental challenges for the new social democracy is to tackle *insecurity* (as distinct from uncertainty) and ensure all have

the resources to cope with change. One goal arising from this should be to grow a critical mass of politicians, business people and teachers, among others, comfortable with uncertainty. A 'confident nation' cannot grow from a belief in the old certainties.

In all of this, we are not alone. The new social democracy need not be wholly 'made in Scotland'. It will be both stronger and more flexible if it draws on progressive ideas and actions in the rest of Britain and beyond. We need to become less hung up on the origins of ideas and innovation, given the smallness and narrowness of policy and civic networks in Scotland. We need to begin to have the confidence in ourselves to borrow from elsewhere – to not dismiss ideas if they come from England, Seattle or Amsterdam.

We also have to begin developing a new notion of Scotland's place in the Union and a new idea of the Union, that goes beyond the old fashioned notions of the Scottish establishment and the Westminster classes about Scotland and the Union.[17] There are many problems in the 'New Unionism' articulated by Gordon Brown, but at least it is an attempt to develop an explanation of the new arrangements that are slowly evolving and the interaction between identities and institutions.[18] This is not about talking endlessly about constitutional politics and processes, but developing a sense of Scotland's place and purpose in a changing Union, the role of its politicians, both in Holyrood and Westminster, how they see themselves, and how the different levels of government can work together for the cause of better governance and a better Scotland.

Finally, for Scotland to make its full contribution, it must wake up to the need to be clear about the sense of purpose and set of values that drive what it does – and the realisation that the 'new politics' demands more than a Parliament, a new generation of politicians and a programme for government.

NOTES

1. D. Miliband (ed), *Reinventing the Left*, Cambridge: Polity Press 1994.
2. Commission on Social Justice, *Social Justice: Strategies for National Renewal: The Report of the Commission on Social Justice*, London: Vintage 1994.
3. J. Cornford and P. Hewitt, 'Do's and Don'ts for Social Democrats', in Miliband, *op. cit.*, pp251-54.
4. Scottish Executive, *Working Together for Scotland: A Programme for Government*, Edinburgh: Scottish Executive 2001.
5. Scottish Executive, *Social Justice Annual Report 2000*, Edinburgh: Scottish Executive 2000.
6. Social Exclusion Unit, *Preventing Social Exclusion*, London: The Cabinet Office 2001.

7. Scottish Enterprise, *The Scottish Enterprise Network Economy*, Glasgow: Scottish Enterprise 1999; Scottish Enterprise and Highlands and Islands Enterprise, *Tracking the Big Picture: Baselines, Milestones and Benchmarks for the Scottish Economy*, Glasgow and Inverness: Scottish Enterprise and Highlands and Islands Enterprise 1999.

8. E. McDowell and J. McCormick (eds), *Environment Scotland*, Aldershot: Ashgate 1999.

9. The condition of the Greater Glasgow area is crucial to the state of the Scottish economy: it is responsible for approximately one third of Scottish GDP, while the City Council's boundaries contain 70% of the most deprived areas of Scotland.

10. Scottish Executive, *Programme for Government, op. cit.*

11. H. T. O. Davies, S. M. Nutley and Peter C. Smith (eds), *What Works?: Evidence-based Policy and Practice in Public Services*, Bristol: Policy Press 2000.

12. P. Lynch, 'The Committee System', in G. Hassan and C. Warhurst (eds), *The New Scottish Politics: The First Year of the Scottish Parliament and Beyond*, Edinburgh: Stationery Office 2000, pp66-74.

13. J. McCormick and G. Leicester, 'Social Democracy in a Small Country: Political Leadership or Managerial Consultancy?', in A. Gamble and T. Wright (eds), *The New Social Democracy, Political Quarterly Special Issue*, Oxford: Blackwell 1999, pp131-41.

14. J. McMillan, 'Will Scottish Devolution Make A Difference', in B. Crick (ed), *Citizens: Towards a Citizenship Culture, Political Quarterly Special Issue*, Oxford: Blackwell, 2001, pp36-46.

15. Davies, *What Works?, op. cit.*

16. S. Stewart (ed), *The Possible Scot*, Edinburgh: Scottish Council Foundation, 1998.

17. G. Hassan and J. McCormick, 'After Blair: The Future of Britain and Britishness', *Soundings*, Summer/Autumn 2001, No. 18, pp118-34.

18. G. Brown and D. Alexander, *New Scotland, New Britain*, London: Smith Institute 1999. See Hassan and McCormick, *op. cit.*, pp125-28 for an analysis of Brown's 'New Unionism'.

Leadership and the Scottish governing classes

RICHARD PARRY

'Leadership' as a concept distinct from political authority is a recent preoccupation of public management. The Scottish Executive, as part of New Labour's drive towards modernised public management, has started to take an interest in the concept and has raised questions about who Scotland's leaders are to be. This questioning in turn relates to two older issues: firstly 'who runs Scotland' and 'who are Scotland's most influential and powerful people' – usually journalistic reproductions of sociological studies of reputation and influence; and, secondly, there have been suggestions that in the pre-devolutionary situation, and possibly beyond it, governmental authority has tended to fall into the hands of a stratum of elite actors in important occupational and intellectual fields, who have co-opted one another into an invisible power structure.[1] Scottish traditions of education and expertise, especially in professional and technical fields, hold out the promise that the quality of this leadership might be high. Indeed, it has become something of an export industry.

However, more pressing now are accusations that a lack of transparency of leadership is a democratic problem. Much of the transitional anxiety during the first two years of the Scottish Parliament has been about the mechanisms for putting in place legitimate leaders as instruments of the public will for policy change.

Throughout the British political system there is currently a search for effective leaders. Tony Blair's search for 'deliverers' to head various parts of his No.10 operation after the 2001 general election is a good example.[2] The role expected falls somewhere between those of politicians and civil servants – more analytical and long-term than the politician, more self-promoting and risk-taking than the official – and is transferable between public and private sectors. Within the British Isles, the authority roles attributed to Scots – doctors, engineers, accountants – have differed from the Welsh and the Irish and are conducive to the assumption of political leadership roles. It is typical that the leading medical and administrative roles in the NHS in

England have recently been held by Scots (Alan Langlands and Kenneth Calman). But the gravitation of Scottish talent to London is a threat to the leadership capability in Scotland. With devolution, there is an issue about how far Scots will continue to fill British leadership roles, whether there will be movement in the opposite direction and whether the Scottish reputation for leadership will be preserved.[3]

THE NEW POLITICAL ELITE – MPS, MSPS AND MEPS

Since devolution, Scotland has more job opportunities for party politicians – with 129 MSPs, 72 MPs and 8 MEPs – a total of 209 elected national representatives.[4] All of the MEPs and 56 of the MSPs are elected from party lists, giving unprecedented powers of patronage to party machines. Unlike many devolved systems (including Northern Ireland) there is no cumulation of mandates in which party leaders seek election at more than one level. Remarkably, all of those with dual Westminster and Holyrood mandates stood down from one level in 2001, and only one MSP (Phil Gallie, unsuccessfully) sought a House of Commons seat.

The quality of Scotland's parliamentary delegation to Westminster has probably improved in recent years. In the past it had been difficult to find enough talent to fill Scottish ministerial jobs, and the increasing numbers of SNP and Liberal Democrat members had reduced the Conservative pool. But under both the Major and Blair administrations Scottish members occupied prominent positions in UK departments, and even the Glasgow tradition received a nostalgic accolade in the election of Michael Martin as Speaker of the House of Commons in 2000.

With devolution, Labour MSPs provide the pool of recruitment for ministers. Labour's selection procedure for Holyrood candidates devalued a normal source of political recruitment – leadership in local government – in favour of broader, non-political experience in third sector organisations. Commitment to gender balance reinforced this theme.[5] Ministerial appointments and style have subsequently followed the trend. Ministers such as Wendy Alexander, Susan Deacon and Sarah Boyack went direct from having no elected experience into the Cabinet.

The leadership issue was thrown into relief by Donald Dewar's death in October 2000 and his succession by Henry McLeish. McLeish was fine as a departmental minister but there were doubts about his leadership qualities as First Minister. There were six members of Labour's 1997 Westminster delegation who became Westminster Cabinet ministers and were of greater political weight than Henry McLeish – Gordon Brown, Robin Cook, Alistair Darling, George Robertson, John Reid and Helen Liddell, with Brian Wilson and George Foulkes on a similar rung to McLeish.[6] Normal federal stratagems of parachuting in leaders from national to sub-national level are very difficult in the Holyrood system even had the political will been present to bring in one of the big six to succeed Dewar. Periodical talk that Cook or Darling might like to move to Holyrood highlights the problem: they would not move to be anything less than First Minister, but how could that be guaranteed? It is likely that only a period of opposition at Holyrood would enable Labour to work through the issue that, in practice, Holyrood is second best to Westminster for its political leaders. The subsequent downfall of McLeish and election of Jack McConnell in November 2001 only served to confirm this analysis.

The Liberal Democrats also have had a Westminster-first approach, with the exception of Jim Wallace. Charles Kennedy is also a British leader with a Scottish seat. Two out of the five contenders for the Conservative leadership in 2001 were English-based Scots, Michael Ancram and Iain Duncan Smith. The Conservatives' heaviest Scottish hitter – Malcolm Rifkind – also opted to seek a return to Westminster when his party's Holyrood leadership was available on a plate and without any electoral risk because of the list system. In contrast, the SNP fields a Holyrood-based first team (though Alex Salmond's decision to relocate himself to the Westminster environment was instructive) and is the one party to have sorted out its position on this issue.

COMPONENTS OF THE NON-ELECTED SCOTTISH GOVERNMENT CLASSES

Categorising political leaders is relatively straightforward. Identifying leaders who are not elected is more difficult. We should be sceptical of the media and cultural personalities whose names fill the '100 most influential' lists. There is real conceptual confusion over where to place Sean Connery and Kirsty Wark, both of whom have become almost civic figures in their readiness to lead social and cultural causes. An important issue here is a readiness to commit to Scotland when a person has an international reputation. But it is possible to go a long way to delineate the kind of jobs whose occupants can be expected to take on a leadership role beyond their formal responsibilities, especially by appointment to public bodies or tasks.

As a rough categorisation, we can include:
- heads of Scottish Executive departments
- local authority chief executives
- heads of major public agencies
- university principals (and other heads of further and higher educa-

tion institutions)
- religious leaders
- judges
- chief constables
- heads of Scottish-based clearing banks and other financial institutions.

An important defining variable is the number of positions in each category. When there were nine regions and four cities, their Chief Executives were a compact elite. With 32 local authorities, the posts and their holders are diminished, and become much less prominent than the eight Chief Constables. Strathclyde Region produced Chief Executives who were considerable figures in Scottish life – Lawrence Boyle, Robert Calderwood and Neil McIntosh. Similar considerations apply to health chiefs, head teachers and university professors: individuals may be prominent and influential, but the generality are not. 'Category creep' is now also affecting judges, whose numbers have increased to 32.

Animating the system are the interstitial figures, especially those who have the capacity to take on portfolios of board memberships – prototypically merchant banker Sir Angus Grossart. The financial orientation of the Scottish business world, with its cross-directorships and cross-shareholdings, has been of prime importance in reinforcing the leadership elite. There is also a West of Scotland engineering-based business leadership, lately typified by the career of Sir Ian Robinson who has moved from the chairmanship of Scottish Power to that of Scottish Enterprise, but it has lost weight to the Edinburgh-based financial institutions. The position of the Scottish clearing banks is central, and they have had to confront the issue of their independence in a globalising economy in which a Scottish-based operation has insufficiency of scale. The Royal Bank of Scotland solved its problems in 2000 through a remarkable takeover of English clearing bank NatWest; the Bank of Scotland, the initial bidders for NatWest, struggled in 2001 towards a merger with Halifax, which preserved head office functions in Edinburgh at the expense of the balance of power in the new company. The greater English exposure of the merged entities potentially reduces the representation of Scottish great and good on their boards, and we are likely to see the end of grandee figures such as Viscount Younger and Sir Jack Shaw, who sustained their banks' roles as patrons of the arts and of Scottish life.

Over time, the influence of the various categories fluctuates. Most judges and university principals now seem more orientated to their own professional worlds than to the public sphere. Stewart (now Lord) Sutherland, Principal of Edinburgh University, has been the most prominent of the latter, and interestingly is a returning Scot with a UK profile as chair of the Royal Commission on Long-term Care of the Elderly.[7] Before devolution, religious leaders were more prominent, especially those of the Church of Scotland, which sought to be a repository of national civil society. The Kirk's leadership structure – with Moderators changing annually and selected to provide a balance of background within the church – is now militating against the building of a profile for its leaders. Even an interesting figure such as John Miller, minister from Castlemilk and Moderator in 2001-02, attracts little media coverage.

Occasionally clerics from other denominations can develop a leadership role – most notably in recent years Richard Holloway, Episcopal Bishop of Edinburgh from 1986 to 2000, whose mastery of the media and taste for controversial pronouncements secured him wide recognition. However the overwhelming religious presence in recent years was that of Cardinal Thomas Winning, Archbishop of Glasgow from 1974 until his death in June 2001. Winning broke the mould of Catholic leaders in Scotland by his attention-grabbing comments on the issues of the day and his fearlessness in mixing it with politicians, virtually none of whom could align themselves completely with his mix of theological conservatism and social radicalism. Winning inherited the power structure of Scottish Catholicism (based upon the school system in central Scotland and the long-term disproportionate loyalty of Scottish Catholics to the Labour Party) and seemed dismayed by its decline. After the Dewar administration advanced the repeal of Section 28/Clause 2a[8] – the bar on local authority 'promotion' of homosexual 'pretended family relationships' – without its having been mentioned in its manifesto, Winning seemed to flirt with the SNP. It was symbolic that his first heart attack, a week before his death, came the day after the UK General Election had confirmed the triumph of New Labour.

With a population of just five million, Scotland's scale produces a much more intimate leadership structure than England's fifty million. The connections between the groups listed above that are accidents of education, social contact or mutual interests are greater therefore in Scotland.[9] The structure may be self-sustaining, but there is a difficulty about reinvigorating it and establishing the correct criteria for movement from a senior position in these fields to the publicly prominent leadership élite. The greatest influence on this process falls to senior civil servants in the Scottish Executive as they advise their ministers.

THE CIVIL SERVICE ELITE
The Scottish Executive represents a fusion of homegrown and UK-based influences. As part of the home civil service, St Andrew's House

has had to follow managerial initiatives – notably Next Steps Agencies from 1988 (which created a significant leadership post of Chief Executive of the Scottish Prison Service) and the Modernising Government policies of the Blair government from early 1999. This latter initiative has now split into Modernising Public Services (branded by the Scottish Executive as '21st Century Government') and Civil Service Reform; improvement is sought around the six broad themes of 'stronger leadership with a clear sense of purpose', 'better business planning from top to bottom', 'sharper performance management', 'a dramatic improvement in diversity', 'a Service more open to people and ideas, which brings on talent' and 'a better deal for staff'.[10] Although this reform programme might be seen as Whitehall interference, the Scottish and Welsh devolved administrations have embraced it without difficulty as it fits the priorities of their own ministers and reflects modern management thinking.

The post of Permanent Secretary to the Scottish Executive – 'Scotland's top civil servant' – must occupy an important place in this discussion. The incumbent, Muir Russell (knighted in June 2001), was inexplicably omitted from Channel 4's list of Scotland's most powerful 100 in 1999.[11] This omission was apparently part of an attempt to show that 'real' power resides away from a formal senior office. In fact great power in animating the system resides here, only partially modified by the more open governmental structures after devolution.

It is only fairly recently that the Scottish Office/Executive as a whole and its head have taken over from component departments as sources of authority. Until 1964 the Permanent Secretaryship was held by the most distinguished of the senior officials, but the position lacked power and direct staff, with the departments having both policy divisions and support services such as personnel and finance. Then, under the authentic 'leadership' figure of Sir Douglas Haddow (1964-73), central functions took shape, first on economic policy and then on finance and personnel management.[12]

Recent Permanent Secretaries have been more clearly 'Scottish' than 'Whitehall' in their orientation to the job. Kerr Fraser (1978-88, later Sir William Fraser) is a pillar of Scottish civil society whose career is a throwback to an earlier age – he went on to be Principal of Glasgow University and then its Chancellor. His wife Marion attained the distinct eminence of being the first non-royal lady member of the Order of the Thistle, after being High Commissioner to the General Assembly of the Church of Scotland. The Frasers wore these distinctions with modesty, and to complete the circle their son Douglas became Political Editor of the *Sunday Herald* in 1999.

Following Fraser, Russell Hillhouse was an unexpected choice, at the expense of the ultra-punctilious William Reid, a Scots returnee from Whitehall, who was rumoured to have fallen foul of Margaret Thatcher. Reid later found his metier, and his knighthood, as an effective Parliamentary Ombudsman, a rigorous Scots keeper of the administrative conscience. For Hillhouse and his colleagues of the time, the increasing non-exemption of Scotland from Conservative Party policies was matched by declining Scottish support for the party. Hillhouse set in train the successful planning of devolution but reached the mandatory retirement age of 60 before it took effect.

With the appointment of Muir Russell in May 1998 we confront the issue of leadership more directly, since the role of the Permanent Secretary to the Executive was going to be different. The other strong candidate was Kenneth MacKenzie, a church elder but also an amateur actor who had a formidable combination of administrative skills, and was widely admired at the top level in Whitehall. Both men were heads of Scottish departments, but the younger Russell emerged as the person for the times, with a smooth style and a cogent and consistent way of speaking equally suitable for a broadcast interview or an address to staff. Also noteworthy is Russell's marriage to Eileen Mackay, another successful Scottish Office official. Their careers advanced in parallel until, in 1996, Mackay took early retirement from the post of Principal Finance Officer and assembled an impressive portfolio career of board memberships, including the Royal Bank of Scotland, the Economic and Social Research Council and the Court of Edinburgh University. The Russell/Mackay partnership is not a double act, but it constitutes a formidable networking presence across public, private and third sectors.[13]

Muir Russell's advancement to the top job – after an external advertisement – repeated his predecessor's leapfrogging over heads of department, all of whom were older and some of whom were former work superiors, and made it difficult to reconfigure departments and hierarchies at the point of devolution. The role of head of department had become a questionable one from a perspective of best business practice, being a potentially redundant hierarchical tier above a range of functions, with little chance for leadership across them. There had been some instances of early departures from the post – for example, two successive industry heads, Gavin McCrone and James Scott, whose careers flourished respectively as university professor and inquiry chair, and head of Scottish Enterprise and later an SNP activist.

Russell is a leader comfortable with the modern management techniques being advanced as part of civil service reform – to which, as a continuing part of the Home Civil Service, the Scottish Executive is committed. Russell has appointed cross-cutting 'champions' from the

Management Team. He is committed to diversity in the workforce and to new forms of performance development. Among the heads of department, Robert Gordon's membership of the Consultative Steering Group on the Scottish Parliament and Holyrood Design Group gave him prominence among politicians and journalists. He became head of a new Department of Finance and Central Services in June 2001, inevitably dubbed the 'Scottish Treasury'. Two recent appointees to this rank, John Elvidge and Jim Gallagher, had both served in the Cabinet Office just previously. Their experience indicates how important still is the Whitehall orientation to top Scottish officials. Sir Muir Russell attends the Wednesday morning meetings of permanent secretaries in London, and is a member of the Senior Appointments Selection Committee that makes nominations to the top 150 jobs across Whitehall. Networks of consultation and mutual briefing remain far more significant than formal mechanisms in making devolution work.

Despite interest in the conversion of departments into 'business units', they were maintained.[14] However, by 2000 senior personnel were changing. There were two early retirements in mid-2000 aided by money from the UK Government's 'Modernising Government' initiative; Hamish Hamill as head of the Justice Department and Colin MacDonald as Principal Establishment Officer. In March 2001 Kenneth MacKenzie also retired and was succeeded by Nicola Munro, the first female head of department. The one Management Group member on a fixed-term contract, health chief Geoff Scaife (formally, and pointedly, not a head of department) found his position not extended in late 2000. Personal factors apart – and there appeared to be some – this lack of extension happened after a decision in both England and Scotland to merge the civil service permanent head of health with the NHS Chief Executive in order to provide an unambiguous official leader of the health service. In both cases the person selected (Trevor Jones in Scotland, Nigel Crisp in England) came from senior health positions, not the civil service.

Although after devolution there have been numerous generalised, gossipy media reports of difficulties between ministers and senior officials, Scotland's top civil servants have retained most of the anonymity associated with pre-devolution days. None of the First Ministers has tried to impose a structure at variance with civil service norms. What is more likely to change is the degree of permeability between the civil service elite and other employment streams in the public sector. The 'bringing on talent' theme of civil service reform fits in well with this possibility, and it is becoming easier to enter the civil service after experience elsewhere – through secondments, external advertising of posts, and open competitions for the Senior Civil Service. It seems likely that the precedent of Trevor Jones's appointment from the health service direct to Head of Department rank may in time be a precedent for high-level leadership transfers. Although it is not always easy to assimilate staff into the civil service at senior levels, the convergence of management practice between organisations and the wish to mobilise senior talent in Scotland could well serve to diminish the Whitehall orientation of Scottish Executive staff. The creation of a Scottish Leadership Foundation in 2001 is part of this process. This Foundation is a cross-sectoral body intended to promote interchange among senior managers, with the Principal Establishment Officer of the Executive as one of its directors. It remains to be seen whether general support for the idea of interchange and best practice across sectors can be fitted within the detailed personnel practices of the organisations involved.

LEADERSHIP IN THE QUANGO STATE

A political system without devolved political authority needs 'quangos' (public bodies outside the civil service or local government) for legitimacy, and public services at all levels may need them for efficiency.[15] These bodies promote endless controversy, with Angus MacKay's cull of June 2001 only one of many attempts to bring them under control.[16] Quangos need leaders, usually with the separation of chair and chief executive roles found in business. They also have the capacity to define a distinctive style and image not found in the civil service, local government or health service.

Operationally, the leadership of quangos is not easy to secure. When the Conservatives launched the internal market in the health service, the volume of board appointments to both Health Boards and NHS Trusts nearly overwhelmed them. The result was an appointments commission (itself another quango) that searched for public-spirited individuals with the right business or voluntary sector background. Competing for chief executives can be a problem when salaries are capped. Lines of quango accountability are unclear: the civil service and ministers operate in an advisory and ultimately supervisory capacity in relation to quangos.[17]

Under devolution, two things have changed. The first is scepticism about maintaining a territorial network of bodies within Scotland. This network has always produced a miniaturised system with potential inefficiency. The tendency has been to collapse structures back to the all-Scotland level, with leadership concentrated at Scottish headquarters – evident in the enterprise network, the health service and in the water authorities. Regionalisation within Scotland, so strong a theme of pre-devolution Scotland, is now weak.

The second change is a renewed legitimacy for incorporating quangos back into the civil service. Until recently, the wish not to increase civil service numbers and to preserve an independent, technocratic status for these functions sustained the quango format. The difficulties of the Scottish Qualifications Agency in 2000 and the impossibility of keeping ministers at arm's length from the issues hastened the change. Now, the emphasis is on shortened lines of accountability and direct support for the responsible ministers. This re-incorporation can be significant for the civil service. The number of staff involved can be quite large in relation to the 14,000 strong Scottish Executive and the styles of work different. Already this can be seen in the Health Department, NHS Management Executive and Communities Scotland.

Related to the quango state and drawing on the same kind of personnel is the advisory state. The use of commissions, committees, working groups and taskforces to promote legitimate policy is an old Scottish theme that has been making a comeback. In the late 1960s, local government reorganisation was taken forward by the Royal Commission under Lord Wheatley (a judge) that included backbench MPs. By the early 1990s, further reorganisation was taken forward within the Scottish Office. The Scottish Executive has used committees to provide policy leadership on some very tricky issues – student finance (under Andrew Cubie, an industrialist[18]), teacher's pay (under former civil servant Gavin McCrone[19]) and local government (under former local authority chief Neil McIntosh[20]). The role of such inquiry chairs is vital, and expanding the pool of suitable talent will be an important task for Executive ministers and their civil service advisers. It is a considerable task to chair these committees and then offer an articulate public defence of their recommendations.

CONCLUSION: SCOTTISH LEADERSHIP POST-DEVOLUTION

Devolution requires leaders who are prepared to be committed to Scotland and not regard the equivalent top job at the British level as the desired career move. The implicit stratification into those who made it in order to leave, and those not quite good enough and so left behind, has pervaded many Scottish institutions and professional worlds. Scotland has always had a high level of inward and outward exchange in proportion to its population, but at the level of political and economic leadership the balance has been in favour of export. Recent political and economic change has corrected this imbalance, and given Scotland the potential to market its life-style and opportunities to outsiders. It may be speculated that Scotland is better than most nations in assimilating those prepared to make a commitment to it.

At the moment, Scottish leadership is influenced by the orientation of the Scottish Executive to British-wide New Labour approaches. Labour's second election victory reinforces the élite that necessarily develops around any administration. But would the élite of an SNP-led Holyrood administration be any different? It would have two aspects – the SNP as the opposition party, providing an alternative administration in combination with other parties, and the SNP as the leader of a movement towards independence. The SNP would like to combine these aspects but in practice they would be distinct. In the nearest international parallel, Quebec, the pro-independence Parti Québecois became a mature party of government over decades of inconclusive manoeuvring on the sovereignty issue. This manoeuvring causes a coalescence of élites into broad groups according to views on the constitutional issue, with the Liberal Party becoming the home of all federalists and even importing the leader of the Federal Conservative Party, Jean Charest, to lead it.

In Scotland, such issues should be easier to manage because of two factors: the absence of a divisive language issue, and the very secure historically based identity of Scotland as a nation. Devolution has made it easier for the unionist-minded to accept this identity, and the anti-devolutionary and anti-Labour sentiments of many parts of the business and professional worlds have largely disappeared. It seems likely that the challenge of providing leadership in the public sphere in Scotland will be faced in the context of political and managerial variables common to all modern systems of government. Already, the younger leading figures of Labour and the SNP seem fairly homogeneous in terms of attitude and personality, almost like twins separated at birth into Montagues and Capulets on the national question but otherwise similar in orientation on the role of government and political leadership.

A final question is of 'old' and 'new' leadership emerging from the Scottish Parliament. However much the old elite categories of Scottish life are used for public leadership tasks, it is to the Parliament that the electorate will turn for instrumental and expressive styles of leadership. The better gender balance at Holyrood reinforces the influence of voluntary sector and social care styles, which as Jackie Baillie (and several of the new ministers in Wales) shows can be highly effective when allied to sharp political instincts. At the moment this development exists alongside a new public management style typified by successive Finance Ministers, Jack McConnell and Angus MacKay. They subscribed to modernisation policies now being taken forward by UK political and civil service élites. Both of these ministers have experience of local authority leadership, as did Susan Deacon at a less experienced level as a policy adviser. Baillie, Mackay and Deacon were all casualties of McConnell's cabinet reshuffle, though not for lack of talent. The style of the SNP's John Swinney and Andrew Wilson invites comparison and is offering something different from the 'amiable professional' style of Jim Wallace and David McLetchie.

Modern political leadership is a search for an optimal mix of personality, background and operating style. It helps to be able to make clear decisions and defend them consistently, to have an awareness of management concepts, and – other things being equal – be of pleasant and equable temperament and sensitive in personal dealings. Management textbooks confirm that old-style thuggery is obsolete. The present Scottish Executive, and the leadership of the political parties, contains politicians likely to meet these criteria. They have been educated by the co-operative working being attempted in the Scottish Parliament, and made resilient by the thoroughly disrespectful tone of press commentary about it. In retrospect, the role of the Consultative Steering Group in offering a model of political behaviour distinct from that of Westminster is likely to have been vital. The prospect is of a continued evolution towards effective leadership styles that derive a positive impetus from both Scottish professional traditions and the new beginning offered by devolution.

NOTES

1. For a 1990s discussion of this co-option see M. Linklater and R. Dennistoun (eds), *Anatomy of Scotland*, Edinburgh: Chambers 1992.

2. P. Hennessy, *The Prime Minister: The Office and Its Holders Since 1945*, London: Penguin 2nd edn. 2001. His chapter, 'Command and Control: Tony Blair 1997-', pp476-538, is an excellent analysis of the Blair style of leadership in government and the problems of delivery. Also see P. Hennessy, *The Blair Revolution in Government?*, Institute for Politics and International Studies, Leeds University 2000; and *The Importance of Being Tony: Two Years of the Blair Style*, London: Guy's and St Thomas' Hospital 1999.

3. Scotland remains intimately bound to the London centre through the Labour Party, which remains highly centralised, and through the structures of UK public administration. See R. Parry, 'The Civil Service and the Scottish Executive Structure and Style', in G. Hassan and C. Warhurst (eds), *The New Scottish Politics: The First Year of the Scottish Parliament and Beyond*, Edinburgh: The Stationery Office 2000, pp85-91.

4. The number of elected politicians in Scotland has more than doubled as a result of devolution. Pre-devolution, Scotland had 80 national politicians (MPs plus MEPs), whereas it now has 209; the experience of Wales and Northern Ireland is similar. Scottish voters are now represented by a total

of eighteen elected politicians – one MP, one FPTP MSP, seven list MSPs, eight MEPs and one councillor. G. Hassan and P. Lynch, The *Almanac of Scottish Politics*, London: Politico's Publishing 2001, pvii.

5. J. Bradbury, J. Mitchell, L. Bennie and D. Denver, 'Candidate Selection, Devolution and Modernisation: The Selection of Labour Party Candidates for the 1999 Scottish Parliament and Welsh Assembly Elections', in P. Cowley, D. Denver, A. Russell and L. Harrison (eds), *British Elections and Parties Review: Volume 10*, London: Frank Cass 2000, pp151-72.

6. On the relationship between Scottish Labour and British Labour see Gerry Hassan in this volume.

7. Royal Commission on Long Term Care, *With Respect to Old Age: A Report by the Royal Commission on Long Term Care*, London: The Stationery Office 1999 (chaired by Stewart Sutherland).

8. On the Section 28/Clause 2a debate see Rowena Arshad in this volume.

9. See the *Sunday Herald* power map on the relationships between politicians and press in Scotland, reprinted in P. Schlesinger, D. Miller and W. Dinan, *Open Scotland?: Journalists, Spin Doctors and Lobbyists*, Edinburgh: Polygon 2001, p20.

10. Scottish Executive, *21st Government Action Plan 2000*, p45.

11. A. Kemp, 'The Scottish Power 100', *The Observer Review*, 18.4.99.

12. On a view of the Scottish Office pre-devolution and the challenges in shifting to the Scottish Executive post-devolution, see: P. Mackay, 'Modernising the Scottish Civil Service', in G. Hassan and C. Warhurst (eds), *A Different Future: A Modernisers' Guide to Scotland*, Edinburgh: Centre for Scottish Public Policy/The Big Issue in Scotland 1999, pp267-74.

13. A. Young, 'Man the money's on', *The Herald*, 12.6.99.

14. R. Parry and A. Jones, 'The Transition from the Scottish Office to the Scottish Executive', *Public Policy and Administration*, 2000, 15: 2.

15. R. Parry, 'Quangos and the Structure of the Public Sector in Scotland', *Scottish Affairs*, Autumn 1999, No. 29, pp12-27.

16. *The Herald*, 22.6.01.

17. R. W. McQuaid, 'The Local Economic Impact of the Scottish Parliament', in J. McCarthy and D. Newlands (eds), *Governing Scotland: Problems and Prospects*, Aldershot: Ashgate 1999, pp149-66.

18. Independent Committee of Inquiry into Student Funding, *Student Finance: Fairness for the Future*, Edinburgh: The Stationery Office 1999 (chaired by Andrew Cubie).

19. Independent Committee of Inquiry into Professional Conditions of Service for Teachers Scotland, Edinburh: Stationery Office, 2000 (chaired by Gavin McCrone).

20. Commission on Local Government and the Scottish Parliament, *Moving Forward: Local Government and the Scottish Parliament*, Edinburgh: The Stationery Office 1999 (chaired by Neil McIntosh).

The Scottish establishment: old and new elites

ALF YOUNG

VILLAGE SCOTLAND

One of the most cherished and oft-repeated myths about modern Scotland is the assertion that the place is still a village where everyone knows everyone else. What those who peddle this myth really mean is that Scotland is a village where everyone who is anyone knows everyone else who matters. In other words, Scotland possesses a tightly-knit and supremely well networked establishment or elite, where all the key players are on first name terms, meet regularly, share a high level of consensus about where Scotland's future lies and have the power and influence to make things happen.

For those who cherish this myth, it represents a source of great national strength. That same strength manifested itself in the 1990s in the Scottish Constitutional Convention and the national Claim of Right, which triggered Scotland's second, successful attempt to achieve its own Parliament and the first legislative measure of home rule since 1707.[1] The common cause this Scottish establishment subscribes to, the manageable scale on which it operates, and the short lines of communication it maintains, all redound to Scotland's benefit, according to the myth-makers. And by implication these self-evident strengths contrast sharply with how things can get so much more messy and confused in larger habitations, such as England.

Others of a more sceptical caste of mind concede the myth has real substance but worry about the parochialism and introspection that allegedly thrives in the hothouse atmosphere of Scotland the village. Knowing everyone else means knowing everyone else's business. And that can drown out any celebration of diversity, choke off fresh thinking and stifle any spark of national dynamism. For more strident critics – those who subscribe to the Andrew Neil school of national doom, for example – Scotland the village and its parish pump establishment is a source of almost unrelieved, debilitating weakness. For them Scotland is the last bastion of municipal socialism, an irredeemably statist, handout culture, where enterprise has withered, envy is rampant, Tories hardly ever get elected and even judges and business executives are not averse to rattling the national begging bowl in pursuit of the latest good cause.[2]

You will already have deduced that I do not wholeheartedly subscribe to either of these caricatures of the country in which I have lived for the past 57 years. In more than two decades in journalism in Scotland I have attended more conferences, seminars, award ceremonies, lunches and black tie dinners, held by more professional bodies, trade associations, state agencies, political parties, companies large and small, universities and colleges, local authorities, charities and lobbying groups than I care to remember. It is certainly true that the same familiar faces pop up again and again at such events. So much so that I sometimes wonder how reputedly influential people have found the time to achieve the things that gave them their power in the first place. But a reservoir of accumulated familiarity with whole constellations of fellow Scots who like nothing better than to talk or eat is not, I would argue, proof positive of the existence of an all-powerful, all-embracing establishment or elite. Rather it is proof that talking interminably about the challenges we face as a nation, eating together in hotels three or four times a week through each and every winter and giving each other awards for qualified achievements in this field or that are national pastimes we all, arguably, pursue to damaging excess.

ELITE SCOTLAND

Scotland is more like one of those diagrams drawn from set theory in mathematics. It consists of a whole series of smaller aspirant elites – in politics, business, the professions, the arts, academia, the media, the public realm, the social economy – that overlap to a greater or lesser extent but seldom coincide. Some barely intrude into each other's territory. One can even chart rival elites within a single sector or across different geographies within Scotland that maintain high levels of mutual exclusivity. For example, the Edinburgh business establishment, traced through who sits on whose board, or who backs whom in contested take-over bids, reveals precisely this kind of establishment fission again and again. And who matters in north-east Scotland, consistently one of the most prosperous Scottish regions, is quite distinct from who matters in the Borders, the other part of Scotland which best typifies the coexistence of both industrial and land-owning classes.

The idea of Scotland the village deserves to be challenged, not least because Scotland's territory accounts for around a third of the entire land mass of the United Kingdom. Within Scotland's borders ancient rivalries persist – east versus west, Glasgow versus Edinburgh, the heavily populated, loyal-to-Labour central belt versus the rest. Such regional and metropolitan rivalries are also present in many other countries. It is their sheer persistence in Scotland that challenges the validity of the village myth. And the parallel idea of a powerful, cohesive Scottish establishment is, I would argue, equally misplaced. Within today's Scotland there cohabits such a rich and diverse variety of would-be elites that no village square would ever be able to hold them. In short, in terms of the distribution of power and influence, Scotland seems to be a much more complex place than the prevalent mythology allows. So any attempt to map out and analyse the changing nature of the elites in a devolved Scotland must expect to come to diverse and complex conclusions. And, given the fresh reality of home rule, the task of understanding must confront another big question.

Even if we can identify an overlapping constellation of sectional and regional elites within Scotland, are they all that powerful? Or does much of the real power continue to reside – notably in the realms of politics, business and some of the professions – in London or further afield? In terms of government, is Scotland's current political elite Jack McConnell, Wendy Alexander and Malcolm Chisholm? Or is it Gordon Brown, Alastair Darling, Dr John Reid and Robin Cook? Can Scotland meaningfully boast an indigenous business elite, if the weekly ritual for aspirant members is the Heathrow shuttle; if some major Scottish companies are routinely run by executives whose principal homes remain in the home counties; and if crunch decisions over which big industrial plants stay open or close are taken in Illinois (Motorola) or Tokyo (NEC)? Does talk of powerful national elites in a small open nation like Scotland mean very much in an age of political power sharing and economic globalisation?

OLD ELITES

Tom Johnston's *Our Scots Noble Families* was published in 1909.[3] It remains to this day the most searing polemic ever launched against Scotland's landed aristocracy.

> Show the people that the title deeds are rapine, murder, massacre, cheating or court harlotry; dissolve the halo of divinity that surrounds the hereditary title; let the people clearly understand that our present House of Lords is composed largely of descendants of successful pirates and rogues; do these things and you shatter the romance that keeps the nation numb and spellbound while privilege picks its pocket.[4]

So wrote the editor of the Independent Labour Party newspaper

Forward, who would eventually become Secretary of State for Scotland in Churchill's wartime national government.[5]

Here is how Johnston dispensed with the twentieth century descendants of King Robert the Bruce.

> Lord Burleigh draws £100 a month, having as an ex-cabinet minister signed a plea that he was too poor to do without some state help. This pension does not, however, seem to have destroyed his energies or his capacity for thrift, for he 'directs' some seven public companies (total capital over £88,000,000), engaged in banking, rails, steamships and telegraphs. In his spare time he amuses himself with the pleasantries of the Anti-Socialist League, endeavouring to revive antediluvian political theories. He was wildly excited over the introduction of an old-age pension of five shillings per week to working class octogenarians, believing that state pensions destroy self-reliance and individuality. He left us to infer that he spoke from personal experience.[6]

Yet when Johnston went looking, in 1943, for the first chairman of his greatest ministerial creation, the North of Scotland Hydro-Electric Board, who should he choose for the job but the 12th Earl of Airlie – Old Etonian, major Scottish landowner, deputy governor of the British Linen Bank and director of Barclays Bank.[7] True Airlie had criticised Johnston's Hydro Bill for not going far enough. True Airlie's son was later blackballed from the Perth Hunt by those landowners who resisted the creation of dams across the highlands to bring power from the glens. And Johnston was operating within the constraints of a wartime coalition. But Johnston, the scourge of privilege, was inviting one of the foremost scions of a system he despised to steer his most cherished political achievement. The incident surely raises important doubts about Scotland's reputation as a cradle of radical, class driven politics, one that has survived into the post-ideological era of Blair and New Labour. Johnston's choice of Airlie – he described the Earl in his autobiography as 'a first rate friend to work with'[8] – also demonstrates both the power of consensus and the deep streak of pragmatism in Scottish life that helped foster and sustain the village myth over the past half-century.[9]

Another element of Johnston's legacy is the Scottish Council for Development and Industry (SCDI), the organisation still around today that best exemplifies that post-war Scottish consensus.[10] Its origins lay in two separate bodies, the Scottish Development Council, set up in 1931 by a group of leading industrialists, led by the influential Clyde shipbuilder Sir James Lithgow, and the Scottish Council on Industry which Johnston himself formed in 1942. The Development Council wanted to attract new industries north of the border and counter Scotland's reputation for shop-floor militancy. But it quickly became a strong advocate of the kind of powerful central planning that was to become such a feature of post-war Labour government strategy. On the eve of war, there were already strong suspicions in London that the Development Council and the industrialists behind it were far too nationalist in their instincts

This was still the era of great family-owned industries in Scotland, some the fruits of the industrial revolution, others of later vintage. Apart from Lithgow, there were also the Colvilles (iron and steel), Coats (thread), Collins (publishing), Alexander (vehicle building), Arrol (structural engineering), McVitie (biscuits), Fraser (department stores) and many, many more. Scotland also had a proud, 250 year-old history of its own distinctive banking industry. When he joined Churchill's coalition government Tom Johnston could see the strategic advantages in exploiting this emerging coalition of purpose north of the border. He persuaded the prime minister to allow him to create a Council of State, consisting of all of his living predecessors as Scottish Secretary, and followed that up with what he called his 'industrial parliament', the Scottish Council on Industry.

It was independent of government and drew its membership and its funding from industry and the unions, from local councils, chambers of commerce and the banks. Through his Council of State Johnston even managed to persuade the chairmen and general managers of the eight major Scottish banks of the time to commit publicly to 'doing everything possible to co-operate with the Council on Industry to promote Scottish industrial interests in the post-war years'.[11] The threat, as Johnston himself described it, has a familiar ring to it:

> We had seen our motor car industry and our calico printing go south. Even the printing of our telephone directories had gone to Harrow. We had seen the rearmament factories being started in England. All we got in Scotland was the storage capacity. Unless drastic and immediate steps had been taken to correct these drifts to the land beyond the Cheviots, the outlook for Scottish industry and the Scottish nation post-war had been bleak indeed.[12]

With such comprehensive backing from capital and labour and the public and private realms, the Council on Industry began to deliver the new funding from the Treasury needed to rebuild Scotland's industrial infrastructure. In less than three years it helped stimulate 700 new industrial enterprises in Scotland, employing 90,000 Scots. Three departments of the UK government were, wrote Johnston, 'induced to expend in Scotland £12m on factories and plant'.[13] Exploiting the wartime consensus brilliantly, Johnston was winning a degree of informal devolution for Scotland from under Churchill's nose. The Scottish Secretary was also giving powerful new impetus to the use of the Scottish card, a tactic that would be played again and again by the Scottish establishment in the decades ahead to considerable effect.

The merger of the two bodies into SCDI in 1946 was designed to reinforce that process. For a time it did. Post-war Scotland benefited from a number of significant inward investment projects from the rest of the UK and from the United States. By 1951, Ferranti, NCR, Honeywell and IBM were all here. Scotland also took state-led corporate planning to its heart with the *Toothill Report on the Scottish Economy*,[14] the creation of the first new towns, and the establishment of the Highlands and Islands Development Board. By the mid-1960s, when the HIDB was launched, it was estimated the SCDI had been instrumental in bringing more than 250,000 new jobs to Scotland.

Thereafter, two new trends – one industrial, the other political – began to undermine this carefully constructed Scottish consensus. One after another the great family-owned Scottish companies began to stumble. Some found themselves taken over. Others simply withered away. They were caught up in a protracted process of deindustrialisation, as the balance in the Scottish economy shifted away from manufacturing towards service industries. An industrial elite whose members bore the same surnames as the companies they ran gave way to a new management elite who, in many cases, were just passing through Scotland on their way to even bigger corporate challenges.

For many years the Scottish card was still played to try the stem some of the consequences of change. In 1980, when the Royal Bank decided to agree a merger with Standard Chartered Bank, only to find itself on the receiving end of a hostile, but financially superior, offer from the Hong Kong and Shanghai Banking Corporation, a great Scottish consensus was assembled to erect a tartan ring-fence and ensure the Royal's independence. One Scottish Tory minister at the time, Alex Fletcher, even suggested that anyone who thought otherwise was a 'traitor' to the Scottish interest.

The same arguments were deployed later in the decade to stop the brewer Scottish & Newcastle falling into the hands of Elders, which was led by the brash Australian John Elliott. S&N managed to persuade the government to refer the bid to the Monopolies and Mergers Commission on UK market share grounds. The MMC decided the bid should be rejected. It must have helped that the man at the helm of S&N at the time, Alick Rankin (Eton and the Guards) enjoyed powerful connections to both the Tory government and the House of Windsor. If proof of that influence were needed, a few years later the tables were turned and S&N acquired Courage, the UK arm of Elders. That deal was given the green light by the competition authorities although the same market share considerations must have applied in reverse.

However, in one of the great contested take-over bids of that time, for Scotland's largest whisky group Distillers, the power of the Scottish card was gravely weakened. Guinness, led by the dynamic Ernest Saunders, had already mopped up Arthur Bell, one of the smaller Scottish whisky distillers. Encouraged by that, the supermarket group Argyll, run by the Campbeltown-born Scot Jimmy Gulliver, launched a much bigger hostile bid for the under-achieving industry leader Distillers. The blue bloods running the Dewars to Vat 69 empire balked at the idea of being taken over by a mere grocer, even if he was a wealthy Scot. In the bitter battle that ensued they turned to Ernest Saunders as their white knight. He, in turn, assiduously cultivated Scottish opinion, inviting two leading business figures, Tom Risk, the governor of the Bank of Scotland, and Charles Fraser, an eminent Edinburgh lawyer and company director, to join the Guinness board if his bid proved successful. Indeed Risk was promised the chairmanship of the enlarged Guinness.

The bid did succeed. But within months fraud inquiries were under way which led to some of the most high-profile criminal trials in City history. Saunders and various other leading figures in the saga eventually went to jail. Their sentences were short. But the impact on Scotland was much longer lasting. Among the casualties were the power of the Scottish card to secure the independence of major Scottish companies and the idea that Scotland's business elite could be relied on to speak with one, consensual voice.

The other trend that began the break-up of the Scottish consensus was political. And, perversely, it centred on the growing momentum for constitutional change that would eventually bring Scotland more power over its own affairs. While Churchill had harboured deep suspicions that the Scottish industrialists behind the Scottish Development Council were closet nationalists, Labour's attempts, in the second half of the 1970s, to counter the growing SNP threat at Westminster by seeking popular support for a devolved Scottish Assembly were not well received by the Scottish business establishment.[15] Most sat sullenly on their hands, but some significant voices, such as Lord Weir of the engineering group that bears his family name, came out vociferously against.[16] The failure of the 1979 referendum to return a big enough majority to endorse the creation of Labour's Scottish Assembly not only ushered in a Thatcher government that most Scots conspicuously did not support; it further eroded the idea that across

Scotland's business and ruling political elites there still existed a strong commonality of interest.[17]

It is no accident that, over the past two decades, the power and influence of Tom Johnston's SCDI has been on the wane. In the early 1980s, when I started attending its annual International Forum, first at Aviemore, later at Gleneagles, you could always guarantee being in the company of A-list Scottish business figures, trade unionists, academics and politicians. Most of the big names stopped going many years ago. SCDI also lost out to new government agencies on some of its core economic roles. Attracting inward investment and stimulating infrastructure investment went first to the Scottish Development Agency (set up in 1975) and then to its successor Scottish Enterprise (in 1991). SCDI was left to organise a few trade missions each year. But even that activity is in decline. More recently it has adopted the role of Scotland's economic watchdog and spawned the Scottish Council Foundation, attempting fresh policy thinking for Scotland's new Parliament. But SCDI, like the all-embracing, single-minded Scottish establishment, is now a mere shadow of what Tom Johnston wanted it to be.

NEW ELITES

The process of deindustrialisation, which saw Scotland lose its steel industry, almost all its deep coal mines and most of its shipyards, also cut a swathe through more modern industries such as aluminium smelting, pulp production and car and van assembly, all of them transplanted north after significant government pressure. The public policy response to their rapid demise was to redouble efforts to win investment in even newer industries from overseas firms. That strategy had existed from the immediate post-war period, but it was accelerated in the 1980s and 1990s, as unemployment soared. The main focus was electronics. Silicon Glen may have been a pale imitation of Silicon Valley, but it created work in the kind of replacement volumes for jobs being lost elsewhere that allowed politicians to sleep at night. One of the reasons multinational firms were attracted to Scotland was the ready availability of moderately priced skills. Part of that pool was a cadre of local management already skilled in these emerging technologies. One company in particular, Ferranti, provided a steady flow of senior managers who went on to run plants for a variety of major American and Japanese corporations. The Ferranti elite and their role in the creation of Silicon Glen is a story that has never properly been told.

The changing nature of Scotland's manufacturing base was matched by massive changes in Scotland's indigenous company base. We have already noted the decline in a whole series of big family-controlled

Scottish businesses and the wave of corporate take-overs (particularly in the 1980s) which replaced a business elite deeply rooted in Scottish society with one with much more transient allegiances. Another significant trend was the privatisation of major state-owned enterprises such as electricity supply, the bus industry and Scotland's ports. Despite the successful defence of the Royal Bank of Scotland's independence in 1981, Scotland's financial services sector was also on the brink of significant change. One by one, the large mutually-owned life and pensions offices surrendered their independence to bigger UK and foreign players. Only the biggest, Standard Life, has resisted that trend. A number of fund management groups, notably in and around Edinburgh, also gave up their independence to join larger UK and international groupings. And most recently Scotland's two largest indigenous banks, the Royal and the Bank of Scotland, became directly involved in this accelerating process of consolidation.

In 1999 Bank of Scotland launched a hostile bid for the much larger English clearer NatWest. Its Edinburgh neighbour, the Royal, quickly responded with a counter-bid. The battle went down to the wire, but the Royal won the day. So far the acquisition has been transformational for the Royal, 9 per cent owned by a Spanish banking group, BSCH. It has propelled Royal into a leading role in European banking. Having seen its prey snatched from under its nose, Bank of Scotland went on to conclude a nil premium merger with the UK's largest mortgage bank, Halifax, creating a new fifth force in British banking to be called HBOS. Although still headquartered in Edinburgh, HBOS will be controlled by senior Halifax executives who have made it clear they will spend most of their time outside Scotland.

In the professions most closely allied to business, notably the law and accountancy, Scotland has long maintained a distinctive tradition. In the 1990s, a proposal that the Institute of Chartered Accountants of Scotland (ICAS), the body that controls entry to the profession north of the border, merge with the equivalent English institute triggered a heated debate and a decisive vote against merger. Since then ICAS has even embarked on an expansionist programme of attracting English trainees from three of the largest accountancy firms to qualify under its banner.

However at the highest levels within both professions, Scottish accountants and corporate lawyers have for a number of years been finding the volume of demanding work within Scotland inadequate. Some have opened offices outside Scotland. Some of the most successful participants have relocated to London or further afield. Others have become very familiar with the inside of a Heathrow shuttle. These business trends are all threads in the ongoing process of globalisation.

One of their consequences has been that the Scottish business elite has become much more fragmented than in the past, its attention much less focused on specific concerns about Scotland and its future.

The relative weakness of the indigenous Scottish business base through take-over and consolidation has triggered a whole new development agenda, built around questions of whether Scotland has lost the spirit of enterprise. In a series of public inquiries since 1993, the nation's main economic development agency, Scottish Enterprise, has focused on Scotland's low business birth rate, the failure of its universities to capitalise on the commercial potential of enough of the research and development work going on within their own precincts, and the comparative dearth of the kind of fast growth companies evident in the US (e.g. Cisco Systems) and elsewhere in Europe (e.g. Nokia).

The new buzz word is entrepreneurship and a new Scottish business elite, composed of those who have built significant Scottish businesses from scratch, is held up as the aspirational role model for the rest of Scotland. These entrepreneurs are, in terms of the roots of their success, a disparate group. Some, such as Brian Souter and Ann Gloag of the bus and rail group Stagecoach, and the Wiseman brothers in milk processing, have made their fortunes from privatisation and related processes. Others, such as Tom Hunter and John Boyle, have achieved considerable success by redefining the most effective business model in traditional business sectors like sports retailing and holidays. And a third group, typified by Richard Emanuel and David Sibbald, have built businesses based on new technologies like mobile telephony and software development.

Seeing themselves as latter-day pioneers (despite the fact that many of the industrialists who created the pre-war Development Council were entrepreneurs before the word was invented), some of this new group have developed their own elite networks, such as the Entrepreneurial Exchange. Networks of angel investors have appeared and some of the most successful individuals have started to recycle their wealth into new ventures using their own vehicles. Notable in this group are Tom Hunter (West Coast Capital) and John Boyle (Hamilton Portfolio). Hunter in particular, who claims Andrew Carnegie as one of his role models, has become evangelical about changing modern Scottish attitudes to enterprise and making money. He has funded a school of entrepreneurship at Strathclyde University and is actively involved in pushing a programme to encourage the spirit of enterprise among primary school pupils. Although Hunter, who sold his original sports retailing business for around £250m, was a significant financial backer of Labour before the 2001 election, he enjoys a fragile relationship with the processes of government, seeing them as far too bureaucratic and cumbersome.

Brian Souter who, with his sister Ann Gloag, exploited the Thatcherite privatisation agenda in transport, to build the Perth-based Stagecoach up into one of the UK's leading people moving businesses, plunged himself into much more public confrontation with the fledgling Scottish Parliament. An evangelical Christian, Souter objected to the New Labour/Liberal Democrat coalition's commitment to scrapping Clause 28/Section 2a of an old Local Government Act preventing teaching about homosexuality in schools. With sections of the tabloid press backing him, Souter launched an advertising campaign against the move to scrap Section 2a (Clause 28 in England), and financed a private referendum of all adult Scots on the subject.[18] He eventually lost, but these episodes, and others, demonstrate that government cannot assume this emerging business elite will always be on its side.

Apart from taking on the government over Section 2a, Souter also had to contend with a significant fall in the Stagecoach share price as some of its overseas ventures failed to deliver on their promise and City sentiment moved against the company. A number of other emerging Scottish entrepreneurs have had to contend with the global reaction against dot.com hype and the steep cyclical downturn in backing for technology and telecoms stocks which started in 2000 and is still in train. Scotland was just beginning to see the fruits of Scottish Enterprise's emphasis on commercialising academic research, with promising advances being made in software development (particularly for games), circuit design and optoelectronics. How well all the young companies that have emerged as part of this process can survive the downturn remains to be seen.

In purely political terms, the creation of the Scottish Parliament in Edinburgh has introduced fresh strains into the dynamic of Scotland's political elite. Throughout the Thatcher and Major years, Scotland stayed much more loyal to Labour than other parts of the UK. During the years of opposition, Labour in Scotland produced a new generation of Westminster MPs convinced of the need for party reform and hungry for high office. This trend was reinforced by John Smith's brief tenure of the Labour leadership. When Labour, under his successor Tony Blair, regained office in 1997, it was almost inevitable that a group of these Scottish MPs would fill some of the highest offices of state. Gordon Brown at the Treasury, Robin Cook at the Foreign Office and George Robertson at Defence were the early beneficiaries. The impression of a Scots take-over of government was reinforced by the presence of Derry Irvine, Scots born and educated but practising at the English bar, as Lord Chancellor. Later we would see Alastair Darling in charge of welfare and benefit reform and Dr John Reid sent to Northern Ireland.

The new Blair government was quick to legislate for the creation of the Scottish Parliament. But among the leading Scots in the new Blair government only the principal architect of that change, Scottish Secretary Donald Dewar, chose to switch his personal allegiance to Edinburgh. All the others chose to continue to pursue their Westminster careers, although George, now Lord Robertson has since become secretary general of NATO. In making that choice they were following the same instincts that have led generations of promising Scots in business, the media, the arts and elsewhere to want to perform on a larger stage. But the reality of devolution and the emergence of a new generation of politicians of all parties at Holyrood have undoubtedly had significant consequences for Scotland's political elite.

In the first two years, the principal focus of media and public attention was inevitably on Holyrood. The new Parliament has not had an easy ride on a whole range of issues. But it has undoubtedly become the principal focus of attention north of the border. That has consequences not just for Scottish MPs and ministers at Westminster but also for some of the leading politicians in local government in Scotland, who now have to adjust to having a Parliament on their doorstep. The partial break-up of COSLA, the body representing Scottish local authorities, is one early consequence of these new tensions.

It is far too early to say whether Jack McConnell, Wendy Alexander and Malcolm Chisholm for Labour and Jim Wallace and Ross Finnie of the Liberal Democrats, the minority partners in the current coalition, will be able to build all this early attention into genuine political leadership in Scotland. Alex Salmond, after all, has given up the leadership of the main opposition, the SNP, and returned to life as a Westminster MP. We need at least one more Holyrood election and several more years of devolved power before we will be able to see how this particular new political dynamic is really working out in practice. In the shorter term, the strains and tensions are likely to go on showing.

THE FUTURE

What will the topography and levels of influence of Scotland's various elites look like in ten years time? I suspect that those who saw the coming of the Scottish Parliament as a great new unifying force in Scottish life, the physical embodiment of an old Scottish consensus, will continue to be disappointed, for two main reasons. Holyrood's existence, albeit with limited legislative powers and even more limited fiscal powers, forces Scotland to confront its own challenges and come up with its own remedies. We can no longer as readily point the finger elsewhere. We will doubtless continue to explore what additional devolved powers the Scottish Parliament needs to make a real impact. The national question will not go away. But the more we are forced to confront what we, as Scots, can do to help ourselves, the more the resultant dialogue is bound to involve forces that will tend to break down consensus rather than reinforce it. One telling contemporary example is the electoral success of Tommy Sheridan's Scottish Socialist Party, which is rapidly filling an ideological void left by New Labour.

The other reason the inheritors of Tom Johnston's vision will be disappointed is that, while the process of political devolution continues to develop and mature, many of the other forces shaping our lives are pointing in the opposite direction. We have already explored the ways in which the process of economic globalisation is tending to break down the power of local business elites. These forces, and related advances in the internet, fast mobile communications and cheap mass air travel, are forging new linkages that render the concept of a national elite increasingly irrelevant. If the current trends of growing political apathy, particularly among the young, and global sourcing of the material manifestations of civilisation, from clothes to computers, continue – and I see scant evidence that they will not – then the significance of national elites will continue to wane.

This is not a counsel of despair. Power will continue to matter. But the process by which it is distributed will become much more dynamic and will depend not simply on political assent but on the exploitation of the new technologies. It will be redistributed in different, innovative ways. The problem with all elites, even entrepreneurial elites, is that, in time, they become complacent and ripe for challenge. Over the next ten years expect more fission within an existing constellation of Scottish elites that is already well into the process of fragmentation. And, for those who survive, expect new challenges to their power bases from unexpected quarters.

NOTES

1. *A Claim of Right for Scotland*, originally published 30.3.89, reprinted in O. Dudley Edwards (ed), *A Claim of Right for Scotland*, Edinburgh: Polygon 1989, pp11-53.
2. For example see: B. Jamieson, *The Bogus State of Brigadoon: What can save Scotland?*, London: Centre for Policy Studies 1998.
3. T. Johnston, *Our Scots Noble Families*, Glasgow: Forward 1909.
4. *Ibid.*, p67.
5. On Thomas Johnston see: C. Harvie, 'Labour and Scottish Government –

the age of Thomas Johnston', *The Bulletin of Scottish Politics*, Spring 1981, No. 2; R. Galbraith, *Without Quarter: A Biography of Tom Johnston: 'The Uncrowned King of Scotland'*, Edinburgh: Mainstream 1995; G. Walker, *Thomas Johnston*, Manchester: Manchester University Press 1988.

6. Johnston, *op. cit.*, p71.
7. On the establishment of the North of Scotland Hydro-Electric Board see Galbraith, *op. cit.*, pp269-77.
8. T. Johnston, *Memories*, London: Collins 1952, p135.
9. Harvie, *op. cit.*, pp16-18.
10. On the role of the now titled Scottish Council for Development and Industry see K. Aitken, 'The Economy', in M. Linklater and R. Dennistoun (eds), *Anatomy of Scotland*, Edinburgh: Chambers 1992.
11. Johnston, *Memories*, *op. cit.*, p151.
12. *Ibid.*, p151.
13. *Ibid.*, p151.
14. *Report on the Scottish Economy: Report of a Committee appointed by the Scottish Council*, Edinburgh: Scottish Council (Development and Industry) 1961.
15. On Scottish devolution and the business community in the 1970s see C. J. Risk, 'Devolution: The Commercial Community's Fears', in H. M. Drucker and M. G. Clarke (eds), *The Scottish Government Yearbook 1978*, Edinburgh: Paul Harris 1978, pp120-128.
16. J. Mitchell, *Conservatives and the Union*, Edinburgh: Edinburgh University Press 1990, p81. Lord Weir was involved in the supposedly cross-party group 'Scotland is British', which was chaired by Sir John Toothill, the author of the 1961 SCDI report which bears his name.
17. On the campaign for a Scottish Parliament and the business community in the 1990s see N. Smith, 'The Business Case for devolution', *Scottish Affairs*, Summer 1996, No. 16; D. Denver, J. Mitchell, C. Pattie and H. Bochel, *Scotland Decides: The Devolution Issue and the Scottish Refendum*, London: Frank Cass 2000.
18. On the Section 28/Clause 2a debate in Scotland, see Rowena Arshad in this book.

Poverty, inequality and social inclusion in the New Scotland

RICHARD MITCHELL AND DANNY DORLING

> A problem is something you have hopes of changing. Anything else is a fact of life.
>
> C.R. Smith, *Publishers Weekly*, 8 September 1969

Everyone who lives in Scotland, whether politician or member of the public, is well aware of the country's high rate of premature mortality, heart disease, cancer and smoking, its 'junk food' diet, crippling poverty and inequalities. However, in the light of devolution and the progression to a different kind of politics, we think it *is* worth looking again at the Scottish experience. In particular, we will look at what has been happening to the health and wealth of Scots in recent years, what is happening now in terms of policy and what might happen as devolved Scotland matures. We see Scotland's inequalities as a problem, not a fact of life.

In this chapter we present a selection of the latest evidence on progress in terms of health, poverty and social exclusion. We question how devolution might affect these issues and we look to possible futures for the health and wealth of the Scottish people.

We start with evidence focusing on health inequalities, poverty and social exclusion in Scotland today. We then consider briefly some historical aspects of Scotland's situation and set devolution in this context. Next we present two sets of 'reasons to be cheerful' about inequalities in Scotland, looking first at the national or macro scale agenda and then the local or micro scale agenda. Within this section we try to show why there are reasons for optimism in Scotland, but also that there are challenges which have yet to be properly addressed. In conclusion will we consider the prospects for a healthier, wealthier more inclusive Scotland.

THE IMPACT OF DEVOLUTION MAY NOT YET BE VISIBLE

Poor public health, poverty and social exclusion are usually the products of long-term socio-economic, structural and political problems. A Scot approaching late middle age, who has spent his or her lifetime in adverse circumstances and been raised in a family and/or a neighbourhood in adverse circumstances, is more likely than others to be on a trajectory leading to an early grave. None of the contemporary initiatives, zones, schemes, campaigns, and recent radical change in parliamentary system has much chance of altering that trajectory very dramatically. It may be a cliché, but the image of the oil tanker which takes a long time to slow down or change direction is a good one when considering issues of health and social exclusion at a population level. The health and wealth of Scots is determined over their whole lifetime. Devolution took place three years ago and at a population level, in terms of health outcomes, socially excluded groups and poverty, almost nothing has changed. However, this does not mean that there are no prospects for change or that change is not beginning to happen. The tremendous efforts that have been going on in recent years have not been, and will not be, in vain, but their impact cannot yet be seen in the statistics that we present here.

THE EVIDENCE FOR POOR HEALTH

Death rates and life expectancy provide a stark and compelling indicator of health and life circumstances. Figure 1 shows clearly that Scotland does badly compared to other countries.

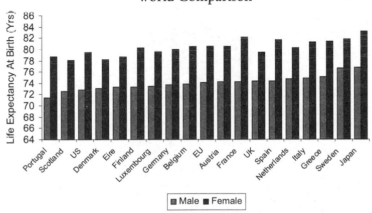

Figure 10.1: Scottish Life Expectancy in a Developed World Comparison

Source: Registrar General for Scotland and World Health Organisation[1]

Rates and ages of death are influenced by levels of affluence, the quality of the physical and social environments in which people live and have lived and, to a lesser extent, the quality of the health care they receive. People's health related behaviours are important too but it would be folly to suggest that these are chosen independently of the social and physical environment in which they live. Far too many Scots smoke and eat junk food. Nearly all of them know that this will damage their health. Knowledge does not often translate into behavioural change because the circumstances in which people live limit their capacity to alter their lifestyle.

Inevitably, a comparison with England and Wales is pertinent to Scotland and one of the most powerful means of making this comparison is with maps. Population level health data are best mapped using a cartogram in which the space on the page is proportional to the population of an area, rather than its physical size. This cartogram is presented in Figure 10.2. Each circle on the map represents a parliamentary constituency in Britain.

Figure 10.2: Inequalities in Mortality Rate Within Britain

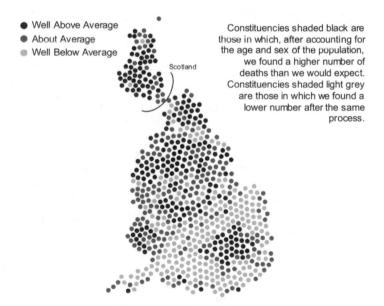

- Well Above Average
- About Average
- Well Below Average

Scotland

Constituencies shaded black are those in which, after accounting for the age and sex of the population, we found a higher number of deaths than we would expect. Constituencies shaded light grey are those in which we found a lower number after the same process.

Data are standardised to English and Welsh averages
Source: Data from Mitchell *et al*, Inequalities in Life and Death, 2000

The map shows rates of mortality at ages less than 65 for each of Britain's parliamentary constituencies. Almost all of Scotland's parliamentary constituencies have mortality rates well above the average for England and Wales; Scots die early at higher rates than their neighbours. This is an often-quoted fact, but it should interest us more than it does. Scotland has poverty, industrial decline, and all their associated social problems, but so do England and Wales. Researchers have struggled to establish what it is about life in Scotland that seems to send people to an early grave but no one yet has the whole answer. This poses an interesting challenge for the devolved nation – to try to 'cure' when the diagnosis is not entirely clear.

Inequalities also persist *within* Scotland.[2] Death rates from coronary heart disease in the poorest parts of the country are more than twice those in the richest parts. The major inequalities in the health of different socio-economic groups within the Scottish population begin even before and just after birth. The perinatal mortality rate in social class V is 11.1 per 1000 compared with 7.1 in social class I, for example.[3] Illness rates, both physical and mental, show vast differences within Scotland, within our regions and within our towns and cities.

The NHS is primarily reactive in its approach to public health. It does a fantastic job curing people and looking after them once they have become ill in some way, but very little by way of prevention. Most health researchers recognise that the key to improving public health is to lessen the rate at which people get ill or injured in the first place. This means that politics and the businesses that control so much of our society hold the key. There is also a paradox here since the general

Figure 10.3: NHS Waiting Lists in Scotland

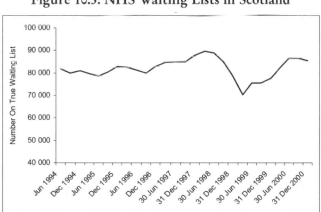

Source: Information and Statistics Division (ISD), NHS Scotland [Form: SMR3] [4]

public tends to equate health issues with the NHS. If GPs are angry or waiting lists are growing, more money to the NHS is often seen to be the answer. In fact many facets of the NHS have changed very little in recent years. The waiting list graph in Figure 10.3 provides some moments of hope, with a considerable fall in 1999, only to be followed by an apparent resurgence of tardy treatment in 2000. By and large, however, the levels in 2000 are the same as they were in 1994.

Figure 10.4 provides an interesting look at the Scottish NHS workforce. The stability of the size and shape of the NHS workforce is the remarkable feature of this graph.

Figure 10.4: The Scottish NHS Workforce

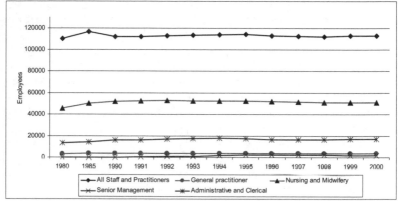

Sources: ISD Scotland (Medical and Dental Census; National Manpower Statistics from payroll; General Medical Practitioner Database)

It is not all doom and gloom however. There has been limited success in the battle against cancer. The battle to detect and treat cancer in Scotland is being slowly won; more people are diagnosed, but fewer die. However, this is not a victory made by the changing administrative systems for Scotland. It has its roots in the early 1990s and in fact, owes its progress to a combination of medical and social advances.

THE EVIDENCE FOR POVERTY AND SOCIAL EXCLUSION

One of the few successes for those monitoring health inequalities in Britain and adverse health in Scotland has been the communication of the basic equation that 'poverty equals poor health'. So, whilst we will present some separate evidence for poverty and social exclusion in a devolved Scotland, it should be borne in mind that these are very strongly related issues.

Quantitative evidence for poverty and social exclusion is abundant within Scotland, but we are wary of its use. We think that the true meaning of social exclusion is hard to articulate using graphs and charts and maps since it is about adversity in everyday life on a personal level. The despair and frustration of life on the bread line, the experience of racism or sectarianism, or the challenge of being illiterate in a complex world is better articulated by qualitative research and accounts of people's day to day lives. In a limited way however, we can at least demonstrate the extent of the problem.

Poverty is not the only cause of social exclusion but it is usually the key component. About 22 per cent of the Scottish population are in a low-income household.[5] This number includes about 300,000 children. Figure 10.5 illustrates the growing disparity between incomes in Britain and within Scotland.

Figure 10.5: Average Weekly Earnings in Scotland and Great Britain

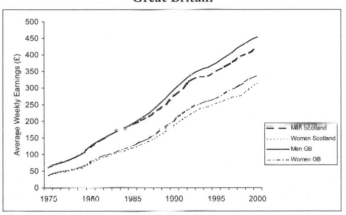

Source: Scottish Executive, Scottish Economic Statistics 2001

The New Labour government in Westminster made much of its attempt to get people off benefit and into work. In Figure 10.6, a cartogram shows changes in income support claims for constituencies in Scotland. Again, the boundaries have been drawn to reflect the size of the population living within each area. The smaller map in the bottom left of the figure has thus been distorted to produce the larger, shaded map. The figures have been standardised for the whole of Britain. Note that Scotland contains no constituencies in the 'best improvement' category and several in the 'worsening category'.

Figure 10.6: The Changing Geography of Want Under New Labour

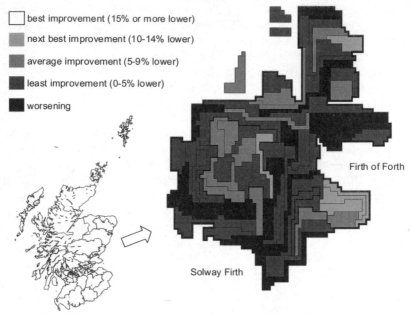

Source: Dorling and Simpson, The Geography of Poverty, 2001[6]

Even those in work may have to contend with low pay. Although the minimum wage has lifted the earnings of low paid workers in a quite radical way, many part-time and minimum wage workers remain on or beneath the breadline. Whilst disposable incomes are rising in Scotland, they inevitably rise further and faster for the richest groups. Low pay results in poor families, childhood poverty and, eventually, pensioner poverty as people cannot afford to pay into pension schemes.[7]

Social exclusion is not just about poverty however. Education, socialisation and integration should be a life long process, but once an individual falls behind in any of these areas it can be incredibly difficult to get back into mainstream society. At the end of the 1990s, about 7 per cent of school leavers had no SCE qualifications.[8] Although this number is falling, a sizeable group still move on into a society in which the basic school education is worthless in the labour market. Many employers now expect vocational or university level education as a minimum (though 36 per cent of 16-21 year olds are not in full or part time education). The myth about increased access to a university education is that it promotes a more inclusive society. In fact, the degree simply becomes the common currency of social advance and the post-graduate or vocational qualification becomes the new marker of the elite. For those struggling to stay at school until 16, the much-trumpeted 'opportunity' for university education is pretty meaningless. The net result is that many more people are better educated, but inequalities between the elite and the rest remain the same or become wider.

Scotland has become an increasingly segregated society over recent years. The housing market contrives to keep richer and poorer folk apart. Few Morningside residents have any idea what life is like in Craigmillar, few of Glasgow's Kelvinside residents know what life is like in Easterhouse and few residents of Harris experience day-to-day life in the cities. The irony is that politicians are amongst the few Scots who encounter and face the divisions of wealth, health and society within the country, because they work in a world where their colleagues bring that geographical diversity alive for them. In this sense, the devolved Scotland is at a tremendous advantage in dealing with its own diversity. It is run by a relatively small group of people dedicated to providing a voice to all those different needs within the country, and ultimately accountable to their constituents.

Many people are of the opinion that Scotland and its devolved government can and must spend its way to a more equal society. Figure 10.7 shows the patterns of spending in Scotland, and in the wider UK,

Figure 10.7: Shares of Public Expenditure in Scotland and the UK

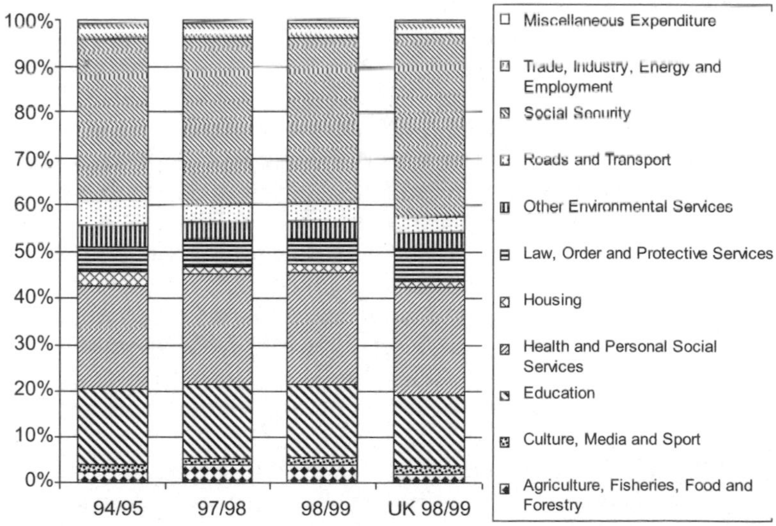

Source: Scottish Executive, Scottish Economic Statistics 2001

as we approached devolution and it is a pattern remarkable in its consistency. The key difference in Scotland today is that the power now exists to make a change to these patterns and to raise the overall budget available through taxation, albeit within the confines of devolution.

HOW DID SCOTLAND BECOME SO SICK?

As far back as records go, evidence abounds that areas within Scotland have had poverty and health problems, with the latter stemming from the former. Battles with cholera and tuberculosis characterised the era of infectious diseases. Scotland's squalid cities provided the perfect breeding ground for wave after wave of epidemics. In more recent history, where degenerative disease has been dominant, Scotland has retained its poor health record. Between 11 per cent and 12 per cent more people died in Scotland between the 1950s and early 1980s than would have done had Scots experienced the mortality rates of their English and Welsh counter-parts. This excess reflected the historical inequalities in material circumstances between these nations, most notably the legacy of the 1930s depression, the failure of the Special Areas Act of 1934 to mitigate 'uneven development' and the continued extreme poverty experienced in many parts of Scotland. Mortality rates were 25 per cent above average in Glasgow county in 1951. For men aged 15-44 rates were 52 per cent above average in the difficult conditions of work and life of Zetland county (now the Shetland Isles) at that time.

However, even these statistics are overshadowed by more recent events. Conditions were relatively good in Scotland in 1951 (following the 1945-50 Labour government) and in 1969-73 (following the 1964/66 Labour governments), when compared to the 1980s. Between 1986 and 1989 excess deaths in the whole of Scotland rose to 13 per cent. In 1990-92 they rose to 19 per cent and in 1993-95 they reached 23 per cent. They have continued to rise in relation to England and Wales ever since. By the late 1990s, men in Glasgow aged 45-64 had an excess mortality rate of roughly 100 per cent. This figure means that *twice* as many men of that age in Glasgow died when compared to the British average. Women of the same age had an excess of 90 per cent.[9] The life expectancy for a man in Glasgow today is 68 years. This is the same as the UK average in 1966. Set against such a strong historical trajectory, changes following devolution pale into insignificance.

DRAWING THE EVIDENCE TOGETHER

Arguments abound as to why Scotland has experienced such a dramatic worsening of its health position, relative to the rest of the UK since the early 1980s. Some evidence exists. Scotland has a poor health record, considerable poverty and social exclusion problems, and precious little has changed in recent years, although the evidence for change post-devolution is patchy at this time. The key questions then are what all this means for a newly devolved Scotland, and what condition a future Scotland might find itself in.

We have identified a number of 'reasons to be cheerful' within a devolved Scotland, based on the possible development of health related social policy within the country in the coming years. These are at two broad scales, macro (including national, international and global factors) and micro (including local authority, neighbourhood and individual factors). We have not felt it necessary to pen different scenarios for Scotland under different administrations since the main contenders for power are all further left on the political spectrum than the Labour-Liberal Democrat coalition. We do not envisage a more left-wing government making reductions in the current attempts to tackle wealth, health and poverty in Scotland.

Reasons to be cheerful part 1: the macro scale
We believe that achieving real change at population level is a matter of ideology, an economic situation which permits delivery of that ideology and, perhaps, partly, the slow but steady advance of medicine (provided it has an equitable application).

The arguments over a 'tax and spend' or a 'tax cut-trickle down' approach to public services within Scotland (and Britain as a whole) have been won. The Conservative Party's policy of 'tax cut-trickle down' was soundly rejected by the whole nation (and especially Scotland) in the 2001 election. We believe the Scottish electorate is unlikely to return to a very Conservative ideology in the near future. We think that fiscal policies which disproportionately favour those most in need, and which favour health, social and education services, will continue to attract electoral support. We believe the single biggest factor that would bring improvements in health enjoyed by rich Scots to poor Scots would be to address the inequality in wealth that exists between them. This includes wealth in people's pockets, in their housing, in their education and in their local environments. We will present some quantitative evidence to back up this claim in a moment.

It seems clear that things are not going to get very much better for those most in need, in worst health and most excluded without radical changes. At a recent policy meeting one of us met a health visitor who works in Glasgow's east end. The conversation turned to wealth and the meaning of and attitudes to poverty amongst some of Glasgow's poorest folk. The health visitor told a story about a young single parent with a child who required home based medical treatment with electrical equipment, on a daily basis. On making a visit and finding the home powerless due to an empty electric key meter, the health visitor moved heaven and earth to obtain an emergency payment from social services to get credit back on the electric meter. On returning to the property at the end of the day she discovered that the parent had spent £5 of the £15 emergency payment on electricity and £10 on treating the family to a special meal. The lesson here is not that this parent was stupid or reckless, it is that they live in an environment where £15 mattered so much and £10 was the most exciting and potentially up-lifting thing in that family's life. Minor changes to benefits and tax systems which amount to a few pounds per week cannot be enough. The trick will be to take this family, and others like them, well away from the situation where £5 might be, literally, a life saving amount of money and where £10 marks a special day. Devolved Scotland has the power to raise taxes.

The bad news is that the radical policies required to achieve a dramatically more equitable distribution of resources and wealth are unlikely to bring their proponents to power.[10] We do not think it unfair to say that the typical Scot believes that wealth, opportunities and resources should be distributed more evenly. We think it very unlikely that the typical Scot would elect a government dedicated to pursuing this policy on the dramatic scale needed to effect a very great narrowing of inequalities.

This is not to say that progressive social and economic policy has not and cannot make tremendous impacts on population health. In a report published in 2000,[11] we demonstrated the implications for health in Britain of New Labour delivering the eradication of child poverty, full employment and a mild redistribution of wealth.[12] For this chapter we have extracted and re-analysed the figures for Scotland's 72 constituencies. Here, Table 10.1 illustrates the figures for Scotland as a whole. Figure 10.8 shows this information mapped on a cartogram of parliamentary constituencies.

Table 10.1: Potential Impact Of Social And Economic Policy On Premature Mortality In Scotland

Policy	Full employment	Redistribution of Wealth	Eradication of child poverty
Lives <65 saved/year	369	672	95

Source: Mitchell et al, Inequalities in Life and Death, 2000[13]

Figure 10.8: Saving Lives in Scotland: The Potential Impact of Current Policies

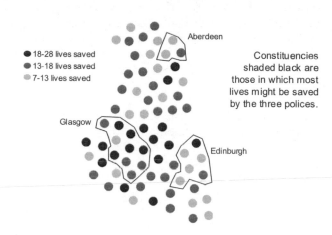

Source: Data from Mitchell *et al*, *Inequalities in Life and Death*, 2000
Figures are standardised to English and Welsh mortality rates per year

These figures were established using a model of the Scottish population in which we knew every Scot's age, sex, social class and
employment status. These characteristics were used to estimate every
individual's risk of dying before the age of 65 and hence estimate population level mortality rates. The risk of dying can then be adjusted in
accordance with the possible impact of each policy. The policies were
defined as follows.

- Achieving Full Employment: the definition of full employment
adheres to the Westminster Government's preferred definition in
which, whilst people may be temporarily between jobs, no one is in
long-term receipt of unemployment benefit. To model the impact
of this policy, everyone in the model who was unemployed is made
employed, thus lowering their mortality rate.
- A Modest Redistribution Of Wealth: a steady widening of the wealth
gap between rich and poor took place in the whole of Britain between
the 1980s and the 1990s. The growing differences in wealth between
the rich and poor were mirrored by differences in their health,
measured by mortality rates (where social class is used a proxy for
wealth). The modest redistribution of wealth referred to here is one
that would return the inequalities in mortality to their 1983 levels.
- Eradicating Child Poverty: the UK government believes that one

third of Britain's children live in poverty and it is their stated aim to bring those children out of poverty. To estimate the effect of achieving that aim in Scotland, the life chances of the 20 per cent of children whose parents work in (had been working in, or were associated with) the most poorly paid occupations were raised to equal those of their peers not living in the poverty which results from low pay. This is a slightly more conservative definition of eradicating child poverty than the UK Government's, but it is one that is more reliably tested.

If, as seems likely, any Scottish Government either supports or extends Westminster's commitments to these kinds of policies, Scotland as a whole should reap a health benefit and, of course, the accompanying effects on wealth and social exclusion. Although this research was only designed to measure the effects in terms of health, getting people into jobs and lifting families out of poverty will have benefits for all poor and excluded communities. These are not unreasonable or outlandish policies (they are, after all, already in existence). If the policies are sustained and shown to have a beneficial impact, we hope and believe they will prompt more radical large-scale policy interventions.

For a chapter principally about health in Scotland, there has been rather little talk about medicine. It was Thomas McKeown who famously demonstrated that late nineteenth and early twentieth century falls in mortality rates were attributable more to rising standards of living than to advances in medicine, but in today's Scotland the biggest killers are degenerative diseases such as cancer and heart disease rather than infectious diseases such as cholera and tuberculosis. Medicine may thus have more of a role to play in driving down death rates. The battle against cancer in Scotland is beginning to turn. A combination of reductions in smoking rates, healthier lifestyles, medical advances and service reorganisation means there is cause for optimism.

With the measures planned for Scotland over the next decade having the potential to reduce cancer deaths by around 1750 per annum (or 11 per cent of cancer deaths) by 2010-14,[14] the Government's target to reduce cancer deaths by one fifth from the 1995-97 baseline by 2010 just might be met. In terms of heart disease, rates are also falling. Capewell *et al* demonstrate the contribution of medicine to falling mortality rates from heart disease. Of the reductions achieved between 1975 and 1994, risk factor reduction accounted for 51 per cent (including 36 per cent for smoking), and medical treatments accounted for 41 per cent, including 10 per cent for initial treatment of acute myocardial infarction (heart attack) and 9 per cent for treating hypertension.[15] Although this is potentially good news for the future as medicine advances further and further, the battle against smoking, poor diet and sedentary lifestyles is being lost amongst younger people (especially women). Those who persist with adverse behaviour tend to be especially resistant to health education programmes and thus changing their behaviour only gets more difficult. The 36 per cent reduction attributable to smoking cessation will have included more of the richest group of Scots than the poorest.

Set against the increasing difficulties of changing adverse behaviour (almost always conditioned by adverse environment), lies the alchemy of 'the new genetics'. It seems likely that this new medical knowledge will bring benefits to Scotland's population. It will be a difficult task for the future governments to ensure that those benefits are evenly distributed and that they do not eclipse the need for a more equitable environment in Scotland.

So, although devolution has not yet made any tremendous changes to the macro factors in control of Scotland's public health, wealth and its inequalities, the *potential* is there to do so and the policies currently pursued will be having some limited effect.

Reasons to be cheerful part 2: the micro scale
Both pre and post-devolution, a large number of zones, schemes, demonstration projects and partnerships were established, each one focused on some aspect of health, wealth and social exclusion.[16] Many were highly experimental and had a local focus. There is an army of professional and volunteer labour working with and in communities to improve health, to tackle poverty, to connect people within communities and to enhance social and physical environments and in that sense, Scotland has established a grass roots culture of action to tackle these problems.

At all levels of government, health, wealth and social exclusion have been installed as cross-cutting concerns to be considered in projects, plans and programmes wherever possible, whether directly health related or not. This is an extraordinary change. The days in which inequality was hidden through terms such as 'variation', and the time when individuals were blamed for their own poor health outcomes, are over (for now). Whether devolution has enhanced these new freedoms or not, we cannot be certain, but it is unlikely to have stifled it in any way.[17]

It is our experience over the last couple of years that a consideration of inequality is being written into local activism and policy and that, encouragingly, the work is well informed and draws on the variety of models that are available for understanding and tackling these problems. As ever, Scotland's greatest resource for working with communities are the communities themselves. They know what is possible and what is not better than any politicians. They also understand the nature of slow or minor progress and are not sidetracked into the desire to see huge-scale change in a short space of time. They often wish for dramatic fiscal change, but know it is unlikely. However, to present community-based action as an unproblematic means to tackle inequalities would be wrong. There is little formal evidence that local and micro-scale action can achieve population level improvements in health, wealth and social inclusion. Even we disagree as to the potential effectiveness of this kind of action. It is true that the richest neighbourhoods tend not to have strong community action forums, and that this suggests wealth, rather than neighbourhood activism, is the better way to achieve health and social inclusion. Nonetheless we will now present two short case studies of action 'on the ground' in which we have been involved and from which we draw some hope that inequalities and adversity are being tackled in a devolved Scotland.

As Scotland designs legislation that will open up access to the countryside, local councils and authorities are preparing by drawing up strategy documents. These documents are designed to guide 'stakeholders' towards mutually acceptable planning and implementation of new routes and better use of older routes. At one level, these documents are about paths; where they might go, and how they might be used. However, in the new Scotland that is well aware of its inequalities and health problems, the advent of access legislation is being set in a much wider context. In the preparation of almost all of these strategies, consideration is being given to the provision of access in relation to needs of communities, trying to make access opportunities available where they are most needed, realising the potential health benefits which recreational opportunities present, searching for economic opportunities which might arise from access, understanding that those who might benefit most from access opportunities might also be those least likely to take them up and setting up mechanisms to reach out to excluded communities and involve them in the process. Explicit consideration is given to making sure that access opportunities do not become yet another mechanism by which inequalities are reinforced in Scotland – between rural and urban communities, between younger and older groups, between car owners and non-car owners, and between richer and poorer people.

We understand that these opportunities are a very small contribution to reduction of inequalities and promotion of well being, but it is significant because once these principles and ideals are built into the operation of policy at a *strategic* level, we can be more confident that benefits will be felt in the downstream processes and implementation. How does this tie in with the macro scale views taken earlier in the chapter? Well, in this instance it is the macro scale views, the terrifying statistics, which seem to provide the determination to act at every available level. Everyone involved understands that if all social and economic policy in a devolved Scotland questions its role with regard to tackling inequalities and promoting well-being, benefits will be felt. It is also a consequence of the directive in the *Towards A Healthier Scotland* White Paper that states:

> The Scottish Office will ensure that its economic and social policies have positive health impact in the drive to tackle inequality, improve educational participation and attainment, boost housing and employment and promote social inclusion.
>
> All Scotland's local councils will be asked to follow the lead that some have already taken by making health improvement a corporate goal and, using community planning, to improve the circumstances in which people live.[18]

The action we have seen on the ground is proof positive that motivation (and instruction) to implement a national agenda can work at a local level.

The second example is at an even smaller scale and is drawn from discussion with a small player in the 'Have A Heart Paisley' scheme.[19] This is a three year scheme running in Paisley and aimed at tackling the area's high levels of heart disease. The project begins and ends in the community. It is primarily aimed at community based efforts to develop awareness of risk factors for heart disease, to promote healthy lifestyles, to promote community cohesion, develop self-esteem and raise expectations amongst younger people. A health worker in Paisley described a new scheme to us in which GPs have been able to 'prescribe' exercise classes to patients as a means of reducing their risk of heart disease. The exercise class is provided and paid for. According to the informant the scheme has been a success, principally because it has constructed a social grouping of patients. This group meet, take their class and then go out and socialise together. Sometimes, the class gets missed, but the socialising never does. They will, of course, be deriving some health benefit from the exercise but the significance of friendship and social contact where previously there had been none, is far greater.

There will be attempts to 'evaluate' the 'Have A Heart Paisley' scheme. Those looking for significant changes in the statistics that describe poverty and ill health in Paisley may not get the results they hoped for after just three years, but we suspect the true value will be in strengthened community networks and better connections between medicine and community. For researchers and policy-makers who are used to dealing with population level statistics, it can be difficult not to dismiss these types of projects as useless. It seems unlikely that large numbers of Paisley residents will be richer or that Paisley's life expectancy will have perceptibly risen at the end of the project. However, weaving the fabric of society back together again by joining previously disparate groups through experience and education must be a good thing. It is important, though, not to lose sight of the reasons by which community and personal bonds were broken in the first place – poverty, unemployment and a neglected social, economic and physical environment. It will be futile to work so hard in the community in Paisley if the macro determinants of population level inequality are not tackled at the same time.

A key reason to be cheerful in devolved Scotland then concerns this last point. We hope for, and to some extent detect, a combination of the macro-level policy base designed to generate and redistribute wealth, opportunity and consequently good health, together with the community level activism which is being allowed to flourish in the new Scotland. Very few people suggest that a simple but radical redistribution of wealth is *all* that is required to stop Scots dying before they should; the community and the environment and support it supplies are part of that equation.

GOOD NEWS AND BAD NEWS – CONCLUSIONS
In a research report based on interviews with a variety of agencies tackling poverty in the new Scotland, the Poverty Alliance states:

> ... it is felt that opportunities offered by devolution include more accessible Government and a more concentrated focus on Scottish issues. The Committee structure of the Parliament is a particular focus for optimism. However, the biggest worry expressed was about the limits to the Scottish Parliament's powers to tackle poverty. Respondents are concerned about confusion and tension over the split in responsibilities for poverty-related issues, and their own feeling of distance from reserved issues.[20]

This is a neat summary of how we see devolution in relation to inequality in health and wealth in Scotland. There are advantages for a smaller, more focused and better informed governing body, in combination with committed local government and community players, struggling within the constraints of a UK and ultimately global economy. However, devolution is not insulation from the jaws of capitalism, which steers money away from the poorer folk and communities, towards the richer folk. The Barnett formula can be changed with positive or negative impact. Scotland might opt for independence and its financial circumstances alter for the worse or perhaps for the better. Trying to narrow the gaps between rich and poor is a long-term, expensive business. We see devolution as having been a significant, but not yet *the* significant, development in achieving the current state where by some redistributive policy is in place accompanied by a commitment to progress.

Assessing the future directions and potential successes or failures of health and poverty policy and how social democratic Scotland's health and poverty status might evolve as the nation's identity and character evolve is fraught with difficulty. Halting, and then reversing, the growth in inequalities in health and wealth are perhaps the most significant milestones Scotland needs to reach but these seem unlikely to be passed in the very near future. A child born in Scotland today immediately begins to accumulate influences on their long-term prospects for health and wealth. The family, neighbourhood and wider economy into which they are born control much of their life's trajectory. These are structures within society, which dwarf the influence of politicians and politics. It would be an arrogant political machine which believed that a change of manifesto, or even party, at the head of Scotland for ten years or so will have much influence on that child's health and wealth in their crucial (and often lethal) later middle age. That said, the emerging schemes, policies and general emphasis on early life circumstances (Sure Start Scotland, Starting Well, etc), numeracy, literacy and citizenship are amongst the most positive developments of this era. It is the politicians who will determine whether those schemes are given the time they need to take root and then whether the successful ones are allowed to graduate from being an 'extra effort to help' to being 'a matter of course' for those most in need. Ideally, the best schemes will eventually have no need for a special status or identity – they will become a part of everyday life. To determine which schemes work best in the long term we would like to see party manifestos which promise to keep funding those started by preceding governments, rather than manifestos which promise new schemes but cut those already in place. How else will we ever learn what *really* helps in the longer term?

We argue then that the opportunity for a radical attack on inequality now exists within Scotland, but we also feel it is not yet really under way.[21] It seems to have been easier to instigate and develop community action under devolution. However, that action will have little effect if it is not backed by macro scale social and economic changes and by long term commitment to make the 'special schemes' of today part of the more equitable society of tomorrow. New Scotland has the power to make these changes. The issue is, does new Scotland have the will?

Richard Mitchell is funded by the Chief Scientist Office of The Scottish Executive Health Department (SEHD) and the Health Education Board for Scotland (HEBS). The opinions expressed in this paper are those of the author(s) not of SEHD or HEBS. All figures taken from the Scottish Executive publications are Crown Copyright. We are grateful for the assistance of ISD.

NOTES

1. Registrar General for Scotland and World Health Organisation, 1998.
2. M. Shaw, D. Dorling, D. Gordon and G. D. Smith, *The Widening Gap: Health Inequalities and Policy in Britain*, Bristol: Policy Press 1999.
3. Scottish Executive, *Working Together for a Healthier Scotland*, Edinburgh: The Stationery Office 1999.
4. Information and Statistics Division, NHS Scotland.
5. Scottish Executive, *Scottish Economic Statistics 2001*, Edinburgh: The Stationery Office 2001.
6. D. Dorling and L. Simpson, 'The Geography of Poverty: A Political Map of Poverty under New Labour', *New Economy*, 2001, 8: 2.
7. See for example, Scottish Executive, Scottish Economic Statistics, *op. cit.* and J. McCormick and G. Leicester, *Three Nations: Social Exclusion in Scotland*, Edinburgh: Scottish Council Foundation 1998.
8. Scottish Executive, *Scottish Economic Statistics*, *op. cit.*
9. D. Dorling, *Death in Britain: How Local Mortality Rates have Changed: 1950s-1990s*, London: Joseph Rowntree Foundation Report 1997.
10. For a UK perspective see J. Hills and Lelkes, 'Social Security, Selective Univeralism and Patchwork Redistribution', in R. Jowell, J. Curtice, A. Park and K. Thomson (eds), *British Social Attitudes: The 16th Report*, London: Sage 1999.
11. R. Mitchell, D. Dorling and M. Shaw, *Inequalities in Life and Death: What If Britain Were More Equal?*, London: Joseph Rowntree Foundation Report 2000.
12. See for a UK perspective on tackling child poverty D. Piachaud and H. Sutherland, *How Effective is the British Government's Attempt to Reduce Child Poverty?*, CASE paper, London: London School of Economics 2000.
13. Further information is available at www.social-medicine.com
14. Scottish Executive Health Department, *Cancer Scenarios: An Aid to*

Planning Cancer Services in Scotland in the Next Decade, Edinburgh: The Stationery Office 2001.

15. S. Capewell, C. E. Morrison and J. J. McMurray, 'Contribution of Modern Cardiovascular Treatment and Risk Factor Changes to the Decline in Coronary Heart Disease Mortality in Scotland between 1975 and 1994', *Heart*, 1999, 81: 4.

16. For a more critical perspective, see R. Ilett and S. Laughlin, 'Devolving Health and Building a Healthy Scotland', *Renewal: A Journal of New Labour Politics*, Winter 2001, Vol. 9 No. 1.

17. C. Nottingham, 'The Politics of Health in Scotland after Devolution', in C. Nottingham (ed), *The NHS in Scotland*, Aldershot: Ashgate 2000; A. Pollock, 'Devolution and Health: Challenges for Scotland and Wales', *British Medical Journal*, May 1999, Vol. 318.

18. Scottish Executive, *Towards a Healthier Scotland, op. cit.*

19. The 'Have a Heart Paisley' Demonstration Project is part of the Scottish Executive's Heart of Scotland Public Health Demonstration Project.

20. Poverty Alliance, *Poverty Related Policy Making in Scotland*, Glasgow: Poverty Alliance 2000.

21. For the UK debate on tackling inequality and government action, see P. Toynbee and D. Walker, *Did Things Get Better?: An Audit of Labour's Successes and Failures*, London: Penguin 2001, pp10-43.

Towards the 'better job': Scottish work and employment in the 'knowledge age'

CHRIS WARHURST

For the foreseeable future, political parties of the left – outside and centre – will, in coalition, govern Scotland. There have been a number of leftist initiatives to develop the 'better job'. Such jobs encompass employees' having greater autonomy, more responsibility and more control in and over their labour. It also includes a capacity for employees to develop themselves through that labour.[1] Initiatives to create such jobs, however, appear to have run into the sand recently. Socialist experiments to create these jobs – whether in communal or state socialist economies – have disappeared or are rapidly disappearing (if they ever existed in the first place in some cases). Within the social democratic capitalist economies, workplace reformers have recast their past efforts. Some involved in the 1970s work humanisation projects, for example, now regard themselves as little more than 'reactionary henchmen to the employers', actively immiserating rather than liberating employees.[2] In any case, Durand believes, many of the better jobs that emerged briefly during this period resulted from historically specific problems for management arising from labour shortages.

In the UK specifically, the Alternative Economic Strategy (AES) pursued by the left during the early 1980s, which included demands for more public ownership, industrial democracy and controls on foreign trade and international capital movements, has long disappeared. In any case, the AES was not really an alternative to capitalism but a safety net for its economic and political crises; sustaining falling employment and living standards – as the renewed, and well-meaning, interest in producer co-operatives within Labour-controlled local council areas exemplified.[3]

The crises, moreover, limited the capacity of trade unions to resist. This would seem to resonate with Durand's point. With labour surpluses, initiatives to develop the better job dropped off both management and trade unions' agendas. Throughout the 1980s and 1990s, employer-led initiatives resulted in mean (rather than just lean) production. During this period, trade unions continued to have little real capacity to resist: frozen out of government, pre-occupied with inter-union turf wars or remodelling themselves to appeal to a declining membership.

By the late 1990s, both the centre-left and outside-left had withdrawn from economic reform and, with it, developing the better job. Even the Scottish Socialist Party seems to have forgotten its materialist foundations. The party that heralds itself as 'the party of the working class' said nothing new or substantive about work in its 2001 manifesto beyond one bland sentence about 'workers control over health and safety and other aspects of working conditions'. Instead its 'everyday is Christmas' manifesto is locked into a pre-new Labour mindset of nationalisation and industrial democracy.[4]

Over the past few decades, real Scottish policy-makers *have* been concerned with jobs. Their focus, however, has been the quantity not the quality of jobs: job creation rather than job content. In the aftermath of economic recessions (and UK Government fiscal policy) that decimated manufacturing across the UK, such a policy was understandable. Although again well meaning, some of the strategies for this job creation have been questionable. Many of the jobs created were the result of foreign direct investment. The companies involved offered labour intensive operations – hence their attractiveness to policy-makers. But, as any business undergraduate knows, such low skill, 'screw-driver' plant jobs are often vulnerable when foreign investors' country-of-origin economics take a down turn or the investors find more amenable locations elsewhere – as the current contraction of the electronics sector in Scotland illustrates. It seems that job content does matter, after all.

At first sight, the recent new Labour-driven 'Third Way', with its desire to join market efficiency and social justice, continues to leave economic reform to the right: seemingly more concerned with workfare than the workplace. The reasons for this myopia are not difficult to discern. New Labour still has difficulty in its relationship with the trade unions; and, in the pursuit of 'flexibility in the face of globalisation', the labour market rather than labour has become its focus of attention. To be fair, there have been some good labour market orientated initiatives, particularly in relation to attempting to tackle social exclusion – the Working Families Tax Credit for example.

Proponents of the Third Way are, however, also recognising the importance of knowledge. A belief exists that a worldwide radical transformation is occurring with the emergence of a knowledge-driven economy. The main source of value and competitive advantage is no longer financial but intellectual capital, according to Blair.[5]

To meet the challenge of this new economy, a consensus has emerged across the centre-left political parties in Scotland, as well as in the Labour Party at Westminster, that what is needed is a highly skilled workforce. Again, skills development is regarded, partially, as a means for enhancing workers' employability in flexible labour markets. But, in addition, 'knowledge' and 'skills' (in this case 'thinking' skills) have quickly become conflated as the cornerstone of the new economy. During the 2001 general election in Scotland, Helen Liddell, as Secretary of State for Scotland, and Wendy Alexander, as Minister for Enterprise and Lifelong Learning, together preached the importance of building up the skills base of the country.[6] It is not surprising, then, that the high skills position has become orthodoxy across the Scottish Executive and Scottish Enterprise, as characteristic of the knowledge-driven economy. (It is also an approach favoured by the Scottish business community, if the Institute of Directors in Scotland is indicative.)

It is easy to be cynical about the claims of policy-makers.[7] Whilst these need to be tempered, it is less easy to be critical of them in terms of engaging with real constraints and choices. This chapter argues that the importance of managing knowledge provides the centre-left with an opportunity to place the better job at the centre of the work and employment policy agenda. The chapter outlines the problems, but also some of the possibilities, that exist with recent initiatives to manage knowledge in the workplace. With caveats, the chapter suggests that such initiatives, if properly facilitated, can create the better job, although that possibility is not pre-determined.

The first section of the chapter outlines past debate and developments throughout the last century about the use of employees' task knowledge. It then outlines current workplace developments to formally manage that knowledge. That possibility is then argued to be best facilitated by formal trade union participation and support. It is argued that managing this knowledge in partnership with trade unions is not only efficacious: in turn a capacity and opportunity exists to enhance work and employment and so create for workers the better job. Finally, the further levers that might aid the creation of the better job are identified and discussed in relation to Scotland and the development of devolution. The chapter thus indicates how work and employment can be enhanced for employees in Scotland, and policy-makers can hitch those employees to their dreams of creating the knowledge-driven economy.

KNOWLEDGEABLE WORKERS

Scientific management – sometimes eponymously called Taylorism, with its utilisation of time and motion studies, had significant negative consequences for workers – summed up by the words 'deskilling' and 'degradation'. Excepting discussions of time and motion studies, what is often forgotten is the process by which this deskilling and degradation occurred. That process featured the appropriation of workers' task knowledge by emergent managers – through, of course, those infamous time and motion studies.

At the turn of the twentieth century owner-managers were keenly aware of the task knowledge possessed by workers and how important that knowledge was to the development of their firms, as Jacques reveals in his historical account of management knowledge: 'It is an important part of [the manager's] duties to find out what [the workers'] ideas and opinions are...and thus to make capital out of their original- ity and their suggestions'.[8] What then happened, through the introduction of scientific management, was the appropriation of this knowledge, so effecting in management and labour a 'complete mental revolution'.[9] Codified and abstracted from workers, this knowledge both enabled a rationalisation of work and functioned as a source of legitimacy and power for managers. This 'knowledge transfer' is part of the forgotten history of the workplace.

Interestingly, however, even Taylor lamented how, even after instruction from 'teachers', workers would quickly return to their own working practices. If disparaged by Taylor, such informal practices were accepted by managers throughout the twentieth century as a form of innovation that enabled the job to be done more effectively than officially recognised and prescribed. In this process of 'making out' workers possess considerable ingenuity, initiative and intimate knowl- edge of their work.

Workers thus retain, and management need, the informal and practical task knowledge of their employees. Even though manage- ment had tried and often succeeded in formally separating thinking and doing, 'knowledgeable practice' could be and was retained by workers.

Moreover, management have also often recognised that toleration of or accommodation to informal working practices can facilitate labour consent and co-operation – the necessary other side of the coin to control and compliance. This might be termed 'peace work'.

However, although tacitly accepting the initiative and informal intervention of employees in the production process, management have generally attempted to prohibit the formal intervention of workers. Knowledgeable practice and the interventions it enabled in the production process by workers had to remain informal or hidden. Management would deny that workers even had to think about work – that was an activity for management. Workers became 'hired hands' and nothing more, at least formally. For these reasons. then, workers' task knowledge was pushed into the shadows during most of the twentieth century; that is, it was manifest as informal working practices and behaviour which, whilst yet vital to efficacious production, was not formally encouraged and only begrudgingly accepted and then accommodated by management.

As a consequence, a valuable source of knowledge was left underdeveloped by management. A notable study of assembly workers quoted one employee: 'I had lots of ideas I could suggest but I have given up. If management doesn't want to draw on my many years of experience, I will say nothing. I'll do just the least amount I can get away with without being disciplined. I'll take my paycheck and forget about the job'.[10]

The knowledgeable worker is therefore not a new economy phenomenon but rather, as Jacques notes, an integral part of the development of industrial capitalism. However, if throughout the twentieth century management attempted to appropriate workers' task knowledge or accommodated any residual knowledge in the form of informal working practices, now management is keen to introduce organisational structures and practices which facilitate initiative and innovation in the form of creativity and continuous improvement on the part of workers.

TRANSFORMING WORK

Things began to change in the 1980s with increased competition and the influence of Japan. Management gurus peddled the idea that Japanese firms encouraged workers to formally intervene in the production process, making suggestions for continuous improvement through such practices as quality circles. Although the gurus' demand for a complete overhaul of British and other Western management and labour practices now seems erroneously exaggerated, there were pressures on management to improve the quality and quantity of labour's input. This did lead many firms to question aspects of the Taylorist separation of thinking and doing.

The practice did not necessarily match the rhetoric. For example, quality circles were characteristic of early stages of work transformation, but were not intrinsically built into a different technical division of labour. In effect, employees continued to be formally excluded from 'thinking' about work, inasmuch as that thinking was not forwarded by management as an intrinsic part of the job – and management and worker cynicism about quality circles seemed justified with their demise before the end of the 1980s.

Recently, knowledge management writers have made much of the need to lever employees' knowledge for product and process innovation. Three assumptions inform this endeavour:

- first, a final realisation and acceptance that 'knowledge is at the centre stage of organisational life'
- second, that management of this knowledge requires a fundamental restructuring of organisations
- and third, that knowledge can be levered to enhance organisations' operations and so competitive advantage.[11]

The task for management is to facilitate the revealing and sharing by workers of their knowledge in the workplace for their firm's commercial utility – what Ichijo *et al* call the '3Cs': creating, capturing and capitalising on knowledge.[12]

In practice, however, the emphasis lies with product rather than process innovation and, as a consequence, there is a continued marginalisation of ordinary employees' task knowledge. Where there is brief mention of employees' task knowledge, the results of this marginalisation and the real concerns of practitioners and consultants become obvious. Nonaka *et al*, in one of their case studies of leading exponents of knowledge management, show how management elicit the task knowledge of their craftsmen. The end result, however, is that these craftsmen are then required to instruct semi-skilled workers using that knowledge.[13] Other proponents, such as Kanevsky and Housel, likewise proclaim that 'the fundamental building material of a modern corporation is knowledge'. At the same time, their case studies reveal this knowledge again being used for deskilling and regulatory employee control, and this is seemingly commended by these authors when they suggest that organisational knowledge has to be reduced to a set of instructions, preferably encoded into automated computer systems. To this end, these authors evoke an efficiency model based on the recalculation of sub-divided organisational tasks or 'component processes'.[14]

These outcomes are familiar to anyone versed with Taylorism and scientific management. Even when firms take the 'high road' and use their employees' knowledge to innovate in production, rather than the 'low road' of employee regulation, horizontal dialogue again supplements rather than replaces vertical command structures, thereby undermining the claim made by Krogh, Roos and Kleine in *Knowing in Firms* that the management of knowledge requires a fundamental restructuring of organisations.

It would be a big mistake to believe that new forms of working have replaced the old. As currently configured and described in mainstream management writing, knowledge management does not create the better job for ordinary employees. The new complements the old. What *is* happening in many workplaces is the emergence of a dual structure that combines the search for employee innovation with enhanced regulation. Methods of co-ordination and accountability therefore become more complex, but vertical structures remain the backbone of firms. Such a development heralds the emergence of a *shadow division of labour*, one that cuts across and supplements vertical structures and hierarchies.

TAKING THE HIGH ROAD

That a desire for levering knowledge within organisations does exist, however, offers an opportunity to enhance work and employment. Given the widespread acceptance of this need amongst academics and business writers, it is not surprising that there has been a policy impact. The priority for governments must now be 'facilitating the diffusion and application of knowledge', argues Graham Vickery of the OECD.[15] Firms must, therefore, be encouraged to pursue employees' knowledge in a more sustained and inclusive manner.

In doing so, there are two possible scenarios, the first of which has already been shown to be pursued by firms.

• **The 'low road' – knowledge for regulation:**
In this scenario, experimental knowledge is used in 'single loop' operations to eliminate errors in existing processes. A past example of this low road was quality circles. Moreover, such elimination, in the form of reduced 'downtime' and the introduction of 'management by stress' further reduces the opportunity for employees to contribute to workplace innovation through experimentation. Hence its label as 'single loop'. If the experience of quality circles provides a marker, then this first scenario will have a limited life span in terms of providing knowledge-driven competitive advantage for both employees and their firms.

Firms must shift from 'single' to 'double loop' thinking, and encourage continuous and systematic innovation on the part of ordinary employees.

• **The 'high road' – knowledge for innovation:**
In this scenario, work is characterised by knowledge-driven experimentation, with trial and error, and in collaborative arrangements

within and across departments, functions and occupations to develop new processes and even products. An example of this approach is the tripartite of production tasks (TPT) that has three features:

- production – learning by doing
- experimentation – reflection, trial and error, innovative capacity
- diffusion, collectivisation of gained experiential knowledge.[16]

Such a system would require support through employees' access to design knowledge (product and process) that is also codified and abstract. Knowledge can be gained through practice and from external sources. As such TPT requires an intra-organisational environment that facilitates, encourages and develops employee thinking, learning, communication, sharing and trust both within and across immediate tasks, functional areas and occupational groups.

In practice, a high road firm might have a form of teamworking resulting from delayering and devolution – though not downsizing. Pursuing such an initiative would require a *new division of labour* with the introduction of strategic, operational and cross-functional team-working, in which management relinquish power so that each team can control money, machines and people in relation to their allocated task. What would follow would be changes in payment systems, selection procedures, labour control, training, career development and task enactment. As a consequence, knowledge management can be affected that transforms work and connects ordinary employees with the desires of policy-makers (and management). To make that transforma-tion, however, requires more than just a reconfiguring of work. The terms of employment too must be changed.

TRADE UNIONS REMEMBERED: A DISTINCTIVE DEVOLUTION AGENDA?

Devolution provides the Scottish Parliament with control of some of the key drivers of modern economic policy – education and employ-ment. The former is direct, the latter indirect, through control of, for example, inward investment and vocational education and training. Much of the learning around the latter has taken place outside the workplace, associated with institutions of further education. This approach is partially correct, and more funding must be made available to further education for this purpose.[17] Learning, however, must also be encouraged in the workplace – and not just through apprenticeships for younger employees. All employees must be encouraged to learn.

Some of the recent claims made for workplace developments are naive in the extreme. Bertels and Savage, for example, argue that we are 'standing with Galileo, realising the contradictions of traditional wisdom, and reaching for a new order'. Again, this new order is one is characterised by the jettisoning of vertical command and control structures in favour of dialogue and trust amongst organisational members who no longer work 'for the boss' but 'with one another'.[18]

Undoubtedly, trust is an important feature of the better job. Trust, as well as learning, is a key element in workers' revealing and offering knowledge in the workplace. Trust facilitates the exchange of knowledge between management and workers. Unfortunately, after a nearly a century of scientific management, work intensification and job losses (often supported by government), that trust is low in the UK and Scotland.

Given these experiences, a key problem will be the lack of trust by workers of management. Workers need to feel that they will benefit, not be punished, by the diffusion of their task knowledge. A form of insurance is thus required. The obvious insurers are the trade unions.

Interestingly, but not surprisingly given employees' previous experience with both quality circles and organisational restructuring in the 1980s, employee involvement is more effective when involving trade unions according to the US Dunlop Commission of 1994. Trade unions' presence tends to:

- lower labour turnover
- increase levels of productivity
- encourage managers to optimise their returns by, for example, investing in training and reskilling.

Thus not only are trade unions compatible with progressive work initiatives: unionised firms are more likely to have such schemes, in the UK and USA. The reason for this is that unions provide organisation, resources, leadership and training, and their involvement assures workforce of mutual respect and partnership with management. Indeed, not only are trade unions compatible, but unionised firms are more likely to have such initiatives, in both the UK and US.[19]

An example from the US is the 'Enterprise Contract' between UAW and GM at Saturn, which heralded a shift from adversarial relations to 'joint venture' between union and firm with employee participation and co-responsibility for strategic business decisions.[20] In Scotland partnership agreements are possible that deliver mutual gains, for example UDV at Leven, which was awarded Britain's Best Factory award in 1997 for its approach to work restructuring, instituting team-working, developing formal initiatives in partnership and, of huge significance, investing in employee learning and development.[21]

Unfortunately, both employers and government have been hostile to trade unions in the UK. This hostility was exacerbated from 1979. During the Thatcher-Major years, the Conservatives 'define[d] themselves unambiguously as hostile to trade unions', as Crouch put it,[22] instituting wide-ranging measures of anti-trade union legislation. At a time of massive economic restructuring, the numerical and political power of trade unions diminished during the 1980s, with union membership declining by over one third from 1979.

However, trade unions have not been eliminated in the UK, far from it. Firstly, despite the traditional confrontational approach adopted by employers towards organised labour, and encouragement in this from previous Conservative governments, it appears that beyond a few well-publicised cases, few employers have seriously attempted to eradicate trade unions.[23] Union density is now fairly settled at around 29 per cent.[24] Variations are apparent, with union density remaining strong in the larger manufacturing plants. Although union membership had declined to around 53 per cent of workplaces by 1998, there is some evidence that this decline has been arrested, with a rise in the number of union members in the UK between 1998 and 1999.[25]

Secondly, with a new administration, there is now the emergence of a sea change in attitudes to trade unions in the UK. New Labour will not repeal most Conservative Party anti-trade union legislation, and the current government has yet to agree to all of the EU Social Chapter. Nonetheless, the administration has adopted the Working Hours Directive and European Works Councils. A now widely accepted minimum wage has also been introduced. In addition, the 'Fairness At Work' initiative enhanced trade union-employer dialogue. The subsequent Employment Relations Act 1999 provided for statutory trade union recognition, made it a duty for management to inform and consult trade unions about training and created a Partnership Fund to contribute to the training of management and trade union representatives in the development of partnership agreements. The number of partnership agreements is increasing in the UK and they are promoted by government. In 2001 a Scottish Trade Union Learning Fund was established by the Scottish Executive to encourage unions' capacity to promote employee development and workplace development. Better relationships with government, plus new legislation, seem to be creating a new mood of optimism amongst trade unions, even though (rightly) disputes remain over the financing of the public sector. The future of trade unionism in the UK looks more assured than for many years. This offers a challenge to progressive trade unionism and the Scottish trade union movement.

Although the control of labour remains important, and flexibility a key strategy, there exist many management styles in the UK, ranging from traditionalist, paternalist to consultative. These styles are not exclusive. Despite human resource management (HRM) initiatives in which management are now more inclined to communicate directly with employees, there appears to be a dualism occurring in some firms. Traditional industrial relations, such as collective bargaining arrangements, are complementing HRM best practice.

The strengthening of trade unions thus bodes well for enhancing work and employment. For workers, it seems that trade unions' presence in the workplace is a key lever in this respect. Trade unions provide insurance for workers against potential exploitation by management; they discipline management to invest in workers rather than shed labour; and they assure workers that initiatives by management have some instrumental benefit for workers. Management too, it seems, also benefits from the presence of trade unions. Little wonder that 'mutual gains' is becoming more common parlance in the workplace.

LIMITS TO THE BETTER JOB
Clearly, the better job can be developed if certain choices are made about work and employment, and doing so would further policy-makers' desire for a knowledge-driven economy. Nonetheless, a note of warning must be sounded. It would be unwise to expect that every job can become the better job. Policy-makers assume that high skill, high wage iMacJobs are the future but, as Thompson *et al* note, the reality is very different.[26] Many jobs today, especially in the expanding interactive service sector of selling, cleaning, guarding and distributing are McJobs: routine, regulated and with low pay and low skill. Such jobs are a key feature of future predicted job growth trends in Scotland. For employees in such jobs, it might not be possible to introduce the type of task knowledge levers being suggested here. Introducing work practices that lever employees' task knowledge tends to be correlated with firms operating in product markets that are high value-added.[27] McJobs are not of this type. The possibility of 'job enrichment', to use the old industrial sociology term of the 1960s and 1970s, is remote. Customers use these services precisely because they are cheap, with standardised product.

For these workers, however, it might be possible to pursue what might be termed 'employment enrichment' in which their work or job content remains unchanged but their employment is enhanced. The most obvious examples here would be the minimum wage and its policing, and fuller trade union activity in these workplaces. Another possibility is the creation of non-work-related learning opportunities through work. Some companies in the UK already offer their employees non-work related study at work, using workplace facilities and resources. Employees study foreign languages, for example. Such study is indirectly beneficial to the firm. Employees in the McJob sector have often had limited learning histories (perhaps having left school at the minimum age), and as 'academic under-achievers' they may be fearful of learning; but learning can enhance both their confidence in doing their work and their commitment to the firm. It must also be said that such learning might also enhance these workers' labour market mobility and so provide an escape route out of McJobs.

An obvious mechanism to encourage this type of learning was the Individual Learning Account (ILA). These ILAs were introduced by New Labour for those who were already in employment (rather than the unemployed), but who had traditionally not continued with education into adult life. An ILA is a voluntary savings account into which an individual, his or her employer and government can deposit funds for the purposes of learning activities. As a complement to work-related training, the objective of ILAs was to:

- encourage employees to individualise their 'personal development'
- raise current levels of investment in work-related learning (for which UK firms are notoriously poor contributors for ordinary employees)
- increase awareness and expectations amongst ordinary employees about the benefits of learning.[28]

Late in 2001, New Labour at Westminster announced a suspension of ILAs because of alleged financial fraud by some providers. However, ILAs did have a positive impact for many workers most in need of enhancing their employment opportunities and prospects. Focus groups run by the DfEE revealed employees in low paid jobs, younger workers and members of ethnic minorities as the groups most likely to want to open an ILA. Interestingly, initial evidence from trials of ILAs demonstrated that the participation of trade unions facilitated traditional non-learners and the low-skilled in opening ILAs. This finding should be of little surprise give the data on trade unions presented in the previous section.

With devolution, the delivery framework of ILAs has varied throughout the UK. Scope still exists therefore for Scottish initiatives to continue ILAs or something similar. Perhaps Holyrood, recognising the need and benefit of ILAs, could find ways of policing them that Westminster could not. The Labour Party in Scotland might also do well to remember that ILAs were very popular amongst the party conference delegates of 1996 as they sought to commit the-incoming Labour government to the concept. Whilst job content is difficult to develop, such that these McJob employees' work remains much the same, their terms of employment can be enhanced with little, if any, cost to their firms. Subsequently, the centre-left can still make a difference to the lives of even these employees, who are so often overlooked in discourse about the knowledge-driven economy.

SCOTLAND AS A TARTAN TIGER?

The Conservative Party, although the sole champions of the right in Scotland, has no foreseeable chance of attaining political power at Holyrood and only a remote possibility of winning power at Westminster at the next election, and possibly beyond. It is the centre-left that will dominate policy-making at UK level. Likewise in Scotland – although the outside-left Scottish Socialist Party may directly influence policy if the Labour Party lose power to a potentially very fractious coalition comprising the SNP, the Liberal Democrats and themselves.

Nevertheless, through its economic (mis-)management, employment and anti-trade union legislation, plus its use of the public sector as model employer, the right significantly affected work and employment in the UK and Scotland throughout the 1980s and 1990s. Given that New Labour sometimes has difficulty in disentangling itself from old Conservative polices, it would be easy, and understandable, for the centre-left to lapse into cynicism about any current possibility to create the better job. Such an attitude would be lazy and, more importantly, it would not serve the interests of those the centre-left (and outside-left) claim to represent – ordinary working men and women.

Although talk of 'planning' has long disappeared, there still exists a need for the centre-left to develop emancipatory theories and initiatives based on best practice. In the UK, the election of the Blair administration has opened that opportunity. This chapter has suggested that knowledge management initiatives can be used to enhance work and employment in Scotland. This outcome is not pre-determined but requires a supportive trade union environment. Enhanced work and employment would significantly contribute to creating the 'better job' for workers, and go some way to addressing, if not ameliorating by reversal, the outcomes of scientific management in the workplace.

There are four recent developments that might act as levers to enhance work and employment in the UK and Scotland. The first is the introduction of evidence-based policy in government. This development does not herald an era of scientifically guided society, rather a belief that evidence should inform 'what works and why'.[29] Acknowledging its past limitations, and in an effort to establish evidence-based policy-making, the UK government is now actively seeking social science research input into its policy-making. There is also the possibility of secondments for academic researchers to government departments, and more seminars through which researchers can directly present their ideas to ministers and senior policy officials. Such processual input, it must be recognised, is not exempt from being politically filtered as output – that is, policy. It may be that, with a few exceptions, evidence-based analysis rather than policy emerges. It should also be recognised that evidence-based policy is not a technocratic panacea – and on its own can lead to an ideologically light, value-free policy. Politics is about choice and change, and as important as evidence-based policy is the need to centre any policies in a sense of vision and values.

An understanding of this debate has happened in some parts of the UK Labour government and Scottish Executive. Wendy Alexander has stated clearly that she thinks that government must change, with different faces and forums involved in the decision-making and delivery: 'We need task forces, mixed background units, more secondments and the use of outside expertise.'[30] The recent establishment of the Scottish Labour Market Intelligence Unit was a model in this respect. It resulted from wide consultation and discussion amongst a range of key individuals and organisations through Scotland – both socially and geographically. In its new guise, Future Skills Scotland, under its new director, Stephen Boyle, a former economist with the Royal Bank of Scotland, external research input will play a crucial role in the unit's contribution to policy discussions with ministers.

Importantly, the engagement of academics, particularly from the social sciences, with government is a two-way process. Government and the civil service must jettison their 'knowledge free zone' reputation and develop a partnership with social science, as occurs in the US and Australia. Social science, for its part, according to Blunkett, must stop being inward looking and ought more often to address issues that are of concern to policy-makers and the public. Under such circumstances, social scientists cannot abdicate their responsibility for attempting social amelioration, or, in the case of this chapter, enhancing work and employment.[31]

The second development is a growing awareness on the part of managers that their firms do benefit from enhanced work and employment. A financial case can now be made for the benefits of management acceding to new work and employment practices, including, for example, problem-solving groups and work-improvement teams. Despite low current take-up of such initiatives, firms should be able to be persuaded to be more inclusive in the operationalisation of their knowledge base for instrumental reasons. Firms would benefit commercially from engaging employees' task knowledge, and should formalise the organisation and managerial structures and practices that would lever that knowledge. Guest reports that there is now a body of research that demonstrates that HRM best practice, including the practices suggested above, does provide competitive advantage for firms.[32] The 1998 Workplace Employee Relations Survey also indicates that high involvement/high performance human resource systems have positive effects on organisational performance.[33] Fortunately, chief executive officers and human resource managers seem to be becoming more aware of the link between human resources practices in training and job design, for example, and business performance.

This point – about particular human resource systems of the kind described in this chapter affecting improvements in firms' operational and financial performance – is one that is applicable to inward investors. Research in Hungary confirms that foreign-owned firms with best practice human resource systems are those firms with leading edge product and process development.[34] This finding is of real significance to Scotland for a number of reasons. Firstly, despite recent problems, a disproportionate number of Scotland's key manufacturing firms remain foreign-owned. Secondly, these firms have adopted these human resource systems whilst in Hungary, with indication that there is occurring a discernible shift from labour intensive to capital intensive operations – a development that has not occurred to any significant extent in Scotland. Finally, with EU enlargement pending, Hungary, of a comparable size and peripheral location to Scotland, is likely to be a competitor nation in some sectors. The lesson is that, to compete, the Scottish Executive should encourage firms in Scotland to also adopt the work and employment being suggested in this chapter.

A third development might act as a lever. Despite cynicism about past management initiatives – the failure of quality circles in the 1980s being just one example – workers indicate that they are aware of the innovations that they can and would be able to make in work, should that opportunity arise. Many workers are aware of the innovative input that they could and should make to their firm's processes and products if only they were able to do so. The quote cited earlier in this chapter from Guest's earlier research is a sad indictment of too many workplaces – even today. Surveys such as the 7th Annual Dibbs, Lupton and Allsop Survey of 1999 demonstrate that employees are also concerned about the poor relationships that exist between trade unions and employers and would like to see improvements. Other research would suggest that, in Scotland at least, this concern arises from the disaffection of employees with the highly individualist orientation of current management practice.[35] Workers would appear to want better relationships with management for themselves and their representatives.

Not surprisingly, partnership agreements involving mutual gains with benefits for workers are, in principle, favoured by workers, as a survey of two companies based in Scotland, conducted by Findlay *et al*, affirms. That partnership must involve more than a formal agreement between managers and trade union officials; it must include equipping workers with 'the appropriate skills and abilities to make partnership work at the level of the shop or office floor'.[36] Whilst this partnership can provide for greater employment security, the importance of which should not be under-estimated, it also includes greater training and development for workers and enhanced task participation for them. As Findlay points out, partnership agreements are possible that deliver mutual gains. To repeat, her and her colleagues' research at UDV affirmed the possibility that established plants could successfully introduce work restructuring, institute team-working, develop formal initiatives in partnership and invest in employee learning and development.

Finally, and not unrelated to the third development – and in spite of employment and industrial relations legislation being a reserved matter – there are grounds for believing that there exists in Scotland a capacity for developing the type of trade union involvement being suggested here. Bill Speirs, General Secretary of the STUC, made three points at a conference assessing the first two years of the Scottish Parliament.[37] Firstly, he believes that the social democratic tradition of Scotland – now foregrounded with the Parliament – will affect and drive how the Scottish Executive views trade unions. Trade unions, he said, are 'voiced as a good thing by politicians in Scotland' and the Scottish Executive is 'an advocate' of trade unions. Secondly, this advocacy can have practical outcomes. Holyrood controls inward investment in Scotland. This control offers an opportunity for the Executive to shape the employment practices of inward investors through contract compliance. The Scottish Executive can suggest that investors 'look favourably on an approach from a trade union', Speirs believes. Finally, he points out that the UK Employment Relations Act 1999 has encouraged firms to seek voluntary agreements with trade unions. Such developments herald the possibility of distinctly Scottish, as opposed to UK, influence on all employment in Scotland, whether provided by domestic or foreign employers.

These four developments signal that it is possible that, with the support of trade unions and encouraged by Government, firms can be persuaded to develop the better job in Scotland. Workers appear to desire the type of work and employment associated with the better job, and would respond positively to it. It is a possibility that Scotland must, directly (in Holyrood) and indirectly (at Westminster), turn into an opportunity. The better job can be created in Scotland. These jobs might go some way to addressing the persisting and significant economic under-performance of Scotland compared to the rest of the UK, not just generally but in relation to the newly devised regional knowledge-based business index[38] – the authors of which argue that new policy initiatives are needed that enhance the stock of knowledge-based businesses in Scotland. This chapter has outlined the possible content of those policy initiatives.

The author would like to thank Paul Thompson for his helpful comments in the formulation of this chapter.

NOTES

1. J.-P. Durand, 'Is the "Better Job" Still Possible Today?', *Economic and Industrial Democracy*, Vol. 19 No. 1, 1998.
2. B. Helgeson and J. Johansson, 'Productivity and the Future of Work: The Lost Debate of Industrial Democracy', *9th Annual Labour Process Conference*, UMIST 1991, p2.
3. On the Alternative Economic Strategy see: S. Aaronvitch, *The Road From Thatcherism: The Alternative Economic Strategy*, London: Lawrence and Wishart 1981; N. Thompson, *Political Economy and the Labour Party*, London: University College London Press 1996.
4. See the Scottish Socialist Party General Election Manifesto 2001, p13. Ironically, the same lack of imagination exists in T. Sheridan and A. McCombes, *Imagine: A Socialist Vision for the 21st Century*, Edinburgh, Rebel Inc. 2000.
5. T. Blair, *The Third Way*, London: Fabian Society 1998.
6. M. Ritchie, 'Liddell's five objectives for Scottish prosperity', *The Herald*, 30.5.01.
7. See, for example C. Warhurst and P. Thompson, 'Hands, Hearts and Minds: Changing Work and Workers at the End of the Century', in P. Thompson and C. Warhurst (eds), *Workplaces of the Future*, London: Macmillan 1998; P. Thompson, C. Warhurst and G. Callaghan, 'Ignorant Theory and Knowledgeable Workers: Interrogating the Connections Between Knowledge, Skills and Services', *Journal of Management Studies*, Vol. 38 No. 7, 2001.
8. T. A. Edison, cited in R. Jacques, *Manufacturing the Employee*, London: Sage 1996, p2.
8. F. W. Taylor, *Scientific Management*, New York: Harper and Brothers 1947, p27.
10. R. H. Guest, 'Organisational democracy and the quality of work life: the man on the assembly line', in C. Crouch and F. Heller (eds),

Organisational Democracy and Political Processes, London: John Wiley and Sons 1983, pp148-49.

11. G. von Krogh, J. Roos and D. Kleine, 'Introduction' in G. von Krogh, J. Roos and D. Kleine (eds), *Knowing in Firms,* Sage: London 1998, p1.

12. K. Ichijo, G. von Krogh and I. Nonaka, 'Knowledge Enablers', in von Krogh et al, *op. cit.*

13. I. Nonaka, K. Umemoto and K. Sasaki, 'Three Tales of Knowledge-Creating Companies', in von Krogh et al, *op. cit.*

14. V. Kanevsky and T. Housel, 'The Learning-Knowledge-Value Cycle', in von Krogh et al., *op. cit.,* pp273, 277, 281.

15. G. Vickery, 'Business and industry policies for knowledge-based economies', *OECD Observer,* No. 215, 1999, p10.

16. Cited in N. D. Ahanotu, 'Empowerment and production workers: a knowledge-based perspective', *Empowerment in Organisations,* Vol. 6 No. 7, 1998.

17. Although some rethinking is required. Too much current vocational education and training tends not to enhance knowledge but merely record and accredit existing knowledge.

18. T. Bertels and C. M. Savage, 'Tough Questions on Knowledge Management' in G. von Krogh et al *op. cit.,* pp9, 19.

19. For US data, see J. T. Dunlop, *Report and Recommendations of the Commission on the Future of Worker-Management Relations,* Washington: US Department of Labor and US Department of Commerce 1994. For discussions of the US and UK, see Allen, *op. cit.;* and N. Millward, *The New Industrial Relations?,* London: Policy Studies Institute 1994.

20. B. Bluestone and I. Bluestone, *Negotiating the Future: A Labor Perspective on American Business,* New York: Basic Books 1992.

21. P. Findlay, 'Creating Partnerships: Challenging Scottish Business and Trade Unions' in G. Hassan and C. Warhurst (eds), *A Different Future: A Modernisers' Guide to Scotland,* Glasgow: Centre for Scottish Public Policy/The Big Issue in Scotland 1999.

22. C. Crouch, 'United Kingdom: The Rejection of Compromise', in G. Baglioni and C. Crouch (eds), *European Industrial Relations,* London: Sage 1991, pp353-54.

23. Allen suggests that the infamous short-termism of UK capital prevented an 'all-out offensive' such as that experienced by organised labour in the US: M. Allen, 'Modernising the Workplace', *Renewal: A Journal of New Labour Politics,* Vol. 3 No. 2, 1995, p65.

24. J. Goodman, M. Marchington, J. Berridge, E. Snape and G. J. Bamber, 'Employment relations in Britain', in G. J. Bamber and R. D. Lansbury (eds), *International and Comparative Employment Relations,* London, Sage 1998.

25. See M. Cully, A. O'Reilly, N. Millward, J. Forth, S. Woodland, G. Dix and

A. Bryson, *The 1998 Workplace Employee Relations Survey*, London: HMSO 1999; Advisory, Conciliation and Arbitration Service (ACAS), *Annual Report 1999-2000*, London: ACAS 2000.

26. Thompson, Warhurst and Callaghan, *op. cit.*

27. See the discussion in E. Keep, *Upskilling Scotland*, Edinburgh: Centre for Scottish Public Policy 2000.

28. J. Warner, 'Individual Learning Accounts: sharing the load', *Employee Development Bulletin*, No. 123, 2000.

29. Then Westminster Minister for Education David Blunkett, quoted in S. M. Nutley and J. Webb, 'Evidence and the policy process', in H.T.O. Davies, S. M. Nutley and P.C. Smith (eds), *What Works?: Evidence-based policy and practice in public services*, Bristol: Policy Press 2000, p13.

30. W. Alexander, 'Tackling Poverty and Social Exclusion' in Hassan and Warhurst, *op. cit.*, pp155-166.

31. D. Blunkett, 'Influence or Irrelevance: can social science improve Government?', Secretary of State's ESRC Lecture Speech, 2.2.00. Nevertheless, to be useful to government and protective of itself, social science should maintain a critical distance, particularly given that 'evidence-based policy' is not necessarily an objective practice.

32. A full outline of these practices, associated with the 'high performance and high commitment workplace', can be found in D. Guest, 'Piece by piece', *People Management*, 20.7.00.

33. Cully et al, *op. cit.*

34. C. Mako, 'Post-Fordism Instead of Hybridisation of Work Organisation', 5th IWOT Workshop, Catholic University of Leuven 2001.

35. J. Millar, and H. Donaldson, 'Setting the Agenda for Human Resource Management', *Proceedings of the 1st Scottish Trade Union Network Conference*, Paisley: University of Paisley 1999.

36. P. Findlay, A. Marks, A. McKinlay and P. Thompson, 'Reluctant Partners? Employee attitudes to company-union partnership agreements', mimeo, Edinburgh: University of Edinburgh 1999; and Findlay, *op. cit.*, p103.

37. B. Speirs, 'Industrial Relations in Scotland: Will Devolution Make an Impact?', *A Different Scotland? The Scottish Parliament Two Years On*, Centre for Scottish Public Policy Conference, Royal Society of Edinburgh, 15.9.01.

38. P. Cooke, N. Clifton and R. Huggins, 'Competitiveness and the Knowledge Economy', mimeo, Cardiff University 2001.

Daring to be different: a new vision of equality

ROWENA ARSHAD

SETTING THE CONTEXT FOR CHANGE

It could be claimed that from the moment that Scotland realised it was on course for devolution, those who managed this change anchored the new Scotland within principles of inclusion and social justice. This was certainly evidenced through the work of the campaign group Scotland Forward that launched their strategy to maximise the Yes, Yes vote for the Scottish Referendum held in September 1997.[1]

The campaign group, with its broad ranging membership (derived from business, trade unions, church, public and voluntary sector), had three conditions that it sought to apply to its short but highly effective campaign. The campaign had to be *popular* (appealing to all sections of society), *inclusive* (drawing in people from outwith politics) and *exciting* (creating a sense of being part of something vital). These conditions were the first signal that Scotland was ready to be different and wanted to be seen to be different.

The people of Scotland, weary of 18 years of Conservative Party policies that promoted individualism, profit and privatisation, wanted change. The turnout at the Referendum of just over 60 per cent exceeded most expectations. One of the most satisfying aspects of the overall result was that there were very clear majorities for the Yes vote in both questions. It could indeed be said that the 'settled will of the Scottish people' was thus declared.[2]

The Scotland Act 1998 which outlined the powers of the new Scottish Parliament ensured that the UK Parliament in Westminster retained the right to legislate and make regulations on equal opportunity issues, but it also enabled the Scottish Parliament to 'encourage' the observance of these regulations and to impose them as a requirement on public bodies. The specific part of the Act that defines equal opportunities for Scotland was in Schedule 5 of this Act.

Significantly, it included for the first time references to sexual orientation, language, age and social origins – aspects of equality that had previously not been explicitly enshrined in any UK legislation on matters of equality. As defined in the Scotland Act 1998, equal opportunities means:

> the prevention, elimination or regulation of discrimination between persons on grounds of sex or marital status, on racial grounds, or on grounds of disability, age, sexual orientation, language or social origin, or of other personal attributes, including beliefs or opinions, such as religious beliefs or political opinion.[3]

Scotland was daring to be different, placing potentially controversial issues such as sexual orientation firmly on the social justice agenda.

The principles of inclusion, equality and social justice were taken forward after the referendum by the Consultative Steering Group on the Scottish Parliament (CSG), which was established by the then Secretary of State for Scotland, Donald Dewar. In its final report in January 1999, the Group recommended four key principles for the Scottish Parliament to adopt: the sharing of power, accountability, access and participation and equal opportunities for all.[4] The Scottish Parliament duly adopted these principles.

The mood of the Scottish people upon receiving their Parliament was captured in the opening words from James MacMillan, Scotland's foremost classical composer, in a lecture to the 1999 Edinburgh International Festival where he stated that:

> There is a palpable sense of optimism in Scotland at this time. Women and men of goodwill detect that the circumstances are ripe with opportunity and challenge ... We are fired by a hitherto unparalleled potential to refresh and renew our society in its politics, in its culture and in its soul.[5]

The Scottish Parliament established an Equal Opportunities Committee as one of eight mandatory standing committees, and ensured that its rules of procedure required all legislative proposals presented by the Scottish Executive (the policy making and governance arm of government in Scotland) to be accompanied by a statement about their impact on equality issues. The Executive committed itself to developing an equality strategy, to doing this through a process of public consultation and to reporting annually on progress. It set up a special unit, the Equality Unit, to ensure momentum was created and maintained.

A CHANGE OF ATTITUDE AND POLICY

I believe that there been tangible change on equality matters following devolution – certainly within public sector provision, which is the priority of this chapter. The business sector, particularly small and medium size business, has, however, been slow to respond to the equality and diversity agenda. But one interesting development within the business world, which may have an impact on future developments in Scotland, has been the creation of the Financial Times Share Exchange (FTSE)4Good. Launched in July 2001, FTSE4Good is an index for socially responsible investment designed by the FTSE, one of the world's leading global index providers. FTSE4Good is a series of benchmark and tradable indices facilitating investment in companies with good records of corporate social responsibility. The FTSE uses three selection criteria for inclusion in the index:

- working towards environmental sustainability
- developing positive relationships with stakeholders
- upholding and supporting universal human rights.

It remains to be seen how the Scottish Parliament will work with business to include equality as part of the agenda for Scottish businesses.

Scotland has committed itself to becoming a country in which everyone matters, and has placed equality at the heart of policy making. It has designated equal opportunities as a key cross-cutting issue that is the responsibility of all departments of the Scottish Executive. It has a Minister for Social Justice.

Key words such as 'social justice', 'equality', 'women', 'racial equality' feature heavily on the Scottish Parliament and Scottish Executive websites. These hits would not have occurred pre-devolution, when searches for words such as 'race' or 'racism' would produce 3-10 hits on the then Scottish Office website. There is hardly a week that goes by without press releases or statements from Ministers and Government officials that relate to the theme of social inclusion and social justice. There is no doubt that the status of equal opportunities has changed since devolution. From a situation pre-devolution where equality practitioners and supporters adopted a 'fire fighting' approach, they now have centre stage where all the work they have carried out for decades is at long last being recognised.

The second bill passed into law by the Scottish Parliament, the Adults with Incapacity Bill, includes the first recognition in Scots law of the existence and validity of same-sex partnerships. The Bill gives a right to the nearest relative of an adult with incapacity to have a say in their affairs, and it includes same-sex partners within its provisions.

There has been sustained effort to improve the representation of women, people with disabilities and minority ethnic groups in the public appointments system. On matters relating to equality, Parliament and Executive have also cast wide the consultative net, taking advice from community groups and local activists instead of simply going to equality commissions and government departments. It is daring to seek guidance from the people for the people, and this connection with community level groups is a tangible change.

Non-departmental public bodies, such as the Scottish Higher Education Funding Council that manages the funding of Higher Education in Scotland, are now prepared to consider including equality of opportunity as an element in the condition of grant offer to higher education institutions. This may seem a fairly insignificant move. However, given Scotland's previous marginalisation of equality issues and the staidness of higher education in Scotland, that such a proposed condition now exists is testament to a change in attitude on equality issues. Being proactive on equality issues is now in vogue. Building equal opportunity targets into organisational business plans is now viewed as good practice.

This commitment to equality and social justice saw the Scottish Parliament (in spite of some vocal opposition) push through the repeal of Section 28/Clause 2a of the Local Government Act 1986 which instructs local authorities not to 'promote homosexuality'. Section 28 has not yet been repealed in England and Wales.[6]

OBSTACLES TO CHANGE

Despite this progress in Scotland, the journey of change has been and remains complex, with two main obstacles to be overcome. The first is the neo-conservative nature of the government machinery in Scotland. Scotland's civil service, and indeed the wider policy making community in Scotland, holds a strong sense of tradition; of the continuity of language (English), religion (Protestantism), political structures and common culture (white Scottish culture). This view of tradition and indeed homogeneity stands as a potential barrier for a new diverse and multicultural Scotland. As Lindsay Paterson argues in this volume, national homogeneity, with its united identity, is too impervious to easily allow entry for those that are different or who choose to reside in Scotland but have allegiances elsewhere. Scotland is still uncomfortable with difference and diversity.

The second obstacle lies in the mindset of the people of Scotland and indeed even those who are non-Scots. As McCrone suggests, 'Few myths are more powerful and prevalent in and about Scotland than that it is a more egalitarian society than England.'[7] McCrone argues that this myth has led to particular forms of Scottish vernacular: the allusion to our common humanity in 'we're a' Jock Tamson's bairns', and in Robert Burn's song 'A Man's A Man For A' That'. It has perhaps been an ideological device for setting the Scots as being different to the English, but this long held myth has now translated into an everyday common sense belief that Scotland has a social ethos and national values that are egalitarian simply because they are Scottish. Scots today subscribe to it very strongly, as evidenced by the singing of the Burns's song as part of the opening of the Scottish Parliament. Scotland and its people wanted the kite mark of justice to be worn explicitly and proudly.

The view of the Scots as inherently egalitarian, combined with a spirit of independence (as demonstrated by the referendum vote), provides a basis from which it is difficult to suggest to Scotland, its people and its institutions that they might be discriminatory and unjust without incurring intense defensiveness and serious disdain.

On the other hand, this myth and self-belief could be harnessed and used as a tool for change. The challenge is whether the politicians of Scotland have the courage to lead on this matter, to rise above their fears and prejudices and to allow for issues to be openly debated.

There are three areas that need to be addressed if equality matters are to be progressed in Scotland. The first area is the question of equality being a reserved matter of Westminster; the second is the matter of skeletons in Scottish cupboards; and the third is the removal of double standards. This chapter does not afford the space to write fully on these three points, but will look at each in brief.

TACKLING WESTMINSTER
Given that equality is a reserved power of Westminster, the London factor must be addressed. Scotland wants to forge ahead with social justice issues and to achieve this through effective consultation with the people of Scotland. Despite devolution, however, there remains a mindset in Westminster that could arguably be described as a 'London' mindset. This mindset assumes that those in Westminster can decide what is best for the rest of the UK. But what happens if the desired will of the people in Scotland differs from that of Westminster? Although a political vision, devolution has not been translated into conceptual or practical vision, either within the civil servant groups of Westminster or the equality commissions that are the guardians of equality legislation within the UK (the Commission for Racial Equality, the Equal Opportunities Commission and the Disability Rights Commission).

Those that create policy in London have tended to roll out one code applicable to all. The differing impact of a policy generated in London on the heavily populated and fairly affluent area of the South-East of England, as opposed to the unemployed and depressed areas of Yorkshire and Humberside or the West of Scotland, for example, has not been given sufficient consideration.

The fact that Scotland has its own education and legal systems is often forgotten or dismissed as inconsequential. It is not uncommon to find that an equality commission will produce a code of practice for schools forgetting that in Scotland the structure and governance of schools are significantly different from those in England and Wales. To add insult to injury, the remedy, when such lapses have been pointed out, has tended to be to add a few lines about Scotland to create an aura of inclusion, or to delete the word 'England' and insert ' Scotland', or to attach a Saltire to the front cover to give it a brand Scotland feel.

It could be argued that this is the type of mindset that has denied England its regional assemblies – one of the promises of the 1997 Labour Party manifesto.[8] On matters such as equality this type of mindset can potentially be highly obstructive, as the recent Census illustrates.

Scotland in common with the UK engaged in the decade count of all people and households. The 2001 Census was the first to be carried out for the Scottish Parliament. One of the key issues to emerge from Scotland as a result of the 2001 Census has been the general disquiet among Scotland's minority ethnic communities, particularly within African communities, about the categorisations currently used within the Census. The central concern revolves around the use of what leaders of Scotland's African communities have termed 'apartheid categories' as headings for the tick boxes. In the Scottish Census Form, in the ethnicity section, there is a mixture of codifications used from colour codes to ethno-geographic codes. People of English, Scottish and Irish descent are offered a choice of White English, White Irish, White Scottish or White Other to select from. Africans and people from the Caribbeans are asked to select from Black African, Black Caribbean and Black Other. Other minority ethnic groups, such as those from the Indian sub-continent, have not been placed within a 'colour box' but defined by geography alone. Africans feel the confused manner in which ethnicity, nationality and colour are used, and particularly the boxing of Africans into a single colour code, denies them the right to identify themselves on the basis of their different ethnic, national and cultural backgrounds.

The term 'Black' was preferred by Caribbeans living in the south of England in the early 1980s because of fear of immigration control.[9] People from the Caribbean preferred not to be identified by ethnonational labels of 'West Indian' or 'Afro-Caribbean' because they felt it would somehow identify them as not being 'British'. Not being 'British' meant their immigration status could be jeopardised. Hence they preferred the term 'Black British'. These categorisations were used for the 1991 Census and have continued in the 2001 Census.

However Africans in Scotland are now arguing that this codification, by and large drawn from consultation with minority ethnic groups in London, is no longer acceptable and that Africans and Caribbeans should not be grouped under one category solely on the basis of colour despite their different national and cultural contexts. The Census question on ethnicity is designed to help counter racial discrimination and disadvantage and provide a sound basis to help central and local government to plan their programmes and resource allocation more efficiently and effectively for a multicultural and diverse society. Africans in Scotland are arguing that classification categories therefore need to be appropriate, consistent and acceptable to all concerned. The categories used should not entrench racial hierarchy and encourage ethnic division, reinforce racial stereotypes that are rooted in a bipolar paradigm, or homogenise ethnic groups rather than to respect their diversity. It is argued that the current categorisations institutionalise racism by continuing to subscribe to the very terms that have been used to oppress people. They most certainly should not be imposed on Africans against their expressed wishes.

These concerns were presented to the Race Equality Advisory Forum (REAF), a short-life working group set up to oversee the implementation of the Scottish Executive's Action Plan in response to the inquiry chaired by Sir William Macpherson into the murder of Stephen Lawrence.[10] These concerns were also put forward directly to the Deputy First Minister and Minister for Justice Jim Wallace. Despite numerous petitions to Scottish Parliament, by the African Community and members of REAF, the 2001 Census ethnic categorisations for Africans stayed the same.

So what choice did Scotland have to react to the concerns of its people on this matter? It should have demanded that the Commission for Racial Equality in Scotland take forward this debate in Westminster, given that equality is a reserved function. It could have refused to implement the current categorisations and taken a bold step against institutionalised racism. It could have issued an immediate guidance notice to public sector services in Scotland that ethnic classifications used in future in Scotland should note the concerns of Africans in Scotland and provide an interim set of classifications for use in Scotland.

Scottish Ministers have acknowledged that the concerns of the

African communities in Scotland are valid and explained that due to timing it would not have been possible for them to change the 2001 Census forms. Ministers have promised that more research will be carried out to find alternative categorisations that would be widely acceptable. Consultations are now proceeding as to the best way forward in resolving this dispute. There is every likelihood that this consultation will kick the issue into the long grass, particularly if members of the African community tire of trying to battle with a system that will not act swiftly.

To respond to the concerns of Africans in Scotland would have required a giant leap into sensitive political waters. The rewriting of census ethnic categorisations in place for the past two decades would have suited neither statisticians nor the technocracy of Westminster. It would have caused a political storm; and on this matter Scotland was not yet prepared to be different.

In the Scottish Census, a new section was also introduced to assess the number of Gaelic speakers. Here was an opportunity to demonstrate Scotland's desire to promote social justice by including key community languages and other heritage languages in daily use in Scotland today, such as Scots, Urdu, Punjabi, Arabic and Cantonese. Parliament chose not to include these languages despite requests from the Commission for Racial Equality in Scotland and various voluntary sector organisations. One of the reasons offered was that adding all these categories would make the document unduly lengthy and cumbersome to the respondent.

Scotland needs to ask itself what message it is giving out if bureaucratic decisions are allowed to override the views of citizens. Is this not a case of business as usual? If Scotland dares to be different, it would ensure bureaucracy was the servant of the people and not vice versa. This is the type of challenge that Scotland must be prepared to take up if it is to become the 'people's parliament' and a champion of equality. Scotland has shown it has the depth and conviction to be different on other matters and it must show the same depth of conviction on equality matters.

Although Westminster controls the statutory levers on equality legislation, Scotland has a Parliament that can choose how to promote and implement it. The Parliament must be more creative in this field.

SKELETONS IN THE CUPBOARD

A Scotland that wishes to be different on equality matters must be prepared to expose the skeletons in its cupboard. The biggest skeleton in Scotland's cupboard is its capacity to deny the existence of prejudice and bigotry. Between 1999 and 2001, we can cite three main examples of this – in relation to homophobia, sectarianism and racial intolerance.

The first example is the debate surrounding the repeal of Section 28/Clause 2a. This was the first time that a public debate in Scotland had taken place about homosexuality, and thus a whole strand of Scottish homophobic opinion was ventilated which had previously been dormant. The debates in the papers were fierce and partisan, with some championing the rights of gay and lesbian people and others finding homosexuality to be immoral, unnatural and intolerable. Despite public uncertainty and often hostility to the topic, the Scottish Parliament took a bold step and pushed forward the repeal of Clause 2a. However, the homophobic skeleton in Scotland had come out of the closet, and egalitarian Scotland's credentials as a tolerant nation had been seriously dented.

The second issue to capture media attention was that of religious bigotry, or more precisely anti-Catholicism in Scotland. In 1999, James MacMillan spoke out about anti-Catholic prejudice in Scotland.[11] As someone who has been working actively in the field of equality in Scotland for the past fifteen years, I was alarmed at the rapidity with which politicians, academics and bureaucrats came together to refute the presence of systematic anti-Catholic prejudice in Scotland. First Minister Donald Dewar responded to MacMillan's comments by stating that 'I don't believe the average Scot is a bigot.'[12] As a consequence, MacMillan's comments were trivialised and portrayed as emotional and over the top in a number of popular and media discussions about his intervention.

Devine's *Scotland's Shame?* contains a range of contributions debating this issue, including one from MacMillan. In the book Finn, among others, attempts to show that religious bigotry does exist, and affects people's life chances. He theorises the situation, drawing parallels with other forms of structural inequality such as racism, and arguing that the new Scotland needs to be explicitly pluralistic and proud of the right of its people to be different.[13] Williams and Walls attempt to show disadvantage on the basis of religion, particularly in the area of health.[14] However, others in the book attempt to downplay MacMillan's challenge, arguing that Scottish Catholics are no more and no less subject to systematic discrimination in Scotland than their Protestant counterparts. Rosie and McCrone, for example, argue that the statistical evidence does not sustain any thesis that Catholics are still systematically discriminated against in Scotland today, stating that, 'Their past is indeed history'.[15]

Statistics and social attitude surveys can provide evidence of changing attitudes over generations, but such research must be used with caution, especially in relation to such complex and tendentious issues.

It is important to accept that discrimination, and in this instance sectarianism, does occur and can take many forms, which may change according to social and economic circumstances. It is important that latent feelings of prejudice and bigotry are exposed, discussed and discarded. In a Scotland where Protestantism has had a dominant position, we must be wary of silent sectarianism, something it is not always easy to identify in attitude surveys and statistics. Silent sectarianism occurs when members of the dominant group see themselves as superior to members of the subordinate group; see members of the subordinate group as inherently different from themselves; sense an advantage over members of the subordinate group; and are fearful and suspicious of members of the subordinate group who they think want to take away their advantage.

Religious bigotry remains an area that politicians in Scotland avoid for fear of unsettling voters. Perhaps Scotland is at last daring to be different on this matter, but it is not clear how far it will it be prepared to take this debate. Politicians from all parties in Scotland are now united in wishing to see a reform of the Act of Settlement, that prevents a Catholic from ascending to the throne, and this would signal the start of the dismantling of institutional sectarianism. But it must be more than a gesture. Moreover, it is the UK Government that is leading on this issue rather than Scotland.

Within the Scottish Parliament, Liberal Democrat MSP Donald Gorrie is calling for a hard line against sectarianism, and for a change in Scots Law to put religious sectarianism on the same legal basis as racism. Gorrie wants incitement to sectarian violence to be brought into the legislation that outlaws racism. He argues that:

> Belting out songs about wading through Fenian or Orange blood should not be acceptable in a civilised Scotland. The Law Society of Scotland have advised me that it would be possible for the Scottish Executive to remove the current exclusion in the law denying protection to those who are abused because of their religion.[16]

Gorrie took this action following the cancellation of a visit to Scotland by the Irish Taoiseach Bertie Ahearn, because of fear that the visit, shortly after a Rangers and Celtic football match, might incite sectarian violence. Sectarianism is one of the biggest skeletons in Scotland's cupboard and is an issue that must be addressed if Scotland is to move forward with difference.

The third series of events has shattered the myth of Scotland as a tolerant nation. In 2001 a young Turkish asylum-seeker, Firsat Yildiz, only recently arrived in Glasgow, was brutally murdered in a racist attack by a white youth.[17] The death of this young man was not an isolated incident. Since the arrival of asylum seekers to Sighthill, an area of multiple deprivation in Glasgow, there has been a significant number of acts of racial abuse and racial attacks on asylum-seekers. A senior Scottish MP, George Galloway, warned that all this should 'have been a wake-up call about race-hate. But most turned over and went back to sleep'[18] – except for extreme right-wing groups who sought to capitalise on the situation to whip up further hatred. Within days another asylum-seeker, Davoud Rasul Naseri, a 22 year old Iranian, was stabbed in the back. He later commented on his adopted land:

> I just feel that I hate Glasgow and I hate the people in Glasgow. I feel that with this recent situation that I just want to stay in my country; it would be better for me because I would be killed because of my aims, not because of nothing.[19]

Michael Kelly, previously a Labour Lord Provost of Glasgow, and responsible for the Glasgow Miles Better campaign, reacted strongly: 'We only smile better when it suits. Glasgow, in its treatment of asylum seekers, has proved itself to be as unpleasant, hard and nasty as all the old clichés defined it.'[20]

It would be wrong to say that all Scots are racist; however, racism in Scotland resulted in the murder of that young asylum-seeker. Scotland has to stop ignoring its racist potential. The largest local authority in Scotland accepted refugees and governmental funds to manage the dispersal scheme, but the elected local politicians ignored warnings from voluntary agencies, anti-racism groups and community groups that adequate support had to be made to ensure that asylum-seekers were integrated into the communities.

Scotland needs to shake off the cloak of denial, and embrace the cloak of truth on equality matters. It must be accepted that sexism, racism and homophobia occur in Scotland. Without accepting that problems exist, solutions cannot be found.

The third, related, area that Scotland needs to address is its double standards, which will be illustrated by returning to the issue of sectarianism, and the issue of state funded Catholic schools.

The Irish were one of the earliest targets of Scottish racism. The Irish (predominantly Catholics) were frequently used as scapegoats for the harsh social and economic times experienced by Scotland in the late 1800s. The Irish were excluded, marginalised and discriminated against economically, educationally and in other aspects of life, such as sports. An excellent discussion on the effects of sectarianism and its links to racism is made by Finn.[21] The Education Act (Scotland) 1918 was passed creating separate schools for Catholics. The intention was to provide young Irish Catholics with a safe place to learn and achieve.

The debates for and against the existence of Catholic schools have continued since then. Paterson and Bradley write that Catholic schools have been instrumental in raising the achievement and attainment levels of working class Catholic pupils.[22] These schools have been so successful, Paterson asserts, that young Catholics today are no longer systematically discriminated against in the labour market. Bradley argues that Catholic schools are able to produce such achievement because the schools draw their inspiration and strength from faith. We need to have an open and mature debate about the place of faith in today's education rather than engage in passionate tirades premised on inaccurate information or raw prejudice. As this debate is suppressed, other faith communities in Scotland are losing out. Kelly and Maan assert that if the new Scotland is to be genuinely democratic and inclusive, it must give practical recognition to religious belief as a basis for Scottish identity and citizenship.[23] In the same way that Scottish Catholics defend their right to have an education curriculum that honours their faith, so should this right be extended to other faith groups.

The debate to date has centred on whether or not Catholic schools should be abolished under the argument that a public funded system should not be paying for segregated forms of education. The current debate assumes that non-denominational schools are neutral and do not practice any particular form of religious instruction, treating all faiths equally. However this is a simplistic and false notion. The dominant hegemony of non-denominational schools remains that of the Protestant Christian faith, whether that be of Calvinistic, Presbyterian, Baptist or other strands of the Protestant Church. It may not be as explicit as those of the Protestant Christian faith would like, but unless the curriculum and school ethos undergoes transformation to acknowledge that other faiths, and Christian strands such as Roman Catholicism, are equal, then Protestantism will dominate silently. Let me illustrate with one example of how this dominance can show through unwittingly. Recently I was working with a local authority to assist them in creating a monitoring form for their pupil population. Under the section on 'Religion', the authority had constructed boxes labelled Christian, Catholic, Muslim, Sikh, Hindu and so on. But are Catholics not also Christians? Where are other major religious and faith groups such as Jews or Buddhists?

If we are to continue to fund Catholic schools then we must also allow parity for other faiths. If it is felt that a publicly funded state system should be inclusive and not fund particular religious schools then this concept needs nationwide consultation. However, the onus is upon the Parliament and Government to convince those who want separate schools as to how a secular system can meet their needs. Kelly and Maan suggest that one way forward might be to bring religious instruction into specific periods within the school week, thus permitting the secularising of the rest of the school week.

Scotland continues to remain silent on the matter of Catholic separate schooling, in the mistaken belief that to raise discussions would exacerbate the situation. This ostrich-like attitude gives in to silent sectarianism and exposes Scotland to accusations of double stands. If Catholic schools are given state funding and other faith groups are refused, then Scotland will be accused of Islamophobia and other forms of religious bigotry. All the signs are that in the new millennium we will experience an increasing diversity of religious movements and, just as there are young people who will be influenced by secular political ideology, there will be those who will be shaped by their religious faith. Scotland's educational system must do justice to all these young Scots of the future.

Devolution has given the UK a plurality of power bases, and by extension a wider range of modes of expression. The existence of a coalition government in Holyrood, and its push on mainstreaming equality into all aspects of Scottish governance, has meant that thinking is no longer trapped within the simple opposition between 'majority' and 'minority' interests. Scotland can now imagine new forms of relationship between representation and participation. Scotland is developing its internal capacity to contain anxiety and to promote diversity.

Since the establishment of the Scottish Parliament in 1999, a number of issues – for example student finance and tuition fees after the Cuble Report, and the long-term provision of care for the elderly after the Sutherland Report – have highlighted the potential divergence of legislation and action in Scotland from what is prescribed by the UK government in Westminster. Prime Minister Tony Blair has signalled that he is comfortable with the new constitutional alignment within the British Isles. Scottish ministers have to be more confident about devolution. They need to lead Scotland to be brave to be different.

The Scottish Executive has recently consulted on whether there should be a specific Scottish Human Rights Commission. In their consultation paper, the Executive suggested that the argument for a separate commission for Scotland might be advanced as justified on democratic grounds against the background of devolution. The fact that Scotland has a separate criminal justice, court and penal system lends weight to this argument. Moreover, it is also said that only a specifically Scottish body could understand and respond to concerns raised in the Scottish context.

On equality issues, if Scotland is unable to progress matters due to equality being a reserved power to Westminster, then two scenarios might happen. Scotland might tire of championing the social justice agenda and back down, deferring to the pace and priorities of Westminster; or it will demand more rights and responsibilities to be transferred to Holyrood using the arguments outlined above for the setting up of a Scottish Human Rights Commission. The Parekh Report already calls for a radical change on how equality is legislated and implemented within Britain.[24] Parekh asks for Britain to come more in line with other countries such as Australia, Canada, Ireland, New Zealand and the United States by having a single Equality Act and a single Equality Commission to enforce it.

The possibility of a single integrated Equality Commission is already being suggested by the UK government consultation paper 'Towards Equality and Diversity', which sets out proposals for the implementation of the European Community Article 13 Race and Employment Directives. It is unclear how Scotland will respond on this. It might be argued that in Scotland, where policy development on equality issues such as race and disability is at an embryonic stage, integrating these issues into one commission might marginalise each equality area. This could create a conceptual and functional mess. However, should Scotland support a single Commission it has to be explicit about where the Commission would stand in relation to the Scottish Parliament. There is a case for a separate Scottish Equality Commission, but Scotland cannot afford a retreat to the mindset that regards equalities work as marginal and irrelevant, as a matter 'reserved' to Westminster.

A Scottish Equality Commission would allow for a new and modern Scottish identity on equality matters to emerge. Such a commission, as with other countries in the Union, would adhere to baseline requirements from the UK Equality Act but have sufficient autonomy for its identity and priorities to be shaped by Scottish people and Scottish issues. What is certain is that Holyrood is likely to remain committed to issues of equality and social justice. The question remains as to how much of that commitment will translate into action. Will some equality issues make it at the expense of others? Will those that support a diversity agenda develop sufficient depth of understanding to move that onwards into a mainstreaming agenda? To move forward means accepting that equality and diversity are a precondition to any real process of democratic renewal. For this to happen, those that have held power this far must be prepared to change or stand aside, dumping grey suits and cloth caps, breaking old alliances for fresh consensual politics.

NOTES

1. P. Jones, 'A New Song to Sing: The 1997 Devolution Referendum Campaign', *Scottish Affairs*, summer 1997, No. 16, pp1-16.

2. The phrase, 'the settled will of the people' was used by John Smith, leader of the Labour Party from 1992-94.
3. Scotland Act 1998, Schedule 5, Section L. 2.
4. Consultative Steering Group, *Shaping Scotland's Parliament: Report of the Consultative Steering Group*, Edinburgh: The Stationery Office 1999.
5. J. MacMillan, 'Scotland's Shame', in T. M. Devine (ed), *Scotland's Shame?: Bigotry and Sectarianism in Modern Scotland*, Edinburgh: Mainstream 2000, p3.
6. See D. T. Evans, '"Keep the Clause": Section 28 and the Politics of Sexuality in Scotland and the UK', *Soundings*, Issue No. 18, pp208-24.
7. D. McCrone, *Understanding Scotland: The Sociology of a Stateless Nation*, London: Routledge 1992, p88.
8. Labour Party, *New Britain: Because Britain Deserves Better*, London: Labour Party 1997, pp34-35.
9. K. Sillitoe and P. L. White, 'Ethnic Group and the British Census: The Search for a Question', *Journal of the Royal Statistical Society*, 1992, 155: 1; R. Ballard, 'Negotiating Race and Ethnicity. Exploring the Implications of the 1991 Census', *Patterns of Prejudice*, 1996, 30: 3.
10. For more information on the Stephen Lawrence case, see www.blink.org.uk/campaign/stevelaw/slmain.html
11. A written version of this speech can be found in MacMillan, *op. cit.*
12. M. Ritchie, *The Herald*, 11.8.99.
13. G. P. T. Finn, 'A Culture of Prejudice: Promoting Pluralism in Education for a Change', pp53-88 in Devine, *op. cit.*
14. R. Williams and P. Walls, 'Going but Not Gone: Catholic Disadvantage in Scotland, in Devine, *op. cit.*, pp231-52.
15. M. Rosie and D. McCrone, 'The Past is History: Catholics in Modern Scotland', in Devine, *op. cit.*, p. 217.
16. D. Gorrie, Website press release 'Call for hard line on sectarianism', 13.2.01. www.donaldgorrie.com
17. *The Herald*, 6.8.01.
18. G. Galloway, *The Guardian*, 9.8.01.
19. *The Times*, 9.8.01.
20. M. Kelly, *The Scotsman*, 7.8.01.
21. Finn, *op. cit.*
22. L. Paterson, 'Salvation Through Education? The Changing Social Status of Scottish Catholics', pp145-58; and J. M. Bradley, 'Catholic Distinctiveness: A Need to be Different?', in Devine, *op. cit.*, pp159-74.
23. E. Kelly and B. Maan, 'Muslims in Scotland: Challenging Islamophobia', in J. Crowther, I. Martin and S. Shaw (eds), *Popular Education and Social Movements in Scotland Today*, Leicester: NIACE 1999.
24. B. Parekh, *The Future of Multi-ethnic Britain*, London: Profile Books 2000.

The identity that cannot speak its name

JANICE KIRKPATRICK

STORIES FROM STOCKHOLM

It is June the ninth, and a grey anaemic dawn fingers the morning's headlines. I start my day in Stockholm with a second-hand copy of the *Financial Times*, filched from a drowsy colleague as we passed in the hotel lobby.

I am in Stockholm at the invitation of both the Design Council and the British Council to discuss the importance of creativity in business with a group of forty or fifty small and medium-sized enterprises. My talk is one of six in a morning workshop that is the last in a series of events focused around Millennium Products, an exhibition of some of the 1012 'innovative and bright new solutions to old problems'. Each one of the exhibits is from the UK, all are excellent and 78 are Scottish.

Between sleep and coffee I pick over the fall-out from the general election graphically illustrated, ink on pale pink. The *FT* puts a ruddy flush on the cheeks of those who decorate its pages, breathing colour and life into the grey faces of spent politicians. I wish it would do the same for Scotland.

As the hungry arrive I gather what news I can find strewn about the breakfast room. What little there is lies buried within the pagan process of prediction and analysis that now passes for proper reporting. Two-in-a-row might be a first for Labour, but judging by the dismal turnout to vote, it has come a distant second in the lives and priorities of the Scottish electorate. This morning I am asked to consider how Tony's kids have grown, whether Blair dyes his hair and the significance of Cherie's frocks. As if any of it really matters to those of us disinclined to ponder horoscopes, checks, florals or stripes in the relentless search for clues to Scotland's future.

Only one paper has bothered to ask what the election might mean for the nascent Scottish Parliament, and it is published in Chicago, Illinois. That our future should be debated in the lofty pages of the *Herald Tribune* preserves my sanity and reassures me that I have not nailed my company colours to the mast of a sinking ship. I still believe I am part of a place that can be bigger and better than the one I left last night. But Scotland's media silence is a salutary reminder that Scottish issues might as well be written with invisible ink as far as the parochial London media, and most of our own papers, are concerned.

I decided some days ago that this would be the point when I would begin to write. At that time I had no idea I would be in Stockholm. But being here, on the morning after the general election, puts me at an advantage because it gives me the chance to place my impressions of Scotland within a wider perspective, not as I remember them from previous trips abroad, but as they actually are, here and now.

In the design business, distance is a precondition for achieving true focus and an understanding of how different cultures manifest themselves. Distance helps me to see more clearly. It helps me to understand and value the things that make me, and others, who are not like me, look forward to the day ahead. 'Design' is a process of controlling creativity. It is a process of understanding and manipulating the elements of culture: our languages, symbols, myths, rituals and values, in order to produce a specific outcome like a book or a building or the desire to walk down a particular street. It is an inexact science, composed of intuition and underpinned with stolen methods, but it is one that works. The hardest part of designing in Scotland is the impossibility of removing myself from the ebb and flow of my own culture in order to see it more clearly. While I try to keep my head above our rich broth of conflict, creativity, history and humour, the lessons it teaches make me quick and incisive when reducing foreign cultural brews to their constituent parts.

Designing is about more than just rearranging the furniture and Scotland is a good place to educate the creative professionals who need the mother of all laboratories in which to test and hone their skills and tools.

In order to understand why things are the way they are, in Scotland and elsewhere, we must view them from different angles. Like precious crystals we hold them up to the light, and slowly rotate them to see how they change shape from one second to the next, sparkling, reflecting and dissolving before once again becoming sharp-edged and diamond hard. It helps to see things close up and then very far away; to achieve maximum contrast and get a feeling for where the edges might be. The most interesting things always happen at the edges, when something becomes what it is going to be, or it dissolves and fades into nothingness: it is the point of resolution or dissolution or devolution. Right now Scotland is in this interesting condition, teetering on the cusp of beginning or ending, and I am a thousand miles away trying to find out which.

I drift away from the black and white certainty of the *Tribune*'s well-thumbed pages and towards my own frustration, anger and shame. I am secretly pleased that somewhere in the world there's a *Herald* that's keeping up the broadsheet end of the business, helping preserve Scotland in the wider world while we prevaricate over its future, if we allow it to have one. Self-loathing washes through me like the premonition of certain failure. This is the Scottish condition, and it would stop me from helping myself, and keep those who would otherwise help me at arms' length, if only I gave it license to rot from the inside out.

Charles Kennedy was right when he said that 'There is still a poverty of ambition at the heart of this government'. But then, we probably get the governments that we deserve.

TALKING IDENTITY

The Blair years, and those of Major and Thatcher before him, are punctuated by much talk of our 'cultural identity', and quite rightly so. The best description of 'culture' I have ever come across is 'social glue', the invisible stuff that binds society together in a special way that makes us unique and distinctive. Culture is not just about ballet and opera and 'high' culture. Culture is everything we do: how we work and play and what we believe in. Culture is part of our economy and our politics, our strategies and our plans for the future. Those aspects of our culture that we choose to display to outsiders colour their opinion of us and affects the regard in which we are held, which in turn influences our balance of trade and our economic growth.

In the past fifteen years I have attended dozens of international forums on the importance of cultural identity, in countries as far apart as China, Egypt, England, Finland, France, Korea, New Zealand, North America and Spain. I have discussed Scottish culture in contexts ranging from creativity in cold climates to furniture manufacturing, innovation, packaging design, alternative arts, food and drink, marketing, sport and education. All of the countries I have visited are searching for new perspectives on themselves that will help them and their product and service industries become more distinctive, desirable and competitive. The message is simple: in the global marketplace Culture equals Cash. In that same fifteen years I have only once participated in a similar international conference in Scotland, and on that one occasion the agenda was set by the London organisers.

It is not that I am peeved at not having been invited to a party, there simply was not a party to go to. Scotland has vast, unrealised cultural dimensions, but when it comes to working out how we use these positive aspects to our advantage we have no forum for their discussion. We do not invite international specialists to help us and we do not use our home grown experts either. Instead we subject ourselves to the kind of tartan and heather asset stripping that we would not tolerate from anyone else.

According the findings of The British Council's 2000 report, *Through Our Eyes 2: How the World sees the United Kingdom*, Scotland remains a land best known (where it is known at all) for its men in skirts.[1] Under pressure we undersell ourselves and opt for the lowest common denominator or the cheap one-liner because we have no plan to construct a more complex, valuable and modern image of Scotland abroad. Instead of promoting ourselves in any number of positive ways – as a teacher, healer or innovator – we create 'Scotland the Brand'. Which in a single brushstroke reduces Scotland to the same level as a tin of baked beans on a convenience store shelf. Without intelligent intervention Scotland will remain crystallised in a nineteenth century commercial script: a faded tartan pattern that is stuck on Marks & Spark's shortbread and Autumn Breaks for the over-fifties.

EXPLAINING SCOTLAND TO THE WORLD

When I am abroad I am from a place that may as well live only in my mind, or in the Brig o'Doon fantasy that persists in the minds of others, or from 'England'. So, when I should be selling my business, I take time to explain that Scotland is the part of the UK to the north of England. I do not do this because I am a rabid nationalist, but because it is unlikely that I will get business from someone who does not know where I am from. There are times when I feel I may just as well be from a remote village in the Amazon basin rather than from the culture that gave us the oldest English language newspaper, telephones and television. Why, with our excellent network of international Embassies and Councils do we still fail to explain our location and the status of our constituent parts? Probably for the same reason that many Americans believe English was their language first.

The *Through Our Eyes 2* report sought to establish current perceptions of Britishness from graduates and young professionals from seventeen countries, with damning results. Many of those interviewed believed that Britain occupied much the same dank corner of the nineteenth century as London smog, Royal Garden Parties and clotted cream teas. Most had heard of the four constituent parts of the UK (85% named England, 80% Scotland, 72% Northern Ireland and 67% Wales), but 'almost no one (only 5%) spontaneously thought that the United Kingdom was the same place as Great Britain' (p49) – which left me wondering what they thought about the British Council. What seemed obvious, not so much from the statistics but from the quotations of those interviewed, was that many confused 'Britain' with 'England'.

If you were from another place, you too might be forgiven for being confused about all this. As the Encyclopaedia Britannica states, 'The names United Kingdom, Britain and England are often confused, even by U.K. inhabitants'[2] (and Great Britain can also refer to the UK minus Northern Ireland). It is therefore not surprising that many people do not understand that Scotland is a nation in its own right, not merely a sub-set of England.

There can be little chance for Scotland to make itself truly known to the world if the old British Empire is allowed to continue its unnatural life. The name 'Britain' will continue to signify the past and the anachronistic, colonial values it represents, while all the time we mouth platitudes about equality, diversity and inclusion. Britain shames us all as well as allowing us to wallow in sickly Merchant Ivory sentimentalism when we should be getting on with the future of all of our Isles. Brits abroad are not an altogether positive force these days. Brits conjure images of insular ex pat communities and English football yobs. As the British Council Chairman David Green points out in his foreword to the Report, 'I am more concerned by the high proportion of young people who associate us British with an arrogant and condescending view of other countries. Anyone who watched, for instance, the scenes at Charleroi during Euro 2000 can easily understand how these perceptions arise'. Needless to say, I am not a Brit when I am abroad.

For now, Scotland remains a silent member of the foursome that makes up the United Kingdom. In law, Scotland may be an unresolved entity but it is a nation and therefore deserves an unequivocal name.

THE ABOLITION OF BRITAIN

There are many reasons I would get rid of 'Britain', not least of which is that it condemns Scotland to a living death on a dusty bookshelf in the British Tourist Authority shop off Trafalgar Square. But the simplest reasons are the best: that it is hard to do business with someone who does not have a name, and it is still harder if you have several names and keep changing them, because no one will trust you. If 'Britain' wasn't prefixed with 'Great' it would have dropped from use a long time ago.

However, meaningful change does not happen overnight. So instead of talking about Scotland 'going it alone' we need first of all to get rid of 'Britain', if only as a prelude to the materialisation of Scotland and the beginning of a structured and informed debate about the UK. Only after we have hacked our way through the years of undergrowth and neglect that have obscured 'Scotland' will we be in a position to see what Scotland really is, and what it might become within the UK, Europe and beyond.

While it is difficult to discuss Scotland and the UK when the names keep changing, it is impossible if there is no forum for discussion. Parliaments may be great places for politicians, press conferences and postcards but they are not where ideas actually happen: that is in the homes, offices, schools and colleges, factories, pubs and towns throughout our geographically challenging country.

What now seems like weeks ago I cast my postal vote, but not before I had wasted hours trawling the Internet and the telephone directory in search of an address for the Returning Officer in my Ward. For the country that has managed to produce Bell, Baird and bits of Lara Croft, eGovernment is not yet virtually a reality – this is a symptom of a much bigger problem.

Despite Scotland's creative and technological legacy, government cannot seem to arrange all of the bits in the right order. Content development, innovative science and technology, publishing and broadcasting should allow us to overcome the disadvantages of our geography and help to create a connected, proactive, informed forum for change. Instead we fund armies of middle managers to produce mountains of reports on 'broadband' and 'sectoral clusters' while the educational institutions and creative industries who can turn change to our advantage remain an undervalued and underused resource.

In the time it has taken us to construct part of our Parliament in stone and mortar we might have laid the foundations of a digital democracy that would have been the envy of everyone.

SCOTLAND THE BRAVE?

Having survived, and even flourished, in the industrial revolutions of the eighteenth and nineteenth centuries, Scotland could quite reasonably be expected to be hustling for a chance to exploit rich opportunities third time around. Uncharacteristically, Scotland the Brave is nowhere to be seen. Some would say that we have transcended our geography and are busy doing business, selling Scottish Power to the US or running banks in other countries. If this were really the case we would have integrated, modern systems of communication and transportation, and we would be much better off.

We are now in the midst of a third industrial revolution, which has come to pass more quickly than anyone but the writers of science fiction could have predicted. Having spent the last fifteen years running a 'design consultancy' I am now told that I actually run a 'creative industry'. It is funny but I had the feeling that something was up when phototypesetting disappeared overnight. My studio changed shape – out went typesetting rules, cow gum and line board, putty rubbers, registration marks, mark-ups and overlays. In the interior design part of our business, designers lost all but one of their drawing boards. Then Applemacs appeared, so we dismantled the process camera that had been craned into our studio and threw it in a skip – once it had been worth fifteen thousand pounds, but six months and one Applemac later, it was worth nothing. Today the place looks less cluttered. I use email, a mobile phone and a laptop that conspire to make me work in corners of my life I never knew existed.

I work for companies thousands of miles away, with people I have never met. We correspond digitally and I get paid electronically. I keep the core business slim, light, flexible and adaptable because I do not know what we will be doing tomorrow and neither does anyone else, including the government.

Why, when my life has changed so completely does the process of government still cling to monuments and wigs and a whole secular vocabulary of strange objects, words and rituals?

Speed, lightness and the ability to adapt to change are characteristics of this latest industrial revolution. In order to keep pace with progress, politicians, like businesses, must get closer to the aspirations and needs of the people they represent. In this Knowledge Revolution no Minister can hope to be master of their brief. They too must form partnerships with people and businesses that can broaden their knowledge and help them to take the decisions and risks that are a necessary part of keeping up with change. It is the quality of our knowledge, and our ability to creatively use it that will put Scotland in the driving seat of this new economy.

In the last year we seem to have lost our vision for the new Parliament. We, like it, have become heavy, weighed down by its gravity. But creativity, science and technology could deliver systems of communication that would allow us to pit our collective wits in designing our future in partnership with government, not in spite of it or in isolation from it. One thing is for sure, if Scotland is to progress, the people who lead it, and participate in every level of the political process, must become connected, decisive, fast and virtual too.

FOOTBALL AND THE HOLYROOD BUILDING: SYMBOLS OF SCOTTISH IDENTITY

Eventually I get to the best bit of the paper, the sports section on the back pages. I am never sure if sport is relegated to the rear because it is of lower value than the political news that hogs the front pages. I prefer to believe that they have saved the best for last in a final attempt to brighten the day with some worthwhile chat and pictures of healthy people.

Frankly, I have had enough of the post-electioneering. I am more interested in how Iain Macpherson does in Sunday's German World Supersport race, or whether Coulthard claims pole in the Canadian Grand Prix. In the absence of fast politics and real action nearer to home, Scots-born motorsport stars grab the attention of the press. They sustain our reputation for daring-do and cutting-edge technical innovation while we blindly await the arrival of our saviour in the shape of a latter-day Bruce. In Sweden, they ask me 'How is Larsson?' and 'How is your Parliament doing?' Mjallby (another Swedish national treasure who plays for Celtic) and Miralles (the Spanish architect of the Scottish Parliament) occupy the same compartment in the minds of educated Swedes. Both are world class players capable of making competitor nations a little envious, and more than a little nervous.

The *Herald* journalist William Tinning has astutely pointed out (in an article about the Californian Lottery) that the Scottish Parliament cost the same as four of the world's most expensive football players. That is not bad value for a building that will undoubtedly enter the international architectural premiership and last a great deal longer than the career of a football player. Our dexterity in culture and sport announce to the world that 'we've arrived', that we have progressed from a hand-to-mouth existence and have the spare time and cash to invest in seeking strategic alliances and business partners amongst those whose values and rituals complement our own.

Buildings and football, like music, dance and theatre are the corollary of nationhood. Not only do they help us appear distinctive and desirable in the global marketplace; they allow us to meet other countries in a civilised manner and on an equal footing. It is for this reason that 'culture' is the first and the last thing on the menu at every international summit. It is the starter and the dessert, the bread that holds the sandwich together, the metaphorical mayonnaise that binds society and stops it from falling apart.

Small countries such as Scotland have limited cash and must put their money where they are strongest to get the best value. Scotland has historical and international credibility when it comes to both football and architecture, but when we want to display our technological and scientific innovation we turn to David Coulthard, Colin Macrae and Jackie Stewart. Mastery of speed celebrates not just velocity and control but also the teamwork and partnerships that are an essential part of modern life and a precondition for business success. Motor sport is an area in which we excel and another wise choice when it comes to signalling our Scottish aspirations and values in the international arena.

Dario Franchitti, Niall Mackenzie and Neil Hyslop continue to grow in popularity abroad, but are known only by a tiny majority at home. Instead we collude with our most negative mythologies, and with the press, feeding our predilection for the pernicious and singular vision of the 'rags to riches' winner: and the stereotype that favours the individual and the 'privateer hero' over most of the rest of us. As a result we prefer to hide amongst our vast army of self-condemned losers rather than risk the ridicule of failure that, in other cultures, is best pals with success. Other countries have many more competitors and chances of winning, while in Scotland we have few winners and lots of losers.

Scotland is not really a team player: we do not like to compete unless we know we can win and that is not a good message for potential business partners. It is at times like this that I wish Jeremy Paxman would write a book about 'The Scots' in the hope that it would save us, and our most potent symbols, from ourselves.[3]

A BRIGHT NEW DAWN?: SCOTTISH IDEAS AND INNOVATION IN THE 'NEW' ECONOMY

Clive Gryner from the Design Council in London kicks the day off by showing an amazing image of a hi-tech silver bridge that's 'somewhere in Scotland between the Firth and the Clyde'. Only later does it dawn on me that this is Falkirk's Millennium Wheel on the Forth and Clyde Canal designed by Marks Barfield Architects. Clive then introduces the work of the Design Council – a Westminster-funded machine with an annual budget of £ 8.7 million.[4] The Design Council works to transform attitudes to creativity and innovation in government, business and education throughout England and Wales, and they also promote UK innovation abroad. If we have a similar organisation in Scotland, I have not yet discovered it, although, thankfully, The Lighthouse, our long overdue Centre for Architecture, Design and the City, champions Scottish creative industries, ensuring that we are represented abroad.

Other speakers at the event include Peter Horbury, who is Head of Design at Volvo in Sweden, who tells me he is originally from Renfrew, and Carol Moore, an American expert in new technologies with IBM Global Services in Amsterdam. Carol knows a colleague of mine, Julie Tierney (who is also from Renfrew). Julie is a product designer with IBM who graduated from Glasgow School of Art in the early 1990s. Since IBM closed their Design Centre in Greenock (which once created and manufactured more computer monitors than any other company in the world) she has based herself at their facility in Raleigh,

South Carolina. Her international reputation is considerable and her products counted in millions of units, and millions of dollars.

For me, this ninth of June is just as depressingly familiar as it was ten, or even fifteen years ago. The day does not herald a bright new dawn and a golden second opportunity to finally get things right in Scotland. The products and the people may be different but the problems are just the same. It is just another great exhibition with lots of good ideas. Some are in production, but too many products and technologies are prototypes not yet fully developed, protected, licensed, manufactured or commercially exploited.

I have known the designers of some of the products on exhibition since they were students. Hamid van Koten and Ian Carnduff formed VK&C who designed and subcontracted the production of their multiple award-winning recycled paper lighting to a Scottish company. There's One Foot Tall founded by Katarina Barac and Will White. They won the coveted Peugeot Design Award at the Milan Fair for their rotationally moulded Chasm chair, which was manufactured by a company in East Kilbride. After several years in business Will White has left One Foot Taller to gain experience in plastics manufacturing that might move the company forward. Ian Carnduff is now in the USA, taking a break from his business and earning some decent cash. I hope they come back, but the sad thing is they are not the only ones.

The economic and social potential of Millennium Products is limited by our inability to exploit our would-be winners. We invest in the education of amazing people with great ideas, but we have no strategy to support them or their businesses as they progress. We have no infrastructure, no vision, no management skill or experience to pass on to them. We even fail to help people convert their ideas into intellectual property: the core asset and currency in the new economy.

Scotland simply does not see the bigger picture: the need for infrastructure and the partnerships that can deliver it; and the need for the mentoring, development and investment that will strengthen our hand. We often cannot tell the difference between riches and rubbish. We also confuse 'money' with 'means' not realising that cash is not always the solution. We have got plenty of cash: half a billion in Scottish Enterprise alone. What we lack is the means to put our cash to good use, and the will to ask others to help us.

In this third industrial upheaval, creativity is our greatest natural resource, our primary industry and our richest national asset. Our history clearly shows us that it only takes one good person to start a revolution. It therefore makes sense to play tai chi, not with 'theoretical sectors' but with the creative individuals and institutions that can help us live up to our greatest myth, that of Scottish innovation.

REINVENTING OURSELVES

At a time when green issues, small countries and cities, unspoiled land-scape and quality-of-life are viewed as advantages, why are we still losing jobs, investment, our best people, our international presence and our credibility? Why are all of these things that mark our country as a probable winner in this third millennium not exploited by our politicians, who continue to argue in analogue while the rest of the world deals in digital?

As every business undergraduate knows, in order to make the most of change and the opportunities it creates you must first of all know who you are, your strengths and weaknesses. If our future depends on creativity, broadcasting, publishing and new media technologies, we need Ministers who can focus on these issues and get the job done.

How, when the world has changed so completely, have we failed to change the methods and manifestations of government? What hope do we have of inhabiting the modern era or of making tomorrow's politics relevant for young people if we still have 'Ministers', 'Lords', 'Chancellors', 'Chambers' and a feudal confection of archaic barriers to understanding, inclusion and progress?

Instead of seizing the opportunity to modernise government, we appear to have crammed Scotland's unique characteristics into a proprietary structure of departments, offices, ministries and agencies, as if one size fitted every country, hot, cold, large or small. We are coasting along on autopilot; going through the motions and rituals of government in much the same way as we have done for hundreds of years, in a place four hundred miles away.

Through this transplanted, and often anachronistic, system we continue to perpetrate our own brand of repression on ourselves, ensuring that we have our age-old excuses for our poor performance, and someone else on which to pin the blame.

It is not every day that a country is given the chance to reinvent itself, but as Westminster slackened our moorings, devolution, far from launching us into a bright new future, has merely allowed us to discover what we have become, which is probably much the same as we were in 1707.

We must break away from our old habits, have the courage to change our behaviour, invent new and relevant rituals and fast forward three hundred years.

For the time being let us forget about Scottish independence. We do not yet know who we are. We have not decided what to believe in, so we are not sure what to throw away and what to keep and value. Only when we have managed to pick the diamonds from the dross will be able to show the world what they have been missing. An Argentinean interviewee summed up the differences in this small group of islands off the coast of Europe:

> The British are one thing and the Scottish and Welsh another, and let's not even talk about the Irish. There are marked differences; in fact, the Scottish are really nice, but it's hard to understand them.[5]

NOTES

1. R. Ratcliffe, *Through Our Eyes 2: How the World sees the United Kingdom*, London: The British Council, 2000.
2. For an Irish perspective on the UK's misunderstanding of itself see J. Coakley and K. Howard, 'Transforming the United Kingdom: The View from Dublin', *Soundings* No. 18, Summer/Autumn 2001, pp184-97. Coakley and Howard point out that the UK is known internationally across a range of forums by the initials GB rather than UK, the world of sport and athletics being an example, while internet domain names are one of the few areas where the initials UK are used.
3. See J. Paxman, *The English: A Portrait of a People*, London: Michael Joseph 1998.
4. Design Council, *Design Council Annual Review 2000*, London: Design Council 2000, p21.
5. *Through Our Eyes 2, op. cit.*, p49.

Disorientations from Down Under: the Old Country in retrospect

TOM NAIRN

Down, down, down. Would the fall *never* come to an end? 'I wonder how many miles I've fallen by this time?' she said aloud ... 'I wonder if I shall fall right *through* the earth! How funny it'll seem to come out among the people that walk with their heads downwards! The Antipathies, I think.

Alice's Adventures in Wonderland[1]

THROUGH THE AUSTRAL GLASS

Everyone arriving in Australia from over the Equator knows the seasons are different – leaving Spring to discover Autumn, and so on. That much is discounted in advance (and is actually quite easy to get used to). But there are deeper levels of disturbance as well, often left unmentioned (perhaps because they are harder to pin down). Regular jet-plane travel has made East-West 'lag' familiar, and accustomed travellers to the idea of the 'body clock'. However, what is far harder to accept is the upset of the body compass. The sun tells you each morning that south has become north and (therefore) that the felt east has turned into the west, and vice versa. As if this were not enough, another sort of disorientation sets in as you leave the airport. Reading the newspapers in the taxi into town, well-known labels show up, like 'the Labour Party', 'the Liberals', 'asylum-seekers', and bothersome 'switch voters' in 'marginal constituencies'.[2] The trouble is, they mean something intensely different, and surface familiarity merely renders that difference all the greater; it is a quite alien state and social fabric that is deploying such counters (though frequently beneath a camouflage of mythic affiliation or descent).

Another unexpected side-effect of this *dépaysement* can be disruption of retrospect. One's own past suddenly feels odd as well. Whole tracts of it seem questionable, even amazing. This effect is particularly powerful in looking back at the United Kingdom general election of 2001, held a few months before the Australian election.[3] From Melbourne, the entire episode now feels like a Lewis Carroll dream. Were such events possible? I mean, can there actually *be* in that other world such a country as the one variously billed as 'Britain', 'Great Britain' or 'The "United Kingdom" of this and that', where around 20 to 25 per cent of the population restored Sovereign Power to the White Rabbit Anthony Blair *with an overwhelming majority*? Where Her Majesty's Opposition then did him the favour of scuttling away down three different rabbit-holes simultaneously, thus awarding him a decade or so of office *after* his present one expires? Where history has fallen down from tragedy, and passed far beyond farce into realms of previously unknown abasement?

THE VANISHING CONSTITUTION

The place to begin a journey to explore these mysteries is the election results map, as published by the BBC on 8 June 2001. This dramatic document followed on from its main 'Vote 2001' page, headed 'The Vote That Never Was: A Labour Landslide and the Tory Leader Resigns'. *So, no change there then.* That same page bore no less than four images of the toothily grinning Blair, in one of which he is kissing a baby (his own), alongside the astonishing statistics of triumphalism: 'Lab 413; Con 166; LibDem 52; others scarcely visible'. The results map which followed had the conventional colours, red for New Labour, blue for the Conservatives, and assorted shades of green or yellow for the Liberal-Democrats, Sinn Fein, etc. But a glance at this showed a picture wildly at variance with the BBC's official complacency – in fact, it showed a picture nobody would have dreamed of ten years ago.

There is just one Tory-blue patch outside England, in the area of Southwest Scotland (the constituency of Galloway and Upper Nithsdale). This was described by the BBC as 'the most agricultural constituency in the British Isles', and also the one worst affected by the foot-and-mouth epidemic which accompanied the election campaign like a howling Greek chorus. Resentment at government mishandling of the crisis, plus some feuding in the ranks of the Scottish National Party, gave Peter Duncan a 74-vote Conservative majority over his SNP opponent. But this was universally viewed as an unrepeatable accident, even by Conservatives.[4] It was that rare event, an exception which actually proved a rule – the rule here being that British Conservatism has abandoned (or been abandoned by) the peripheral countries of the United Kingdom. The initial desertion took place in 1997, and 2001 simply confirmed it. Nobody now expects it to be reversed.

The former 'natural ruling party' of Great Britain has given up, in other words. Toryism in that old sense is extinct in Scotland and Wales, as well as being on the retreat in England.⁵ (Of course it was never present in Northern Ireland, but I will come back to that later.) What's more, I cannot resist drawing attention to another normally overlooked internal frontier of the Old Country: the Tamar River separating Devon from Cornwall. This part of the UK is now also 'Tory-free', and thus part of the Celtic-affiliated common trend.

However, the 'red' of New Labour still pervades throughout the country (except in Ulster). This is what now holds the United Kingdom together. The land of the White Rabbit depends upon the Crown and a single political party – that manic grin again and its *overwhelming* majority. But what of the British Constitution? Surely the indestructible fabric still stands, unaffected by the eddies and accidents of mere parties? Well ... no, it does not. What fabric there was has quietly gone into the dark, for reasons I will go on to explain. All that remains of it is the toothy smile of Lewis Carroll's Cheshire Cat – the grin which hung round in the air long after the actual animal had vanished. 'The Cat vanished quite slowly, beginning with the tail, and ending with the grin', wrote Carroll: '... wasn't that a curious thing, a Grin without any Cat? Would you like to see one?' British voters see one all the time now – it appeared, for instance, in an extraordinary war dance at the 2001 Labour Party Annual Conference (shortly after a declaration of war on Afghanistan and, more ambitiously, on terrorism and – in Blair's 2001 conference speech – on world hunger, hardship and general badness).

The British Constitution was only a virtual Rock of Ages. Its true being consisted in the belief of its worshippers, and the way they acted out such convictions. Its chief boast was that it did not need to exist in any vulgar, modern sense – written down for the rabble to peruse. No, it was simply the agreed power structure, carried forward by 'conventions' and the profoundly shared attitudes of a class-structured 'system' – carried forward,⁶ and then, in the nineteenth century, crystallised as world-empire. These shared assumptions covered all the territories involved, and were consecrated by the Crown – enabling different parties and policies to succeed one another by tacit agreement rather than formal 'holy writ'.

But there is a downside to this system, heavily underlined by the recent UK election. Once the shared psyche and 'conventions' evaporate, *there is nothing left*. From that bourne, no traveller will return indeed. The cat can never come back to retrieve his smile. All that the great repositories of Statehood then do is *pretend* that he has not really gone – 'put on a show' as it were. That is what 'Blairism' mostly is. Its

British 'Third Way' is pantomime smoke and strobe-lights, designed to bolster audience conviction and keep them in their seats for as many repeat performances as may yet be possible. The non-written 'system' depended upon *the system*: in truth, that is, an actually working two-or-more party-and-policy continuum capable of alternation, and embracing the whole turf. Without that embrace, the sole remaining continuum is just New Labour's increasingly hysterical one-party performance, with the Crown wobbling uneasily on top of it.

As time passes, this performance has to be constantly intensified – it demands ever more primary colours and tabloid decibels. Reckless populism becomes its substitute for both democracy and reform. Thus the Millennium Dome 'tent' at Greenwich was a mega-circus meant to hammer home all-British rejuvenation and conviction. However, it proved the most expensive flop in entertainment history, largely because (most commentators agreed) it was impossible to think up suitable 'content' for the display. The wellspring of Britishness was exhausted, and nothing worthy could be found to install under the great common roof. Such a failure should have brought the common government down. But instead, the guilty party was awarded a land-slide election victory. How was this possible?

THE NON-VOTING PARTY

It was possible because the non-Will of the People prevailed. Society had, in the interval, resigned from the political State. There had already been ominous signs of growing indifference in the 1997 election, when only 28.6 per cent of the enfranchised had supported New Labour. This was a mere two points behind what David Mackie has called 'the Non-Voting Party'.[7] But as the 2001 election approached, Mackie was predicting that the Non-Voting Party might be set for its best result ever. Never was prophecy so quickly borne out. The NVP won a sensational 15 per cent victory over its New Labour opponents: 40 per cent as against 25 per cent. It had been widely feared that participation might slump down from the seventies into the lower sixties; in fact it fell to 59 per cent – clearly within sight of current US norms.[8] By 2005, if present trends continue, the UK will quite clearly be leading the West in apathy.[9]

I will spare readers any references to post-modern and other *Zeitgeist* alibis about this phenomenon. It goes without saying that the profound conceit of New Labourism found no culprit other than the universal decay of Western culture, and the shifting sands of globalisa-tion. It was simply inconceivable that such a lapse might be due to the blinkered, parochial ineptitude of one particular out-of-date state struggling to survive – to remain its grand and integral self, as it were, with the maximum of flourishes and a minimum of changes. Blairite blabbering about their 'revolution' has been a way of avoiding the constitutional changes which could have had the effect of normalising Great Britain, of making changes that acknowledged contemporary realities; these would not have constituted a 'revolution' exactly, but would have involved a number of quite mundane modernising reforms. But this is what no true Westminster junkie can stand: being reduced to the ranks of the ordinary, the unexceptional, those abandoned by a deity whose attention has been unfairly (but permanently) distracted elsewhere.

Historically, United Kingdom identity has rested upon a purloined Hebraic confidence in 'Providence' – that sense of occupying a central throne as Heaven's chosen ones. The subsequent passage from the ranks of Elect to those of the un-Chosen has been, subjectively speaking, a terrible experience. Divine meaning snatched away is the bitterest of medicines – in some ways possibly worse than military and political defeat. The losers of World War Two reinvented themselves as the non-imperial principals of a great recovery. But for a state elite facing *cosmic* demotion such ruptures have no appeal: better to hang on to the greatness one has, or to try and refloat it by association with a successor Elect like the USA.

FOR WORSE, FOR BETTER: THE SELLING OF BRITLAND

Surely (some will object) Great Britain plc cannot be doing all *that* badly? Government PR regularly offers glowing tableaux of a prospering and forward-looking country. Beset by problems, of course – like the rural apocalypse of foot-and-mouth, the failures of the National Health Service, or the near-collapse of the national rail network – yet simultaneously striving to improve things, and not wholly without success?

The objection is quite justified. The publicists of Britland should be accused of exaggeration, rather than outright mendacity. The real trouble is that they are talking about something quite different. What they normally choose to depict is the progress of United Kingdom *society*, rather than the downfall of its *state*. The latter goes on being 'taken for granted', and is deemed immutable. However, the stories of society and state have now become not simply different, but widely divergent.

British 'civil society' (a convenient shorthand) has indeed been prospering in the circumstances of post-cold-war globalisation – albeit very unevenly, chaotically and with pathological side effects. (But then, such contradictions are standard. Free-trade capitalism was ever thus. It was immortally described that way in a great poem of 1848, *The*

Communist Manifesto.) Thus a Southeast England survey in 2001 showed people on the whole rather cheerful about their prospects and looking forward to better times 'for me and my family'.[10] But the survey also indicated that the same people were quite indifferent to 'politics' in any broader or ideological sense, and if anything hostile to, or cynical about, leadership and state. It depicted a population severed from the ruling class of former times, rather than 'liberated' from it – if liberation is taken to mean a new start, or a more representative or democratic replacement. 'They' had disappeared, and (like Mrs Thatcher) nobody wanted them back. The controlling caste has vanished. Yet only self-serving poltroons and chancers seem to have stepped into their shoes – and somehow nothing could be done about this. New Labour self-servers were merely less corrupt (as yet) than their predecessors – the implication being that such was the way of all political flesh, curable only by some future popular mutiny, or rejection-shock (i.e. not by political reform, let alone 'revolution').

Thus, things getting better at an individual or atomised level serves to reinforce their getting steadily worse – I would argue, incurably worse – at the Alice-in-Wonderland level of Her Majesty, Black Rod, the House of Lords and the Mother of Parliaments. The 2001 election was a new low in this disintegrative process. The existing electoral system, a first-past-the-post conjuring trick, now functions like a wedge splitting off the social order from a genuinely decadent state elite. The latter's decadence comes not simply from failure, or from the series of disasters that have shaken the British realm over the last decade. It is rooted in the impossibility of that realm's embedded will and enduring purpose.

However, do not take my word for this. Take Tony Blair's. When he got back to London from the Nice Conference of the European Union at the end of 2000, he reported to Parliament:

> It is possible, in our judgement, to fight Britain's corner, get the best out of Europe for Britain and exercise real authority and influence in Europe. That is as it should be. Britain is a world power. To stand aside from the key alliance – the EU – right on our doorstep, is not advancing Britain's interests; it is betraying British interests …[11]

Greatness is all. For a world power, making use of Europe is a necessity, but remains one tool among others. There is no question of joining in the sense of merging, or identifying the national interest with such a wider project. No question (that is) of being like the Danes, the Irish, the Portuguese, the Italians or the Scots (forever whinging about 'Scotland in Europe'). Different standards apply. But, again, do not take my analysis for it. The *Economist*, that most unbending critic of Blairism, commented two days after the vote:

> Mr. Blair is no 'declinist'. He believes that Britain can lead in Europe, not just take its place as a loyal member ... He does not accept that leading in Europe implies weakening Britain's bond with America. He argues that Britain has a 'pivotal' role in world politics (and) Mr. Blair relishes cutting a dash on the world scene.[12]

'Declinism' is old hat – the long period of ill-managed retreat and graceless withdrawal from the 1950s to the late 1970s. Mrs Thatcher put a stop to that in 1979. The 'Great' was drummed back into Britain again, by a combination of neo-liberal economics and iron determination: decline gave way to outright redemption. Soon, the formula appeared to be confirmed by the foundering of the Soviet imperium and the misfortunes of social democracy in the West. British 'redemptionism' gained impetus in the early years of globalisation, and won over Labour completely when Tony Blair became leader in 1994.

The problem is that decline-management *was* a possible strategy, though profoundly uninspiring; and making a political break, building a reformed UK system, federal or confederal, might also have been possible, albeit difficult. But redemption is not possible at all – or at least, it is possible solely on a basis of pretence and increasingly absurd assertiveness, or of self-important servility towards a helpful outside force. There is no real way in which 'Great' can be re-enacted or maintained, or even convincingly displayed (as the Dome farce revealed). On the other hand, the inherited institutional structures of the state can still *prevent* changes from taking place. This is what Westminster politics is now about – and what the 2001 election was about. Triumphalist Immobilism is the *Leitmotif* of end-game Britain.

IMMOBILISM AT WORK: LIVING IN LATE BRITAIN

The laws of redemptory Immobilism work like this. (Here I am merely recapitulating long and sobering analyses made by academics such as Jim Bulpitt and others.[13]) The 1688-1832 state was an aristocratic creation devoted, like the Venetian oligarchy of early-modern times, to the exploitation and supervision of a sprawling commercial empire. It evolved a two-party 'electoral dictatorship' which valued centralised stability above all else. There was no other way of controlling the disparate, sometimes centrifugal, elements of such a ragbag enterprise. The home archipelago was disparate enough, and as the maritime imperium swelled in the nineteenth century a formidable institutional core became both consort and controller – the world conceit of the

Imperial Crown, and of Blair's present-day determination to preserve its 'pivotal' role.

As Paul Kennedy's chronicle *The Rise and Fall of the Great Powers* shows, no other former world-power has ever been able to withstand defeat or revolution (or both).[14] But Great Britain was spared this standard fate by its 'finest hour' in 1940.[15] However, escaping that fate has invited another and less spectacular one, which Kennedy does not encompass. It has produced the tragi-comic parameters of a sole survivor – an albatross-state forever unwilling to settle for life as a coastal sea-gull. One should also keep in mind how strong are the self-reproducing traditions of such an institutional or 'civic' nationalism. It may be that in some sense such traditions are always 'compensating' for the absence of British ethnicity; but in that case, the implication must be that civic-political identity, at least in some places and over important periods of time, may be understood as being more powerful than the ethnic variety.

Post-1979 Britain shows a power-system bent on re-modelling society, in order to preserve or reconstruct such an inherited 'identity'. This project (which of course became Blair's self-conscious 'Project' in 1997) may be hopeless in the longer term, but it still keeps going today for a number of important reasons. One of these is economic. Most arguments about late Britain have concentrated on neo-liberal economics, and the acceptance by New Labour of Mrs Thatcher's de-regulatory programmes of the 1980s. Though justified in its own right, this focus has also served to divert attention from the *national* conjuncture involved. One particular – indeed genuinely unique – state problem was at least temporarily resolved by Thatcher's resolve to swim so strongly with the tide of resurgent post-cold-war capitalism. She was quite right to see 'there was no alternative' to this – and Blair in his turn had to accept and even hype up the only show in town.

The only show (that is) for this threatened polity. The initial decade of globalisation generated plenty of alternatives elsewhere – in Scandinavia, for example, or in Ireland. Smaller democratic countries almost immediately benefited from the great thaw, and their souls as well as their budgets were the better for it. At the same time, the European Union (essentially a co-operative of such nobodies) prepared for longer-term advance with a common currency. But not Great Britain. The latter retained the main economic armature of its former imperium, in the form of the City of London, whose institutions of trade and exchange had in the 1970s managed a somewhat lumpy transition from the Keynesian welfare state to globalisation. The umbilical cord had been strained but not broken. And then, in the 1980s and 1990s, the City found new prosperity in a recreated free trade universe.

The United Kingdom state had never depended upon industrial leadership, let alone 'supremacy'. Its continuity lay with the pre-existent 'globalism' of finance and trans-oceanic exchange – a fabric which of course was now flourishing as never before, and has provided the lifeline for British state continuity.

Certainly, a transition of elites took place within that development, from aristocracy to the present stratum of exchange-billionaires, mediocrats, ennobled pundits, and duly-rewarded civil servants and generals. But this change was largely favourable to the preservation of the archaic state and all its trappings. Only industrial capitalism had ever been guilty of democracy and conspiracy with the plebs. By contrast, financial capital was either tolerant of or positively favourable to the pomp and circumstance of Monarchy, populist pantomimes and pageantry-politics. It was awfully keen on the Millennium Dome, for example, and cruelly disappointed by its unexpected failure and abandonment. It is 'outward-looking', since this is where its business interests lie – and hence quite well disposed to outward-posturing, and to all-purpose-busybody governments pretending to be pivots. For an exchange-nexus, 'Great' just means being everywhere at once, and having a right to have its finger in every pie. Occasionally attired these days as 'cosmopolitanism', the essence of Britishness lies in being far too big for tiresomely national boots. But that has suited the new, globally-adapted south-eastern England quite well. The City always detested 'little England'; now its hegemony has acquired the splendid post-imperial costumes of globalisation, as well as a New party of political servitors.

SOVEREIGNTY: THE IRON LUNG
The preservation of 'sovereignty' is crucial for the servicing of this system. And this implies reliably vast majorities. Which entails keeping the lethal 'first-past-the-post' election system. This alone can conjure crushing majorities from shrinking minorities of voters, and thereby guarantee onirically decisive authority: no fudging and fumbling coalition would have a hope of redeeming the British day and securing Greatness. Democracy would have it by the throat in no time. This is why the object of late-British constitutional reform is to prevent constitutional reform. Blairite 'modernisation' has aimed at tidying up the inherited anachronisms of both government and state, the better to conserve them. It aims to replace the old blue-blood House of Lords with a new 'appointed' House of Lords: aristocracy reborn as cronyism. New Labour is also keen to see Prince Charles installed as the new-century Monarch, one capable of finally dispelling Republicanism. Thus the ancient Unwritten, customary order will continue indefinitely, without tiresome disturbance of the British iden-

tity ('all we hold dear', etc). The 2001 election was an outstanding victory for this campaign of systemic obfuscation and reaction.

Twenty-three years ago, the late Lord Hailsham suggested that Britain was becoming an 'elective dictatorship'.[16] Party rule had turned into Cabinet rule, which then mutated into dominance by the Leader. Elections would be transformed into referendums, staged by Leadership whim, at which the people would periodically renew its prostration – whether eagerly or sullenly did not matter very much. The *effective* electorate would shrink to the small number of 'floating voters' who had to be cajoled or bullied into casting their ballots, thus maintaining the credentials of the Mother of Democracy. If most voters abstained from that honour, it would be a pity, but not fatal. If people were not bothered about 'politics', it could only be because they were content with their lot. And this was, in fact, the most widely pronounced verdict on Britain's non-voters of June 2001: a perverted idea of 'the politics of contentment'.

These rules of the redemption-polity are of course self-perpetuating. Simple-majority voting supports a two-party order, which makes it practically impossible for new or third movements to muscle in, which in turn reinforces the two-party order. Voter-fatalism intensifies, as does acceptance of the 'regime' and its stay-as-we-are political identity. Elections become periodic reaffirmations of the faith, and proofs of the futility of constitutional reform. In this quaint Ukanian version of the 'end of history', only egg-headed fanatics fail to see that Britishness is forever, in the best of all possible worlds.

Society will go on changing, naturally, and this is why think tanks have replaced stately homes as the shrines of British *mentalité*. Mrs Thatcher discovered the things, and Blair has elevated them into a clerisy. Their task is to generate smart *policies* that will ensure painless change (painless to the state, naturally). Who would deny that politics has to be about policies? But what the politics of immobilism encourages is the *fetishisation* of policy-making, as utterly brilliant ways of going round in neo-liberal circles and 'delivering' the minimum of alteration needed to stay out of trouble, with the maximum of profit for whoever assists 'the Project'.[17] Westminster has a practically bottomless wardrobe of stuff to help with these charades: David Hume's waistcoat, Edmund Burke's breeches, W.E. Gladstone's old watch, Churchill's finest-hour hat, etc – all regularly deployed whenever the New falters or starts to rub off.

GREAT STATE, TROUBLESOME PEOPLE

If we return once more to the 2001 election results map, a somewhat broader interpretation now seems in order. The old Westminster system has effectively withdrawn from the periphery of devolved government, in Scotland, Wales and Northern Ireland. But the hidden third dimension of the map is that, simultaneously, its multinational state order has become 'hollowed out' in England as well; less than a quarter of the electorate supported the 'winning party' and government. Now add on a fourth dimension: by these indications, in 2005 or 2010 landslide-style victories could result from the ballots of a fifth or even less of eligible voters, with results even more like the Mad Hatter's tea-party in *Alice*.

Closer scrutiny of the results map will also show that the still-serried ranks of English blue are not what they seem. They increasingly represent EU-subsidised fields, not people. Surveys like Anthony Seldon's *The Blair Effect* have made clear how strongly the existing system now favours urban constituencies.[18] Demographic movements mean that it takes fewer votes to put in a New Labourite than a Conservative.[19] At the same time, suburbs formerly 'staunchly Tory' have gravitated over to Blairism, above all in the resurgent South. The abysmal performance of the Conservative Party in the 2001 election expressed a tidal movement pushing Toryism back into 'the Shires' – a patchwork of depleted rural provinces, smaller towns and half-ruined industries. It would be serious enough if Conservatism had become 'an English party', as so many have said since 1997. The fact is, it shows signs of becoming the party of non-metropolitan England – a far more serious fate.

Just how serious was demonstrated in the election aftermath. The standard reaction would have been for Tories to 'rally round' a successor Leader who looked capable of bearing Mrs Thatcher's redemptionist mantle – that is, somebody who could be ready by 2005 or 2010 with a plausible 'alternative' scenario, appropriate think-tank artillery, new European alibis, ingratiating visits to court in Washington, and a reasonable number of new money-bags in tow. There was even a plausible candidate to hand, in Michael Portillo. But it all went hopelessly wrong. Feeling the rug being tugged from beneath their feet, the Shire Tories insisted on having one of their own sort, a ramrod-backed military gent.[20] As the American Republican journalist Hans Nichols noted:

> At a Duncan Smith meeting in Harrogate, a former MP joked: 'If you spot anyone under the age of 40, you'll know they've come to the wrong place.' Of course, he wasn't really joking, because the average age of a dues-paying Tory is 65. Like most of its members, the Tories are on the brink of extinction.[21]

Probably nobody in Scotland or Wales would have supported any new Tory Leader, whoever he was; but it is now plain that almost nobody south of Watford or east of Reading will support this character either. The 'middle ground' in the Tory Party has been not so much lost as fled from, in pursuit of yesterday. Thus 'Middle England' is no longer what it was – and again, in ways not visible on the Westminster results diagram.

The dilemma of 'non-metropolitan' England lies in the way that the metropolis has itself changed. Since Mrs Thatcher won office a generation ago, London has evolved into a cosmopolis. The 2001 census will probably show around a third of its population as comparatively recent immigrants. A veritable deluge of incomers overtook both it and its adjacent area in the 1990s, generating the largest 'black economy' in Europe alongside the City's refashioned prosperity. The successes of Thatcherism had reconfigured England, in fact, at the same time as they completed the destruction of the old ruling elite. Both of these big changes were quite unintended, and completely irreversible – and largely explain both the force and the probable longevity of Blairism.

'England' has become the place you have to get across, in order to reach London: DuncanSmith-land, as it were, where time has stopped and the clocks now run backwards.[22] In her *Nationalism: Five Roads to Modernity*, Liah Greenfeld sees England as the original forge of the nation-state, the template of modernity.[23] But fate is now turning heroic origins into a zone of indeterminacy, the *terrain vague* of an identity partly lost to Empire and now further drained by the southeastern city-polity – possessed by its own 'great wen'. Again, no-one should read condemnation into this judgement: I remember London as it still was in the 1960s – the capital of England, and theatre of the mercifully brief efflorescence of Powellite Anglo-nationalism. Each time I disembark these days, I feel grateful for the transformation. But at the same time, the structural dilemmas posed by such a shift must be recognised.

Referring to the recent work of the great Canadian urbanologist Jane Jacobs, Kevin Pask points out how theory has 'increasingly turned to the idea of the nation as defined by a single metropole', with the accompanying presumption that:

> ... the nation is a unit of metropole and periphery, the former now thoroughly dominating the latter. Each great city requires its own hinterland (already a stunning demotion of the 'heartland' of classical nationalism) and the nation becomes the city-state writ large ...[24]

Post-1988 globalisation has undoubtedly reinforced this trend, just as it has promoted the emergence of nations, and the formation of regional alliances or groupings of states. Capitalist expansion in the nineteenth and twentieth centuries resulted in the creation of protective breakwaters – primarily, as Pask suggests, those of ethnic or 'heartland' nationalism. Today, the breakwaters are more varied, and even less predictable in their effects.

For nations to become 'city-states writ large' may work in a few cases; but there are some nations incapable of following this route, and England is one of them. There was never the smallest chance of Britain becoming a 'hinterland' of the South-East; but we must remember that 'England' represents about 85 per cent of Britain, and contains several other vast conurbations, like Manchester, Merseyside and (above all) the post-industrial valleys of the Tyne and the Wear, around Newcastle. These are in the long run more likely to become European competitors than appendages of any Southern 'city-state'. But they are currently prevented from finding political voice by the Westminster counter-revolution – the mummy-case of the Windsor Monarchy, and the ceaseless parade of Great-Power pretensions. In typically sleekit style, the Blairite bauble-bearers have taken to half-advocating 'regional assemblies' for these left-behind indigenes of the North, secure in the knowledge of how weak 'popular demand' for such bodies is likely to be. As they smugly point out, strong regional government 'has never been a feature' of historic England.

Well, *of course* demand for this, as for other, constitutional changes is weak. It is kept weak by the system, and its metropolitan media carpet-bombers. This is the essence of the Britannic palsy: a system just democratic enough to prevent farther democratisation, while laying it on thick about its own superiority. The Unwritten Constitution remains sacrosanct, to prevent or constrain the release of new voices – both class and territorial – that should be the normal accompaniment of a rapidly developing civil society. But here the whole point is to keep 'normal' at bay. Like the Thatcherites who pioneered the Redemptionist Way, Blairites believe that Britain already has as much democracy as is good for it. We have already seen how the fact that over half the population had given up on politics was presented after the 2001 election as a proof of this wisdom. The people were too happy to be bothered voting. Furthermore, repoliticising them is seen as simply leading to trouble – as it did in Wales and then in London.

The growing divide between society and state that I referred to earlier has this consequence. State-fostered populism generates a society which abstains from voting responsibly, and becomes capable only of mutiny. Mutiny against the Poll Tax destroyed Thatcher. The Welsh would not have a perfectly sound (but Centre-inspired) candidate imposed upon them. Londoners rebelled against New Labour and clamoured for an actually popular candidate who then had to leave the Party to get elected. In the 2000 'fuel protests', the regime was twice paralysed by inexplicably popular movements against properly sanctioned tax increases. The 2001 election campaign itself was shaken by ugly 'race riots' in non-metropolitan badlands, where natives and incomers alike demonstrated total mistrust of state intentions and parties. The people are a bad lot: in fact, many of them may soon be as deserving of transportation as they were back in 1788.

A POLYGRAPH OF DISINTEGRATION

It follows that the break-up process is more many-sided and unforeseeable than appears from the election results map. 'Devolution' is only the most visible part of it. It is widely believed abroad that New Labour 'gave' Home Rule to Scotland, Home representation to Wales, and then a new consociational government to Northern Ireland. Well, this is correct; but the term 'gave' hides an unusual number of ambiguities.

Extensive regime blarney was devoted at that time to the virtues of wise decentralisation and healthy local government – as if British Socialism had always longed for these things, but (alas) had been unable to do anything about them when previously in power. But a more accurate reading of the 1997 runes would be that by 1997 it was no longer possible to escape from doing *something* about all three parts of its domain. Blair's incoming administration owed important debts to the Scottish and Welsh battalions of his party.[25] Mafias take debts seriously. It was those soldiers who had enabled it to survive the humiliating defeats of the 1980s. But the same provincial cadres had simultaneously been battling against advancing nationalist movements in their own countries. They understood that some concessions were now needed to help them (as they hoped) win such wars. And movement in a Home Rule direction was the very least they would settle for. This was both aided and complicated by the figure and persona of Gordon Brown, co-architect with Blair of New Labour, and head chieftain of the clan known as the 'Brownites'. The Scottish part of this saw Scottish Labour as its own fiefdom, promoted devolution from a very Westminster world-view and articulated a narrow, antagonistic idea of British unionism.[26]

In Ireland the situation was simpler: Blair was pursuing a strategy begun even before Thatcher's time, and continued by the Conservatives over the 1980s and 1990s. This was for an agreement with the Irish Republic on cautious disengagement, accompanied by a consociational (or cross-community) government in Ulster. Quite reasonably, all Westminster governments have calculated that a successful and peaceful withdrawal would enhance Britain's international standing, while a civil war and forced retreat would seriously damage it. Blair and his then Foreign Secretary Robin Cook thought that a new drive was needed to implement this strategy. And the result was the Belfast Agreement of 1998 – Northern Ireland's 'peace process'.

These 'devolutionary' initiatives are now, however, in wild disarray – a disarray which has been justified on the grounds that discrete policies were 'made to measure' for each different situation. But this is only the David-Hume's-waistcoat rationalisation of the Mad Hatter's party (where, it will be recalled, the clocks all misbehaved themselves and the argument ended up down a treacle-well). There has been no constitutional plan that might risk making sense. There has been no question whatever, for Blair, of the United Kingdom Constitution being reformed – as distinct from having some new bits tacked on to it: Ukania is terribly flexible about such add-ons and plug-ins, but completely rigid about Sovereignty, the unswerving essence supposed to preside over the Centre of Things. A constitutional plan which made sense would thus be little better than a suicide note: the anguished farewell from his bed of rags of a wretch doomed to normalcy – proportional representation, plurality of powers, democracy, creeping Republicanism, the dank humiliation of being 'quite important', and pivotal no more.

This is not to deny for a moment the value of such initiatives 'in themselves'. Of course Scotland is better off advancing towards recovery of statehood, as is Wales with its own representative voice. The Northern Ireland constitution and Assembly is arguably the most important achievement of the 1997-2001 New Labour government, voted for (we should remember) by decisive majorities in both the Republic and the North itself. However, 'in themselves' is another deceptive phrase. None of these changes are as yet 'in themselves', or self-standing. All continue to depend upon the United Kingdom's non-constitution – upon a collapsing structure of authority that rests on a dwindling basis of real allegiance, and yet persists in identifying all its incorrigible weaknesses as wondrous strengths. David Hume's waistcoat has turned into the straitjacket of terminal Britishness. The inmate has given up figuring a way out and settled for just being himself: 'British through and through'.

During the 2001 election campaign, quite different campaigns were fought in the devolved and Tory-free countries of Her Majesty's state. The Ulster contest was about the future of power-sharing government there. The Scottish and Welsh votes were rehearsals for the next elections to their own parliaments, due in 2003. These will almost certainly be marked by further advances for the SNP and Plaid Cymru respectively, increased resentment in the English hinterland, and a beefing-up of the Save Britain campaign.[27] In other words, the UK will be moving on from the Hatter's tea-party of 2001 to the insane croquet competition of 2005 to 2007 (the latter date being the third centenary of the Treaty of Union with Scotland, the architrave of the existing state).

There is an old blueprint for the post-British Isles, which runs like this: four nationalities simultaneously recover from the colonial addiction and resume their separate, or partly separate, ways. Scotland, Ireland, Wales and England will in the end agree amicably on forms of independence, and the big new population of incomers to the archipelago (who are mostly in England) will swap 'British' for 'English', and before long hardly notice the difference (aided by the near certainty that a reconstructed England would be more democratic than Britain ever was). 'British' would then become a loosely ethnic label in something like the old Greek sense, denoting certain cultural traits common to the archipelagic tribes. Though politically independent, the latter would be most unlikely to abandon such traits overnight – any more (for example) than the Irish Republic did in 1922 or 1947. Civil society would remain (so to speak) mainly 'British-Irish', at least until someone thinks up a smarter term than 'archipelago'.

Unfortunately, this is a formula for an intelligible or standard game of croquet, played on more or less level ground by the contemporary rules of nation-statehood. In *Alice in Wonderland* things unfold differently. They are much more like what seems presaged by Her Majesty's general election of 2001:

> Alice thought she had never seen such a curious croquet ground in all her life; it was all ridges and furrows; the balls were live hedgehogs and the mallets live flamingos, and the soldiers had to double themselves up and stand upon their hands and feet, to make the arches ....[28]

All the players play at once, 'quarrelling all the while' and fighting for the hedgehogs, who constantly unroll themselves and crawl away, while the soldiers get tired of waiting and wander off, and the Queen works herself into a furious passion, stamping about and shouting 'Off with his head!' or 'Off with her head!' Alice confides in the Cheshire Cat that she has understood the real point of the confusion: 'The Queen is so extremely likely to win that it's hardly worth while finishing the game'. Hearing her, 'The Queen smiled and passed on'.

It will be clear that there must be something else wrong with that tidy old blueprint. The assumption it encourages is that all the problems of devolution and fragmentation must arise from peripheral nationalism. They do not. It was of course a necessary condition of the collapse that national movements and claims assert themselves; but the sufficient condition of Britain's end lies within the core itself.[29] The underlying motor of disintegration is in the contradictions of a state which has now grossly outlived its historic day, but would rather fall apart than cease being itself through reform. The finest hour gave it a new lease of life; but when that lease ended in the 1970s, nothing would persuade the title-holders to relinquish their tenure and make an honest end to the grandeur of a departed age. Thatcherism and Blairism have been at bottom strategies of state-salvation, in which their own societies are ceasing daily to believe. Loyalty survives solely in the Protestant last ditches of Ulster, or the blatant self-interest of the neo-British managers who now squat in the abandoned mansions of the former ruling class. Willy-nilly, all the *societies* of this heirloom-state find themselves driven towards the true salvation of exit.

Under such conditions, exit will naturally assume different forms, and there has been prolonged debate about this in the echo chambers of post-modernism. The one that concerns me most, however, is distinctly pre-post-modern. The Scots really know what has to be done to the Treaty of Union. When asked whether they want independence *now*, a majority of them still haver about putting it off or hanging around in case some ineffably better offer turns up. On the other hand, one survey after another has also shown that most of them think independence is inevitable. If something is inevitable in a reasonably foreseeable future, would it not be best to anticipate it now, or as soon as possible? But the ghostly *persona* of Britishness still appears to walk abroad, even in Scotland, defying democracy, outliving genuine loyalty and conviction, with the 'Exit' door near at hand. Let it soon be laid to rest.

NOTES

1. L. Carroll, *Alice's Adventures in Wonderland* [1865]; references in this chapter are to R. Gasson (ed), *The Illustrated Lewis Carroll*, London: Jupiter Books 1978, p8.

2. I arrived in Australia during the run-up to the 2001 Australian election, which was dominated – to an extent even unimaginable by UK standards – by the issues of asylum-seekers, immigration and race. This was symbolised by the international news event of the Norwegian freighter carrying asylum seekers which was refused permission to land.

3. I followed the 2001 UK election quite closely, from the beginning of the year until after polling day, for a book project I was writing at the time: T. Nairn, *Pariah: Misfortunes of the British Kingdom*, London: Verso 2002.

4. See David Seawright's chapter in this book on the post-election reaction to the Conservatives' solitary victory in Galloway and Upper Nithsdale.

5. See S. Walters, *Tory Wars: Conservatives in Crisis*, London: Politico's Publishing 2001; A. Seldon and P. Snowdon, *A New Conservative Century?*, London: Centre for Policy Studies 2001; D. Seawright: *An Important Matter of Principle: The Decline of the Conservative and Unionist Party*, Aldershot: Ashgate 1999.

6. See R. H. S. Crossman, 'Introduction', to W. Bagehot, *The English Constitution*, London: Fontana 1963, for an informed labourist analysis of the supposed democratisation of this mystifying structure.

7. See D. McKie, 'The non-voting party', in J. Glover (ed), *The Guardian Companion to the General Election 2001*, London: Atlantic Books 2001, pp122-24.

8. The official figure was that '25 per cent of voters' supported New Labour in the 2001 general election. However, the UK electoral roll is notoriously out of date. Nobody knows how many potential voters have absented themselves from registration over the period since Mrs Thatcher's Poll tax, at the same time as many immigrants have failed to enrol. 'Keeping out of trouble' has become a way of life, possibly for millions, the implication being that the 'NVP' is a lot bigger than statistics recognised – and therefore that 25 per cent of voters represents less than a quarter of the real voting-age population.

9. There is a widespread consensus that voting participation is irrevocably failing across Europe and the West, but this hides disparate trends and turnouts. In 2001 the Italian general election produced an 83 per cent turnout, whereas the Polish election, after a decade of non-communist government, produced a derisory turnout of 47 per cent.

10. *Basildon: The Mood of the Nation*, London: Demos 2001, p11: 'The Basildonians ... see their own prospects for self-improvement as good, but not the future of society as a whole.'

11. *Hansard*, 11.12.00, Col. 351.

12. *Economist*, 9.6.01.

13. J. Bulpitt, *Territory and Power in the United Kingdom*, Manchester: Manchester University Press 1983.

14. P. Kennedy, *The Rise and Fall of the Great Powers*, London: Unwin Hyman 1988.

15. A. Barnett, *Iron Britannia*, London: Allison and Busby 1982. Barnett's essay, subtitled, 'Why Parliament waged its Falklands War', is a wonderful polemic about post-imperial decline, the meaning of 1940 and the creation of 'Churchillism'.

16. Hailsham's remarks were representative of right-wing fears and fantasies about democracy and ungovernability. See: A. King (ed), *Why is Britain Becoming Harder to Govern?*, London: BBC 1976; R. Moss, *The Collapse of Democracy*, London: Temple Smith 1975.

17. J. Freedland, 'I think we should do ...', *Guardian*, 18.6.01.

18. I. Crewe, 'Elections and Public Opinion', in A. Seldon (ed), *The Blair Effect: The Blair Government 1997-2001*, London: Little Brown 2001, pp67-96. Crewe explains the key significance of 'depopulating industrial and inner-city areas' for reinforcing New Labour dominance.

19. D. Butler and D. Kavanagh, *The British General Election of 2001*, London: Palgrave 2001.

20. See Walters, *op. cit.*

21. Hans Nichols, 'The Extinction of the Tory Party', *Guardian*, 8.10.01.

22. Post-1997 there was an avalanche of books on the theme of the death of England and Britain: J. Paxman, *The English: A Portrait of A People*, London: Michael Joseph 1998; R. Scruton, *England: An Elegy*, London: 2001; S. Heffer, *Nor Shall My Sword: The Reinvention of England*, London: Weidenfeld and Nicolson 1999; P. Hitchens, *The Abolition of Britain: The British Cultural Revolution From Lady Chatterley to Tony Blair*, London: Quartet Books 1999; J. Redwood, *The Death of Britain: The UK's Constitutional Crisis*, London: Macmillan 1999; A. Marr, *The Day Britain Died*, London: Profile 2000.

23. L. Greenfeld, *Nationalism: Five Roads to Modernity*, Cambridge: Harvard University Press 1992.

24. K. Pask, 'Late Nationalism: The Case of Quebec', *New Left Review*, No. 11 (Second Series), September-October 2001, pp49-50.

25. G. Hassan and J. McCormick, 'After Blair: The Future of Britishness', *Soundings*, No. 18, Summer/Autumn 2001, pp118-34.

26. G. Brown and D. Alexander, *New Scotland, New Britain*, London: Smith Institute 1999. See Hassan and McCormick, *op. cit.*, pp125-28.

27. It is no accident that the demise of two-party Ukania 1945-70 has seen the development of more pluralist political systems in Scotland, Wales and Northern Ireland. Northern Ireland has a highly competitive four party system at both Westminster and Stormont, while the Scots and Welsh have four party systems at a devolved level, but the continuation of Labour one party rule at Westminster. England – at the 2001 election – has a political system where Labour predominates – but which currently sits with ill-ease between a two-party system and one party dominance, neither one nor the other. The interaction between these different political systems – the tensions, dynamics and evolution – will have a major influence on the future shape of the UK.

28. L. Carroll, 'The Queen's Croquet Ground', in Gasson, *op. cit.*, pp64-71.

29. On this theme see my *The Break-up of Britain*, London: New Left Books 2nd edn. 1981, the original version of which was written twenty-five years ago.

Contributors

Gerry Hassan is director and co-founder of Big Thinking. He has produced and contributed to a number of books and publications on Scottish and UK politics, was co-editor of *A Different Future* (1999) and *The New Scottish Politics* (2000) and co-author of *The Almanac of Scottish Politics* (2001). He has worked with Demos and the Fabian Society, and edited issues of the journals *Renewal* and *Soundings*.

Chris Warhurst is Director of the Scottish Centre for Employment Research at the University of Strathclyde, Glasgow and co-founder of Big Thinking. His research and writing focuses on work in the global economy as well as Scottish policy-making. He has co-edited and authored a number of books and articles including *Workplaces of the Future* (1998) and *The New Scottish Politics* (2000). He also commissions public interest reports funded by Scottish Enterprise.

Nicola McEwen is a lecturer in politics at the University of Edinburgh. Her doctoral thesis was a study of state and sub-state nationalism in Scotland and Quebec. Her research focuses on territorial politics and comparative sub-state governance and she is author of a number of book chapters and articles in this field.

David Seawright is a lecturer in British Politics in the Institute for Politics and International Studies (POLIS) at the University of Leeds. He is the author of *An Important Matter of Principle* (1999), and co-editor (with David Baker) of *Britain For and Against Europe* (1998).

Peter Lynch is a lecturer in politics at the University of Stirling. He is the author of *Minority Nationalism and European Integration* (1996) and *Scottish Government and Politics* (2001), co-author of *The Almanac of Scottish Politics* (2001) and co-editor of *Out of the Ghetto? The Catholic Community in Modern Scotland* (1998). He is currently writing a history of the Scottish National Party.

Lynn Bennie is lecturer in the Department of Politics and International Relations at the University of Aberdeen. Her research interests include elections, political parties, environmental politics and political participation. Publications include *Understanding Participation: Green Party Membership in Scotland* (2002) and (with Jack Brand and James Mitchell) *How Scotland Votes: Scottish Parties and Elections* (1997).

Lindsay Paterson is professor of educational policy in the Faculty of Education, Edinburgh University. He is editor of *Scottish Affairs* and author of *The Autonomy of Modern Scotland* (1994) and *A Diverse Assembly: The Debate on a Scottish Parliament* (1998), as well as co-author of several books.

Jim McCormick is Research Director of the Scottish Council Foundation and was previously a Research Fellow at the IPPR. He is author of a number of books and publications on social policy, welfare and the implications of devolution. He was a contributor to the IPPR study *The State and the Nations* (1996) and co-editor of *Welfare in Working Order* (1998) and *Environment Scotland* (1999).

Richard Parry is senior lecturer in the School of Social and Political Studies at the University of Edinburgh. His main interests are in Scottish and British public policy. He is the co-author of *The Treasury and Social Policy* (with Nicholas Deakin, Macmillan 2000) and is currently researching the impact of devolution on the civil service.

Alf Young is Policy Editor of *The Herald* and a regular writer and commentator on economic, social and political affairs. He has also worked for *The Scotsman*, *The Sunday Standard*, Radio Clyde and the Scottish Labour Party.

Richard Mitchell is a research fellow at the Research Unit in Health, Behaviour and Change, University of Edinburgh. His primary research interest is health inequality with recent work focusing on geographic differences in mortality rates within Britain and incorporating health and social inclusion issues into wider social policy.

Danny Dorling is Professor of Quantitative Human Geography, School of Geography, University of Leeds. He was previously Reader and Lecturer in Geography, University of Bristol, Joseph Rowntree Foundation Fellow, British Academy Fellow and Senior Research Associate, University of Newcastle upon Tyne.

Rowena Arshad is the Director of the Centre for Education for Racial Equality in Scotland based in the Faculty of Education, University of Edinburgh. She has recently been appointed Equal Opportunities Commissioner with responsibility for Scotland. She writes here in a personal capacity.

Janice Kirkpatrick co-founded the inter-disciplinary international design consultancy Graven Images with her partner, architect Ross Hunter, in 1986. She is a broadcaster, and curator of several exhibitions including *UK Style*, *UK PackAge* and *Connecting Cultures*. She recently wrote and presented *Designing Our Lives*, a six part series on the history of creativity for BBC2, broadcast in 2000. She is a Visiting Professor at Glasgow School of Art, a Director of The Lighthouse and a Governor of Glasgow School of Art.

Tom Nairn is Research Professor in Globalisation at the Royal Melbourne Institute of Technology, Australia and one of the leading commentators on Scottish and UK politics and the decline of Ukania. He is author of several books including *The Left Against Europe?* (1973), *The Break-up of Britain* (1977; 2nd edn. 1981), *The Enchanted Glass* (1988), *Faces of Nationalism* (1997) and *After Britain* (2000). His latest work is *Pariah* (Verso 2002).

Index